Rituals. Killers. Wars. & Sex.

Tibet, India, Nepal, Laos, Vietnam, Afghanistan, Sri Lanka & New York

RICHARD S. EHRLICH

Copyright © 2020 Richard S. Ehrlich

World rights reserved. No part of this book may be reproduced or transmitted in any form or by any means, electronic or mechanical, including photocopying, recording or by information storage and retrieval system, without the written permission of the author, except for small quotes used during reviews of this book.

ISBN: 9798635164013

Cover & design by Richard S. Ehrlich

I am a Bangkok-based journalist from San Francisco, California, reporting news from Asia since 1978 and winner of Columbia University's Foreign Correspondent's Award.

This book elaborates on my published dispatches from Tibet, India, Nepal, Laos, Vietnam, Afghanistan, Sri Lanka and New York.

These stories portray fragments of people and their distant voices, mixed with unique and rare events. Slices, starting at random moments and ending in bleak locations.

Many of these transcribed handwritten notes, impressions and exclusive interviews have never appeared in print until now.

The person who never dreams,
always hunts and kills the person who does.

But dreaming is not the cure.

Because the person who dreams one dream,
will hunt and kill the person who dreams another.

This book is for the innocent on all sides, slain without mercy.

Special thanks to Tom Vater for deciphering
the blurred graffiti inside the top of the minaret,
and to Kanchana Chanawong for saving my life.

RITUALS. KILLERS. WARS. & SEX.

Chapter 1 ~ Rituals

Sky Funeral Vultures in Tibet

The Dalai Lama & the Dead

Holy Sadhus in India & Nepal

Calcutta's Dom Caste Undertakers

Chapter 2 ~ Killers

Jampa Phuntsok & Tibet's Armed Rebellion

Tony "Poe" Poshepny, CIA in Laos

James "Mule" Parker, CIA in Vietnam

International "Bikini Killer" Charles Sobhraj

India's "Bandit Queen" Phoolan Devi

Jonathan "Jack" Idema in Kabul

Chapter 3 ~ Wars

Americans, Soviets & Mujahideen in Afghanistan

India's Kashmir

The Liberation Tigers of Tamil Eelam

Chapter 4 ~ Sex

Peri, a New York Stripper

Michelle, in Peepland on 42nd Street

CHAPTER 1 ~ RITUALS

SKY FUNERAL VULTURES IN TIBET

On the rocky outskirts of Lhasa, Tibetan mourners whispered prayers while hungry, brooding vultures circled overhead.

Cawing.

"This is our sky funeral. We let the vultures eat the bodies of dead Tibetans," a mourner told me at the beginning of the somber rites. "I personally think it is too gruesome. But this is our Buddhist tradition."

Cremations and burials are difficult to perform. Firewood is scarce throughout much of Tibet. The ground is often frozen or rocky. In 1984 a gray boulder looming 30 feet high, served as the cold altar for Lhasa's Tibetan corpses. The flat boulder's 20-foot by 20-foot surface could be used every day except Sundays.

Sky funerals -- bya gtor or "alms for the birds" -- began at dawn with attendees moaning prayers.

"Today, four bodies," the mourner quietly explained.

"You can see, three of the dead are village women. Also a merchant. He is a murder victim. He was killed two nights ago in the Lhasa market at a card game. Stabbed. We are all friends of the dead. The brothers, sisters, parents and children don't come to these funerals."

This morning was chilly and clear.

The sun smoldered behind snow-covered mountain peaks while four Tibetan undertakers -- rogyapa or "body breakers" --

and two assistants laid the four corpses face down on the boulder. The undertakers pulled off the bodies' shoes. Mourners glanced at the slumped, immobile humans, then looked away. More friends arrived to honor the deceased.

Visitors came in battered, dusty, green Chinese trucks. The vehicles veered off a dirt road, rattled across a small, flat garbage dump, and splashed through an icy, shallow brook. The trucks stopped near the blood-stained boulder.

The all-male passengers climbed down and solemnly trudged towards the rock which rested amid treeless lunar foothills dotted with ragged Buddhist prayer flags on the northern outskirts of Lhasa below the stone wall of the 15th century Sera Monastery. Vultures swooped and spiraled, or simply loitered atop a nearby cliff. The birds of prey looked down upon the living and the dead, waiting for the ritual to begin.

Six undertakers, reeking of cheap Tibetan chang beer, used thick ropes to noose the necks of the bodies. They attached the ropes to a very heavy stone. This prevented the bodies sliding off the boulder's slightly angled surface.

The mourners were becoming increasingly miserable. They clustered around small campfires a few yards away, below the boulder. Some used dented aluminum tea pots to brew hot tea laced with yak butter and salt -- a popular nourishment.

Overhead, more vultures circled and cawed.

Some of the birds hopped unafraid onto the boulder and inspected the cadavers. A few of the two dozen mourners quietly joked and gossiped among themselves. The undertakers, in filthy, blood-splattered aprons and knee-high boots, pulled out their whetstones.

They sharpened vicious, 18-inch knives and heavy cleavers.

Someone tossed a mixture of dried yak dung, roots and seeds onto eight small campfires below the rock and five tiny fires on the boulder's surface. The heaving smoke was to signal distant vultures that a sky funeral had started. A noisy flock of about 150 vultures now swooped above the boulder but didn't land.

The drunk undertakers appeared numb to the slowly

unfolding horror. With heavy, grabbing gestures, they unceremoniously ripped the clothes off the corpses. The bodies were now completely nude. Face down.

As a grim backdrop, Tibet's dreaded Drapchi Prison sprawled nearby.

The butchering was terrible to watch. It had all the rawness of a medieval slaughterhouse. Each of the four undertakers quietly worked separately on a single body. They chopped off flesh. Cut away the dark red muscles down to white bones. Dismembered limbs. With bare hands, they scooped out each heart. They yanked out internal organs, briefly inspected the ugly tangle, and tossed it aside.

Hacking sounds made by their blades, pierced the silent dawn.

Amid the gore, the undertakers revealed efficient techniques. With knives and cleavers, they chopped the flesh and muscles into chunks and tossed the pieces from all four corpses into a central pile on the boulder's surface. They discarded the bones into a separate pile. The two attendants, with heavy hammers, sat and pounded the bones into a powdery gruel while chanting Buddhist prayers of emancipation.

They eventually made a tasty mash by mixing tsampa -- roasted barley flour and yak butter -- together with the corpses' minced meat to entice the vultures. They sprinkled the powdered bones over the entire meal, to ensure the bones would also be eaten. The result resembled a huge, bright red, sinewy, chunky, raw hamburger on the dark gray boulder.

One mourner placed a handkerchief over his mouth to filter the stench. From time to time, assistants brought the undertakers large containers of chang barley beer and steaming tea to drink.

Saved for last were the four severed heads. Cheap earrings dangled from the three women's ears.

Undertakers inspected the heads before proceeding. One by one, they gripped each severed head by the hair and held it high up, watching as the shredded blood vessels, neck muscles and connecting flesh dangled from the skinned neck. In the early morning light, each undertaker appeared as if portrayed in Italian Baroque artist Caravaggio's painting of David with the Head of Goliath or as Judith with the Head of Holofernes, painted by Allori.

The undertakers stared at the heads and the drooped faces. Most of the blood had coagulated, but some dripped onto the rock into shallow circular puddles. Mourners watched transfixed, gazing up from below the boulder. Most mourners then looked away.

The undertakers casually placed the four heads on the boulder's surface and used the sharp points of their knives to cut into the flesh, forming a big circle around each person's face.

They deepened the slices across the foreheads, at the hairline. With blood-splattered fists, each undertaker clutched the hair above the corpse's sliced forehead and pulled it backwards while hacking two gashes along the sides near the ears. They chopped off most of the heads' hair and lobbed those chunks away from the boulder.

The undertakers then grabbed each grimacing dead face at the forehead using their right hands, and also stuck the fingers of their left hands into each corpse's mouth. Strongly pulling in opposite directions, they began yanking off each scalp.

It was as if they were removing a stubborn, glued-down wig.

After a final pull, they tore away the scalp, exposing the skull's dome, glistening white and flecked with red gristle.

An assistant silently laid out a white cotton sheet onto the boulder's surface. The undertakers cut each scalp into hand-size chunks and tossed the pieces onto the cloth along with any remnants of flesh.

The undertakers then picked up the scalped heads and, with several hard, downward tugs, skillfully yanked each face completely down and away. Each removed face formed a bloody, pouch-like, rubbery mask.

The exposed skulls displayed macabre red and white skeletal

expressions rendered with small shreds of the remaining muscle and bone.

Another assistant offered the undertakers hot tea. Some mourners, each holding a handkerchief over their mouth and nose, clumsily climbed onto the boulder for a brief closer look before climbing back down. The two assistants then sat and continued hammering any remaining bones into powder while softly singing.

Suddenly, all work stopped.

One of the undertakers jumped off the boulder. Searching nearby, he found the heaviest rock he could carry and climbed back up onto the boulder's surface. He stood over a bloodied skull which he had laid on its side. The other undertakers stared at him. Slowly, he raised his heavy rock above his head, as high as he could. Then, with all his strength, he hurled the rock down onto the skull.

The skull cracked with a sharp, breaking sound.

But it did not crack completely open. So he retrieved his rock, stood above the head once more, and hurled it down, smashing the rock onto the oval skull. Finally, on the third attempt, the skull cracked open wider, partially exposing an encased brain.

The delighted undertaker smiled. He proudly and delicately picked up the cracked skull and, with a shout and wave of his hand, told all the mourners to pay attention.

While they silently watched, he carefully held the skull high in the air so everyone could see and, with his large hands, opened it like a giant breakfast egg.

The brain dropped onto the smooth boulder with a quivering plop.

Everyone gawked at the soft, round brain.

The undertaker nonchalantly discarded the skull's two broken pieces onto the pile of bones to be hammered. He then gently tossed the brain onto the other pile of tsampa-flavored flesh.

A nearby undertaker picked up the heavy rock and laughingly

pretended to try and smash the now-exhausted undertaker's head.

Another undertaker jumped off the boulder, found another heavy rock, climbed back up and smashed another corpse's skull, following his colleague's assault technique.

The other undertakers repeated the process with the remaining skulls.

When an assistant offered one of the undertakers a glass of tea, he replied, "My hands are too bloody. Hold and tilt the glass and I will drink from it."

Only one of the undertakers wore gloves. The hands of the three others were soaked in blood.

Soon, all six men climbed off the boulder.

"Come! Eat!" an assistant called out, throwing a small piece of human flesh off the boulder to attract the vultures.

The other assistant shouted at the mourners, "Sit down! You are scaring the vultures away!"

More than 100 huge birds swarmed down from the sky and landed on the boulder's surface. They displayed sleek, white feathers around their beaked heads and long necks. They were fat from frequent funerals. But the vultures soon became frenzied and competed for whatever they could eat. They battled each other, ripping chunks of stretchy, sinewy flesh and organs out of each other's beaks. They squawked, tearing at their feast. Devouring everything.

Soon only small puddles of blood remained on the boulder's surface in pock-marked, cup-sized dips created by centuries of brutal weather. The corpses' discarded clothes lay scattered below. These crumpled garments would be picked over by the undertakers, leaving the worst tattered rags to rot.

Sky funerals, the most common method for disposing human corpses throughout Tibet, usually cost about $25.

"Before the Chinese liberated Tibet in the 1950s, sky funerals were the only way to dispose of bodies," a Chinese communist official told me in Lhasa.

He wrinkled his nose at the thought.

"But now, cremation or burial is available for anyone. Of course, we Chinese in Lhasa do not feed each other to vultures. But most Tibetans still do."

China, which controls Tibet, tried to hide the ritual from foreigners' eyes. Throughout Lhasa, Chinese security forces posted English-language signs in hotel rooms and other places where foreign tourists gathered, warning:

"It is forbidden to visit and photo the sky burial site, according to the local government's regulations for the minority nationality's habits and customs. The tourist who breaks the regulation will be punished strictly."

In some monasteries, wall murals detailing the life of Buddha depicted Tibet's sky funerals with paintings of Egyptian-looking vultures munching people's internal organs -- reminiscent of Hieronymus Bosch's art.

A Tibetan lama told me about the funeral's origins:

"Buddhism teaches you should give yourself to others and to nature during your life. So it is natural to give yourself to the birds when you die. Also, many Tibetans believe if the body has been buried, the ghost of the dead can return to haunt the family. Some Tibetans say doorways are built low, to force you to bow down upon entering, because a ghost walks with its body stiff and cannot bend. A low doorway will prevent a ghost from entering. With the sky funeral, the body does not remain to haunt the family."

Lamas, including dalai lamas and panchen lamas, were not fed to vultures.

Instead, their bodies were embalmed and covered in aromatic spices and encased in a stupa -- also known as a chorten -- a bell-shaped structure. To honor dead dalai lamas and panchen lamas, the stupa's external surface was then covered in gold. For lamas of a lesser rank, silver, copper, wooden or clay stupas were constructed.

Cremations might be performed for other senior monks. Sometimes, their ashes were thrown into the wind from a mountain top. Beggars and poor people who could not afford a sky funeral were sometimes given a water burial. Their bodies, chopped to pieces, might have been tossed into a river to be carried away by swift currents and ultimately eaten by fish.

Some people who witnessed a sky funeral did not understand its sacredness. One day an American tourist in Lhasa, bent over a large sink in our hostel's main washing room, was frantically scrubbing his Levis jacket with bubbling shampoo, desperately trying to clean a large splotch of blood. He had defied the undertakers' ban on photography during the ritual. The American discreetly kept his camera partially hidden under his jacket, but its loud "click" gave him away.

"An undertaker picked up a chopped-off human leg and began chasing me, swinging it and trying to hit me! I couldn't run fast enough. He chased me and hit me with the leg here on my shoulder. Look at all this blood!"

The distraught tourist was on the verge of tears. He kept scrubbing at the dark red stain.

"He hit me with a human leg! And I'm a vegetarian!"

Death rituals in Tibet had other surprising ways of affecting living people.

Some dying Tibetan Buddhist mystics claimed to have entered other people's corpses, animating the dead flesh and living happily ever after inside their revived bodies -- even better than a zombie or a Frankenstein monster. These mystics were said to keep their own personalities and memories while residing under someone else's skin.

The Tibetan-English Dictionary of Buddhist Terminology defined how to extend your life by inhabiting a dead person:

"The Practice of Entering a Corpse. An exalted Tantric practice through which a yogi, having gained control of his energy winds and mind, purposely abandons his body and transfers his consciousness into another serviceable corpse.

"This enables him to maintain his life even after the break-up of his original body, in order to fulfill the purpose of other sentient beings. The great yogi Dharma Dhode, the son of Lama Marpa, is said to have demonstrated this practice."

THE DALAI LAMA & THE DEAD

The Dalai Lama was intrigued by these possibilities. He believed when his tutor died, the teacher was able to prevent his own corpse from decomposing for almost two weeks.

Experts from Columbia and Berkeley universities and elsewhere, fascinated by the Dalai Lama's insights into the afterlife, spent one week with him in 1987 researching the possibility of living in corpses and other inconceivable behavior.

The Dalai Lama told the group:

"Through Tantric technique, the meditator is able to transfer his consciousness into a dead body. Because the meditator hasn't actualized the 'clear light' state of death -- meaning he hasn't gone through the process of death -- he is able to retain the knowledge gathered during his lifetime.

"Memory is not brain. Anyway, it's a mere hypothesis from the Buddhist point of view. So it has to be experimented with," the Dalai Lama said, chuckling.

No one, however, can achieve immortality by jumping from body to body.

"A total change of the [dead] physical body takes place, but the lifespan of the [living] person is said to be the same," the Dalai Lama told group.

Participants in the spirited dialogue included Columbia University's computer sciences professor Dr. Newcomb Greenleaf, plus Berkeley University's cognitive scientist Eleanor Rosch, and San Diego University's brain development expert Dr. Robert Livingston. Naropa Institute's Dr. Jeremy Hawyard, along with French neurobiologist Dr. Francisco Varela of the Ecole Polytechnique in Paris, also attended.

Deep meditators can "see the events of their past lives," the Dalai Lama said. Ordinary people can at least attain low-level near-death awareness and "clear light" -- through meditation or during sex.

The Dalai Lama also told the experts:

"There are four ordinary occasions when a very gross form of 'clear light' arises: at the moments of yawning, sneezing, falling asleep, and orgasm. Orgasm is the strongest of the four ordinary occasions in which 'clear light' appears, and so it is used in meditation to extend the experience of the emergence of 'clear light,' to clarify the experience and make it more vivid."

Some lamas who die, keep "very subtle consciousness" in their corpses, to prevent their bodies spoiling after expiration.

"As a result, the body doesn't decompose while the self is in the 'clear light' [of] final dissolution," the Dalai Lama said. "Some people can remain in that state for a week or more. For example, the late Kyabjey Ling Rinpoche, my tutor, remained in the state of 'clear light' for 13 days, and his body remained very fresh."

Over the centuries, death and dying became attractive career choices for some Tibetan mystics. The "Ten Innermost Jewels" of Tibetan Buddhism's Kadampa tradition defined by the Tibetan dictionary include "entrusting yourself to death as the extreme consequence of poverty" and "entrusting yourself to an empty cave as the simplest place to die."

To do that, a Tibetan Buddhist ascetic was instructed to wear special garments, depending on where they lived.

"An ascetic who dwells in a cemetery" should be "crowned with human skulls. He wears a rosary of human heads carved in crystal [and] an elephant skin as an upper garment."

Alternatively, "he uses the skin of a human."

To mark a red dot of devotion on his forehead, "he uses blood for the tilika between his eyes." Whenever he is near a campfire, he can gather some of the white burnt ash to ensure "his body is covered with ashes".

Some Tibetan lamas also practiced "Nine Points of Meditation on Ugliness."

They would meditate on a human's "swollen corpse" or

"worm-eaten corpse," "festering corpse," "bloody corpse," "bluish corpse," "a corpse being devoured" by maggots or other creatures, "a scattered corpse" dismembered or broken apart by rotting, "a burnt corpse," or "a poisonous corpse."

Gods could suddenly drop dead or be murdered by other gods, so they too needed to heed various omens.

"The Five Signs of Imminent Death for a God. Number one, they lose luster and brightness of their body. Number two, they dislike to sit on their cushions. Number three, their garlands fade away. Number four, their robes are worn out and smell bad. Number five, their body is covered with sweat."

Tibetan death rituals sometimes utilized human bones as musical instruments because the sounds they produced were perceived vital to mystical realizations.

These include a "human thighbone trumpet" and "femur trumpet" which are "used as a ritual implement in certain Tantric practices of exorcism to remind one of death and impermanence."

Even laughter can reveal the unspeakable.

"Among the terrifying laughs of a wrathful deity" are the deceptively ominous, "Ha Ha as the threatening; He He as the pleasing; Hi Hi as the elegant; and Ho Ho as the outshining laugh."

Lamas, ascetics and others deep into Buddhist revelry were also able to protect parts of their body being burnt during their own cremation, so devotees could use them for future rituals.

"Some of the highly realized masters leave their heart, tongue and eyeballs untouched by fire at their cremation as a source of inspiration and devotion, symbolizing their blessings of body, speech and mind as relics for their followers," the dictionary said.

The sacred Tibetan Book of the Dead, Bardo Thodol, or Liberation by Hearing During the After-Death Plane, warns everyone they inevitably face reincarnation -- even if they do not believe in the concept -- so it is vital next time to select the best womb.

The book dates back to the 9th century, describes the "after-death experiences on the bardo plane" and includes "testimony" from holy men who "claim to have died and re-entered the human womb consciously."

They determined that after you die, "thou wilt see thine own home, the attendants, relatives, and the corpse [of yourself] and think, 'Now I am dead! What shall I do?' and being oppressed with intense sorrow, the thought will occur to thee, 'O what would I not give to possess a body!' And so thinking, thou wilt be wandering hither and thither seeking a body. Put aside the desire for a body."

Instead listen to the attending Buddhist "officiant" who should be whispering instructions into your dead ears for up to 49 days -- even if you died deaf -- to help you avoid entering the wrong "womb-door" or, worse, going to Hell.

Only enlightened people will be able to free themselves from this next cycle of rebirth. In your case, however, female wombs all over the world will be attracting you, wherever any two people's sperm and ovum happen to be uniting during the 49 days after you died.

According to Lama Kazi Dawa-Samdup's English rendering of the Tibetan Book of the Dead, edited by W. Y. Evans-Wentz and published in 1927:

"Thou wilt see visions of males and females in union. Remember to withhold thyself from going between them," because then you will be conceived by people who you later might not want as your parents.

Instead, be extremely choosy. And don't get suckered by illusionary tricks.

"Do not enter into any sort of womb which may come by. In selecting the womb-door thus, there is a possibility of error: through the influence of karma, good wombs may appear bad, and bad wombs may appear good."

Even more confusing, some gorgeous visual lures displayed by wombs may be sinister tricks and not really belong to a human mother. If you mistakenly choose one of those, you could be reincarnated as a beast.

If you fail to heed this advice, ancient teachings predict:

"Encased in oval form, in the embryonic state, and upon emerging from the womb and opening its [your] eyes, it may find itself transformed into a young dog. Formerly it had been a human being, but now, if it has become a dog, it findeth itself undergoing sufferings in a dog's kennel. Or perhaps a pig in a pigsty, or as an ant in an ant-hill."

Worse is to be cast into a Buddhist Hell.

According to The Princeton Dictionary of Buddhism, "This Hell is said to be located 20,000 yojanas below the continent of Jambudvipa and is the destination of beings whose 'wholesome faculties are eradicated' -- samucchinnakusalamula -- or who have committed the most heinous of acts which, after death, result in immediate rebirth in the avici hell: patricide, matricide, killing an arhat [saint], wound a Buddha, and causing schism in the sangha [clergy].

"Because being reborn in this Hell, they are being constantly burned alive in hot flames, with no respite in their torture, the agony they experience is said to be 'interminable'.

"Avici and its seven companion Hells each have 16 -- four in each direction -- neighboring Hells, pratyekanaraka, or sub hells, utsada, where supplementary tortures are meted out to the unfortunate inhabitants, such as plains of ash that burn their feet; swamps of excrement and corpses in which maggots eat their flesh; roads and forests of razor blades that slice off their flesh; and rivers of boiling water in which they are plunged."

In 1983, The Dalai Lama was living in comfortable self-exile in McLeod Ganj town, nestled just above Dharamsala amid India's tranquil, forested Himalayan mountain peaks. He was protected by armed Indian guards and surrounded by a bustling Tibetan refugee community.

During our interview, the easy-going Dalai Lama said he worried whether Tibetan Buddhism and its rituals, wisdom and meditation techniques would survive under China's control.

"If the Tibetan people get more benefits with the unity and

good marriage with China, all right. There has been some improvement regarding food and Tibetan culture," during the past five years, he said.

"But profound religious teaching is not allowed. The Chinese say that Tibetans can simply recite prayers. That is the most generous freedom allowed. But that is not sufficient. To practice Buddhism, you must study volumes of books and meditate. This the Chinese do not know. They do not know what Tibetan culture is."

When I asked the Dalai Lama if he had reached nirvana, he replied:

"No. I would need complete isolation. In order to achieve nirvana, I must have deep meditation. You must spend at least a few months, if not, then a few years to qualify for that state of consciousness. Now I am 49, although that is not too late. But 10 years back, I expressed a desire to begin a three-year retreat, but the Tibetan people complained" because they wanted him to campaign worldwide for human rights in Tibet.

In 1986, during our second interview in McLeod Ganj, the Dalai Lama sat barefoot with his legs folded underneath himself on a chair. Next to him was a large model of his former Potala Palace, wired to light up. He appeared happy, with his head freshly shaved, wearing glasses, a wristwatch and a dark maroon robe.

Tibetan Buddhist wisdom and rituals were vanishing, he said.

"The most unfortunate thing today is there is no proper place to learn [Buddhism], and teachers also are not available because the learned are almost gone. The remaining few are either very old or physically not healthy due to torture and many difficult experiences and events. And also, those learned ones are sort of discouraged to teach others because it may look from the Chinese side, it may look like propagating dharma, propagating something that was prohibited. In Buddhism, unless you study quite a number of years, it is difficult to understand. And without knowledge, it is difficult to practice."

When I asked the Dalai Lama again if he had achieved

nirvana, he now replied:

"No, no, no, no. My own spiritual stage, I think I can say, is at a developing stage. Unfortunately, for the practice of Tantric teaching or Tantric practice, age is also an important factor. The best time is below 40. Now the Dalai Lama, poor Dalai Lama, has already reached his 50s. But the only thing which gives me inspiration is whether you personally develop satisfactorily or not.

"Now I have a strong desire to spend more time on meditation. In the next 20, 30 years, suppose I live, how much time can I achieve on the spiritual path? I don't know. But one thing I can say, up to now I've made quite a sound foundation which easily I can now build on. Now the most important factor is time. My main practice is altruism and understanding of Shinya. Do you know Shinya? Perhaps you have heard? Emptiness. Voidness. That's a difficult subject.

"Next year, I am hoping to spend a few months in a longer retreat. Usually, I can't spend more than a few weeks. If someone is just waiting to see me, I feel it difficult to send them away. In a more remote place, I hope people may not come unless something very serious, so I can spend a few months."

Where?

"Confidential!" he replied, laughing. "I think maybe next year, maybe Ladakh [in northwest India]. Monsoon time."

Meanwhile, life for Tibetans in Lhasa focused on the crowded Barkor "middle circuit" circumference lane in the center of town where people strolled clockwise around the Jokhang Temple, the most sacred Buddhist shrine in all Tibet.

During China's 1966-1976 Cultural Revolution, fanatic Chinese communist Red Guards lived in the Jokhang Temple and used it as a headquarters, according to some Tibetans. Later, China lifted their ban on Tibetans who wanted to pray at the 7th century Jokhang and surviving monasteries.

During my one-month stay in Lhasa in 1984 -- the first of three visits to Tibet between 1984 and 1999 -- hundreds of worshippers flocked daily to the Jokhang, repeatedly prostrating in prayer, often for several hours or several days at a time.

Many Tibetans walked here from distant villages.

In a painstakingly slow stroll, they repeatedly threw themselves forward, face-down onto dusty, rocky roads, then stood up, took one step forward and again threw themselves onto the ground. They did this again and again to complete each step, in an obsequious and physically painful style of praying.

Their grueling, rugged ritual appeared almost mechanical.

They did this during the entire route, for miles and miles, sometimes for several bruising weeks, from their villages to Lhasa.

They were body surfing into the harsh, gravel and dirt. They rarely bothered trying to avoid the random garbage, crud, or sharp stones which littered their paths. Obsessed and in deep meditation, they dove onto the ground even among busy traffic, forcing vehicles and crowds' scurrying feet to dodge their horizontal torsos every time the pilgrims flattened themselves on the roads.

Many of the Tibetan pilgrims wore crude, hand-stitched, raw leather overalls to protect their bodies from being grated into bloody shreds by the ground. To save their hands from severe injury, they usually gripped big, makeshift, leather-and-wood blocks in each hand so the wood covered their vulnerable palms.

When they arrived in Lhasa, they followed a traditional linkor pathway for several miles, drawn on some maps, which meandered around Lhasa along its earlier city limits. These sanctified dusty lanes led along turquoise, icy waters of the glassy Kyi Chu River, and alongside huge prayer wheels and hand-hammered Buddhist rock carvings.

Finally, it led them to the Jokhang, where pilgrims continued prostrating themselves for several hours each day. But they now remained in place each time they dove and stood up in front of the temple on a worn, smooth stone courtyard.

The ringing of brass bells and chanting by devotees and monks mixed with smoke wafting across them from nearby bonfires of auspicious juniper branches which had been shoved into huge, flaming, egg-shaped holy ovens in front of the temple.

Devotees purchased these juniper twigs in the surrounding market to burn.

Maroon-robed monks sat along the Jokhang Temple's outer white-washed walls droning incantations which they read from woodblock-printed texts written in Tibetan script. All around them bustled Barkor Square's market, stuffed with rolled lengths of dyed wool, Buddhist icons, and bloody hunks of yak meat laid on open, fly-infested tables near shops selling rare leopard skins, Chinese-made down jackets and local hand-forged metal tools.

Back in India, the Dalai Lama was grappling with another problem involving rituals and rebirth.

Looking vexed during our third interview at his Namgyal Monastery in McLeod Ganj in 1992, the Dalai Lama revealed that secretive investigations indicated his long dead arch-enemy, China's Chairman Mao Zedong, had been reincarnated.

This was the Dalai Lama's first mention to any journalist about Mao's reincarnation, or anything about an investigation.

A reborn Mao was alive and well?

Somewhere in China?

Reincarnated as a child?

The Dalai Lama's surprise disclosure about the possibility of a reincarnated Mao emerged when I asked what happens to people who do not believe in Buddhism, or reincarnation, and then die?

And what punishment in the afterworld would these people suffer if they committed acts of evil while alive -- I randomly tossed out Mao's name as an example -- according to Tibetan Buddhism?

Frowning slightly, the Dalai Lama leaned forward and replied:

"According to some indications, Chairman Mao has already emerged as one Chinese boy. According to some mysterious investigations. Usually when somebody has passed away, we start to investigate where they'll be reborn. According to some indications, Chairman Mao may be reborn three times among the Chinese. Three times."

Were these investigations into Mao's reincarnation being conducted by Tibetan Buddhists?

The Dalai Lama nodded and replied while repeatedly laughing:

"Oh yes, of course, of course. No Chinese sources. Certainly not Chinese communist sources. But really I don't know where. Also I have no interest to recognize the reincarnation. Unless we create an institution for Mao Zedong's reincarnation."

According to Buddhist teaching, all people whether they are Buddhists or not, are reborn after they die either as a human or a creature. It is difficult to be released from these repeated rebirths because all people, including Mao, are trapped on the Wheel of Life.

Each dalai lama is believed to be a reincarnated manifestation of Avalokita, also known as Avalokiteshwara, the Bodhisattva of Compassion. A bodhisattva is a person destined for enlightenment, reborn to serve other people. The Dalai Lama said he could not remember his 13 past lives as previous dalai lamas.

As usual during our interviews, I again asked the Dalai Lama -- who was older than me and now 57 -- if he achieved nirvana.

He replied:

"I think you may achieve it first, or before my age. Even a one month retreat is almost impossible now. When I recite some prayer, or remain in a secluded area with no contact with anyone for 24 hours, I still feel a mixture of happiness and sadness," because longer meditations are impossible. Since 1983, I don't think I've had much spiritual progress."

Despite Chinese efforts to control and crush Tibet's elaborate forms of Buddhism, many beliefs survived in Tibetans' daily lives.

When I rode a public bus across central Tibet on the

Chinese-built Friendship Highway during a one-month visit in 1999, the majority of passengers were Tibetans who occasionally burst into soft devotional singing, reminiscent of Native American Navajo chants. When the bus crossed a bridge over a river near the journey's mid-point between Xigatse and Lhasa, some Tibetans excitedly chanted, "Om mani padme hum" while others' prayers sounded like a sobbing of souls.

Most of the Tibetan passengers had planned for this moment.

They pulled out colorful rectangular tissues illustrated with woodblock-printed yantra illustrations and phrases to echo their prayers. They flung the printed tissues out the windows from the speeding bus, so the wind would spiral their prayers into the air and downward into the steep stone gorge below, where the river flowed.

Earlier that morning when we boarded the bus in Xigatse -- Tibet's second-biggest city, also known as Shigatse -- the passengers purchased inch-thick stacks of colored tissues from a Tibetan woman who was covered in sweaters against the chill. She sold paper prayers along with popcorn, soft drinks and other treats for the eight-hour journey.

While the passengers chanted, a filth-encrusted Tibetan mother repeatedly slapped her baby's forehead, trying to smash a fly. Failing to squash the bug, the mother pinched her wrinkled breast and shoved it into the baby's mouth. As the bus sped across dramatic, barren flatlands two miles high and wedged by gigantic mountains displaying vivid, geological traumas along the turbulent Brahmaputra River, the mother inspected her infant's stain-blackened T-shirt for lice. She scratched away tiny, hardened clusters of dirt and mucous from her child's nose, until one nostril bled.

Such poverty was quickly degrading some Tibetans' spiritual beliefs and rites.

In Lhasa, Tibetans wearing monks' robes wandered or sat on rough-hewn, gray stone-slabbed streets, chanting ancient scripture and asking for cash.

"Money, money, money," they begged while holding up fists of Chinese currency notes.

"Koochie, koochie, koochie," some asked in Tibetan language, describing a little charitable gift.

Some of these purported monks attracted cash by squatting in the street and blowing a horn made from a leg bone -- animal or human -- and twirling a drum constructed from a small skull. Others held up a cylindrical prayer wheel and gently made it spin.

"Some of the monks you see begging are not real monks, because real monks will never beg like that. There are some people who just put on robes and pretend, but at night they have a girl or gamble," a Tibetan said while standing next to the Jokhang Temple.

"They should not be turning a prayer wheel. A monk is supposed to know the prayers himself, and not have the prayer wheel say the prayers for him."

The Tibetan began describing his own life and said he stopped being a monk after five years because his monastery's senior lama beat novices with a stick during scripture examinations.

Tibetan Buddhist monasteries often meted out such child abuse.

During the Dalai Lama's time before he fled Tibet in 1959, head lamas in his Potala Palace beat errant monks for gambling or other naughty behavior. Today, some young monks in other monasteries in Tibet displayed scabbed bruises on their head.

In Drepung Monastery on the outskirts of Lhasa, I asked about the dark red, vertical scabs on a young monk's forehead. The robed young man nervously touched the gashes and replied sadly, "My teacher."

Despite all the emphasis on rituals, sacred texts and other spiritual lessons, in many ways Tibet's monasteries were often simply boarding schools. Sons were sent -- especially if the parents were too poor to properly feed, clothe and educate them -- whether or not the sons wanted to be clergymen. Many would drop out due to the beatings, the austere existence, or harassment by Chinese police.

"I quit the monastery because the Chinese were coming around asking the monks to say bad things about the Dalai Lama," the former monk said.

"Most monks would rather go to jail than say bad things about the Dalai Lama. Now there are many monks because Tibetans are very religious people, and when Tibetans pray, they offer food or money. When I was a monk, we had everything we needed. But now the Chinese don't let young children become monks. The Chinese say the children must go to school first and learn things. Only later can they be a monk. That is a good idea, but the Chinese actually just say that, so the Chinese can teach the children about Chinese politics and other things. So it is like a trick."

Free from his religious confines, he was now more interested in looking for "beautiful girls." Here in Lhasa, he was pursuing foreign females.

Suddenly, a Caucasian woman walked by, eagerly chatting with other travelers.

The former monk ecstatically whispered, "Do you think she can fall in love with me?"

He grinned and eased closer to her. He tried to talk to the group of tourists. He asked if they needed anything.

"Tibetans usually don't marry Chinese," he told me later. "Tibetans can marry Chinese, no problem. But if we do marry a Chinese girl, all the other Tibetans will say bad things, because actually we Tibetans hate the Chinese. But if I marry a foreign [non-Chinese] girl, the Tibetans will say that you are a lucky man.

"Tell me something, do the American girls like if the man talks to her about love? I had a European girl once and she was kissing me all over, here on my mouth and my neck and everywhere. Actually, Tibetan girls want to be sexy, but they are too shy. So I hope a foreign girl will help me. I left the monastery after five years because I wanted to live a more successful life. I wanted to do more things than just pray and study religion. I want to escape Tibet, but I don't have a lot of money. But at least now I have a good job.

"If I leave and go to Nepal or India, my life might be much worse because I wouldn't have any money at all. And I don't want to try and leave and get caught and be put in prison. Before [the Chinese invasion in] 1959, Tibetans were poorer. But they were happier. Now some have money, but they are unhappy. They are already thinking how to cheat the other one, or how much more money they can make.

"Tibetans are still poor. But some merchants have become rich. Tibetans who work with the Chinese, they can make some money. In some ways, things are better now because before 1959, Tibetans would just stay in the room and talk and talk. But now the market is open. Now Tibetans wake up early because they can sell things. They can do business."

Some Tibetan Buddhist nuns were also abandoning their strictures of how they should behave. During a visit to Lhasa's Ani Sangkhung Convent in 1999, four robed Tibetan Buddhist nuns in one of their residence chambers were so intrigued by my body hair that they loosened their vows and -- knowing no one else could see them -- repeatedly pet my forearm while offering cups of hot milk.

The nuns theatrically posed while trying on my hat.

They playfully engaged with me for hours and allowed me to photograph them reading my Tibetan-English language booklet.

Delightful, surprising, but politically extremely dangerous for all of us. It was evening when I left their chamber, strolled out the convent's entrance, and wandered into the night.

Several days later, a lama in a tiny rebuilt monastery near the center of Lhasa, tumbled three dice around in a cigarette box.

"I am telling this woman's fortune," the lama said, nodding toward a middle-aged Tibetan woman who gazed at him with eager, black eyes.

"I roll the dice to tell which prayer she should read, in this book, which she should say."

The lama pulled out another book and asked for help with his English lessons. His latest English vocabulary, written on a list in his own writing, read:

"Buddha. Temple. Prayer. Prostitution."

Prostitution?

The lama replied, "To bow down like this." He performed a typical Tibetan Buddhist prostration for praying.

Some Tibetan monks in Lhasa occasionally glided by as taxi passengers. Many monks who resided at big monasteries in and around Lhasa now wore new wool robes and strong shoes. They frequently displayed a carefree casualness, joking among themselves or with an occasional foreign visitor. A pair of young monks played with squirt guns on the flat roof of the Jokhang. Three monks at the Drepung Monastery teased each other, sometimes painfully, with a battery-powered shaver.

Cash crashed into their religion in other ways.

Chinese currency notes were plastered on Tibetan statues, shrines, temples, and monasteries. After receiving donations for telling fortunes, giving advice or offering blessings, monks were often seen counting stacked currency with the manual staccato dexterity of bank clerks. One of the most elaborate displays of money appeared inside the Potala Palace at the 5th Dalai Lama's stupa tomb where local and international donors plastered currency notes from various nations on its large circular platform.

The Dalai Lama fondly remembered the Potala as his center of power in Tibet. But by 1999, China had turned the stunning 1,000-room structure into a slick corporate logo.

In Lhasa's street markets, delicious jerky made of "yak meat, sugar, salt, cooking wine, sesame, chili and vegetable oil," appeared in hand-size packs illustrated with the photogenic Potala Palace above a picture of a hairy yak.

The label of Lhasa Beer included the Potala which also appeared on the brew's cardboard packing crates.

Department stores in front of the Potala sold attractive desk ornaments, including a plastic-framed photo of the palace, in matching design.

Chinese-made computers attracted customers by flashing advertisements showing a high-resolution picture of the sparkling, colorful Potala filling the screen.

Shops also sold big posters of the Potala alongside portraits of Hollywood film stars and Mao Zedong.

The ultimate blasphemy -- or commercial success -- appeared deep inside the Potala Palace where Tibetan Buddhist lamas formerly received religious offerings from devotees: the Potala now boasted a tacky, spacious, Chinese-run gift shop.

"When visiting the Potala Palace, the Sitting Room of the Red Palace is an ideal place for you to have a rest, as well as to do some shopping," said the store's sign, erected near exquisite Buddhist murals.

"Originally, this Sitting Room is used for laying offerings. Now it is used as a Sitting Room for the tourists to take a break." Glass display cases highlighted trinkets for sale.

Postcards published by China described the Potala Palace as "an awe-inspiring sight, a gem in China's cultural heritage and manifestation of the Tibetan laboring people's capability."

In official statements, the Chinese government heralded the Potala Palace as a magnificent trophy, "liberated" from Tibet's theocracy which had enabled generations of "reincarnated" dalai lamas ruled through a repressive, "superstitious" system.

All the palace's treasures and "Tibetan cultural relics" which had escaped looting were now displayed as evidence of how a wealthy "elite" of Tibetan Buddhist clergy and their political collaborators -- known as regents -- enjoyed unimaginable splendor while the Tibetan people suffered horrific poverty.

Chinese security forces watched visitors inside the Potala via CCTV. A similar system gazed into the Dalai Lama's nearby Norbulingka Summer Palace. A Chinese official sat in a nondescript, whitewashed stone annex of the Norbulingka told me, "I like living here," while he glanced at eight Panasonic screens.

Six of the screens showed rooms inside the Norbulingka,

including the ornately decorated main room and some halls. A seventh screen spied on an open doorway where ghostly black-and-white blurred imagery of a man appeared to chat with someone off-screen. The eighth screen displayed China's nationwide government TV broadcast.

Other monasteries, such as Sera near the sky funerals, allowed some traditional rituals to continue, including dramatic outdoor performances by monks engaging each other in loud, animated, Tibetan-language debates to test their rational and meditative wisdom.

Questions and answers between two excited, competing monks included:

"There is a horse with white hair. What is the color of that horse?"

When the other monk's answer was rejected as wrong, the first monk clapped his hands once and replied:

"No, the horse is not white. Inside it is red blood, and other colors!"

As a demerit, he gave the mistaken monk a gruff, mocking head rub.

On the other side of Sera Monastery's stone wall meanwhile, a few scattered vultures circled above, waiting for the next sky funeral on the flat boulder below.

HOLY SADHUS IN INDIA & NEPAL

"Soon, probably he starts smoking hemp -- for it is a curious fact that a large proportion of Indian mystics are addicted to this form of intoxication. Later, he becomes a paramahansa, which means a 'great goose,' and is the highest order of holy man."

~ Lowell Thomas, 1930

In India, some rituals occur deep in people's minds. Ash-covered sadhus twist their bodies into pretzelled positions or undergo grueling physical and mental stress to rapidly change their physical and spiritual perceptions. Sadhus try to free their imprisoned spirits from the shackles of their mortal bodies. They aim towards bliss. Unity with Hindu gods.

Along the Ganges River, a holy man will astound or repulse passersby by coiling his penis around a big stick, stretching all erogenous nerves past their breaking point, and brutally destroying his erotic fervor. The painful goal is to permanently banish sexual obsessions from causing distractions during deep meditation.

Aghori sadhus dwell in cemeteries and at cremation ghats, eating the flesh of human corpses and sometimes wearing a necklace made from an adult's or a baby's skull and bones. Other sadhus may claim that every 50 years they change into birds and fly to the Himalayas' highest caves to meditate.

Devotees say they witnessed a sadhu who awoke from deep meditation to discover birds nesting in his hair. He allowed them to live there and hatch eggs in the nest until they all flew away.

Countless sadhus sleep on nails, stab themselves with spikes, live in caves, or walk half-naked across India's cities, deserts, forests and glaciers. Survival is difficult. Family, fortune, physical comforts and ego must be abandoned. They wander as beggars in a land already swarming with desperate people pleading for alms.

Spiritual traditions of renouncing the material world can be traced back more than 4,000 years ago before the Vedic religion and Hinduism.

Sadhu Swami Jayaprakash Puri in the holy Hindu town of Hardwar along the Ganges River told me how to become a sadhu:

"You should have a guru who will give you every cultural

guidance, and teach you the way of eating, sleeping, living, preaching and worship. A guru will tell you not only about peace, but will give you protection. You will reside with him. He will know everything about you. You will know everything about him. I have been a sadhu for 15 years. Before that time, I was a student of economics in Dehra Dun. I completed my studies, but felt I was not a special man. I felt I was just like everyone else. I was cut off from humanity. Now, because I'm a sadhu, I am a special man."

Puri, 35, sat barefoot, bearded and wrapped in a long, pumpkin-colored cloth. When he spoke, nearby sadhus nodded in agreement. Sitting in a circle, they began passing around an upright, funnel-shaped, clay chillum pipe packed with hashish mixed with tobacco so the drug would burn with billowing smoke.

Many sadhus smoke hashish every day. Puri gestured towards the smoke-bellowing chillum, grinned, and said, "This is our enjoyment. You must be clear in your heart. I wander all over India. I also get food from other sadhus. I like being a sadhu."

He cheerfully took a massive hit from the pipe, held his breath, exhaled, and smiled. Proudly, he proclaimed:

"I smoke hashish, this is my need. Hashish is God's gift. God is faith."

He brought the pipe to his mouth again and inhaled more of the resin's bluish smoke.

"I am going for salvation. I think to myself, 'What is our soul? What is our heart? Our feet? Hands? And why do we feel angry and sleepiness?' These questions are the path to salvation."

Completing a third deep drag from the chillum, he passed it to the next sadhu.

After gazing at the tumbling water of the rushing Ganges, Puri said, "Our soul? From where all the light is coming, that is our soul. The destruction and creation of the universe, that is our soul. We do not know about everything. The one thing in possession of God is, we do not know what is 'time'. But time will come."

In earlier centuries, sadhus massacred each other by the thousands.

Some sadhu cliques fought each other to be the first to bathe in the Ganges at exact auspicious moments. The worst of these sadhu wars erupted in 1760 here in Hardwar. Worshipers of the Hindu god Shiva battled devotees of Vishnu, another Hindu god. Historians say thousands of sadhus were slaughtered before Shiva's side won.

As victors, Shiva Sadhus got to dip themselves in the Ganges' fast-flowing waters at special, foretold moments during the massively popular Kumbh Mela festivals. All the other holy men and everyone else had to wait until the Shiva Sadhus finished.

Devout Hindus believe bathing anywhere in the Ganges cleanses their sins, with startling effect. Bathing at Hardwar's fabled Har Ki Pauri human cremation ghat during a Kumbh Mela festival is said to bestow soul-purification equal to 1,000 horse sacrifices.

Unfortunately, after washing away so many people's sins, the Ganges retains too much evil from humans. The river's waters must then be spiritually cleansed. To purify the Ganges and make it sin-absorbent again, sadhus -- often naked -- and Hindu saints immerse themselves at key moments each year.

American author Mark Twain was stunned when he saw sadhus in India in 1895.

"There was a holy man who sat naked by the day, and by the week, on a cluster of iron spikes, and did not seem to mind it," Twain wrote in More Tramps Abroad.

"And another man who stood all day holding his withered arms motionless aloft, and was said to have been doing it for years. All these performers have a cloth on the ground beside them for receipt of contributions, and even the poorest of the poor give a trifle and hope that the sacrifice will be blessed to them. At last came a procession of naked holy people marching by and chanting, and I wrenched myself away."

In 1915, Mohandas "the Mahatma" Gandhi became irritated

at how sadhus had degenerated from Hinduism's lofty spiritual ideals and had formed decadent gangs competing with each other for power.

Gandhi wrote:

"The swarm of sadhus who descend on Hardwar seem to have been born to enjoy the good things in life."

During an auspicious time in 1954, sadhus were blocked from reaching the Ganges by the chaos of thousands of other pilgrims and devotees vying to wade in the river. Determined sadhus shoved their way forward with increasing force. People panicked. The resulting stampede killed at least 500 people, though many believe the toll was much higher.

To prevent such fatalities occurring again, police then began guarding the Ganges at specific sites in Hardwar and elsewhere during large gatherings, especially festivals which attract millions of Indians from across the nation. Police also try to keep sadhus from squabbling among themselves. Some sadhu factions however occasionally hurl cowshit or rocks at rival sadhus for the coveted right to bathe first.

No one knows how many loin-clothed sadhus are rambling across India. According to some Indian statistics, there appears to be more than one million. Most sadhus are male.

Anyone can declare himself to be a sadhu and worship in their own style. Such freedom means that the ranks of sadhus include schizophrenics and psychotics fueled by insane, manic inspiration and delirium. Other sadhus appear crazy simply from smoking so many chillums. Devious beggars loiter around Hindu temples, masquerading as sadhus to get fast cash from naive and pious believers.

The public is often shocked when they see a sadhu's head laying in the dirt. On closer inspection, witnesses realize he has buried his entire body up to his neck, in an effort to attract coin-tossing viewers. Is he a real sadhu? A fake? A madman? During eclipses, some sadhus ignore government warnings not to stare at the sun. They defiantly gaze up at the celestial corona because they fear the sun is being devoured by Rahu, a Vedic astrological planet that appears as a severed head in Hindu tradition. As a result of staring at an eclipse, some sadhus become permanently blind.

Near Puri and the others, a sadhu with his hair in matted tangles casually reclined on a bed of thick iron nails. Silently, he gestured to indicate baksheesh could be dropped in his coin-filled, dented aluminum bowl.

A few naked holymen, known as naga sadhus, soon arrived at the riverside and began smearing their skin with sanctified white ash. Naga means "snake" in Hindi and Sanskrit. When sadhus were warriors, naga sadhus were the fiercest. If nude nagas decide to plunge in the Ganges, nearby women are ordered not to look.

Another group of sadhus soon arrived, carrying aluminum bowls filled with dried cow manure. Each sadhu arranged several bowls of manure in a circle around himself. Someone lit a match and ignited the dung in each bowl. Each sadhu then sat cross-legged in the dirt in the center of his own flaming circle.

An extra bowl filled with dung was balanced on each sadhu's head and also lit. The sadhus then closed their eyes and meditated, surrounded by flames, capped by the flaming bowl atop their heads. The purpose of the ring of fire is to create intense heat, akin to being baked alive in a big oven.

Sadhus swear this extremely hot meditation is similar to a fever and, coupled with a deep religious trance, produces paramananda or "supreme pure bliss".

But despite smoking hashish and performing countless rituals to Hindu gods, some sadhus experience problems achieving any spiritual revolution at all.

"I am trying to be a sadhu but it is so difficult," a middle-aged Bengali holy man told me while sitting in the shade under a big tree, watching circles of fire being lit by other sadhus performing their extreme heat meditation.

"I tried walking barefoot. But I hurt my feet. So now I wear these tennis shoes. I pray to Shiva. I get money from begging. I even smoke hashish with the other sadhus so I can witness

God. But still I feel no liberation. And now I must make a pilgrimage up the Himalayas. My feet are killing me. My head hurts from the hashish. Mosquitoes bite me all the time. And I'm always hungry. Other sadhus are just laughing at me. I was a shopkeeper for 22 years in Calcutta, and now I am seeking. But I cannot transcend so easily."

Meanwhile in Kathmandu, the capital of Nepal, half-naked sadhus are so highly respected that they were allowed to join privileged guests witnessing the cremation in 2001 of nine murdered members of Nepal's royal family and the princely assassin.

"I saw them burn the king and queen and the others," Rada Kris Mudari, a 40-year-old sadhu told me at the Pashupati Temple complex where the cremation took place amid Hindu pagodas, shrines, and sadhu caves.

"It was not good when they burned them because the public was not allowed. Only the government people and the army people and us sadhus were here" during the mass royal cremations.

"But all people become like this," Mudari said, gesturing at a bleak row of flame-blackened cement funeral ghats.

The ghats are raised, rectangular platforms along the Bagmati River where most of Kathmandu's deceased -- royals and commoners -- are brought and cremated according to Hindu and Buddhist rites.

"The rich, when they die, do not take anything. They lose everything. Even the royal family do not take their palaces. They don't even take their names. They only take their karma," said bearded, turbaned, barefoot Mudari.

Another sadhu sitting nearby, white-bearded Bogindra Das, 55, told me:

"Unlike royal people or rich people, we sadhus don't need anything. We give up everything and are always in a peaceful place. Rich people live with money. Poor people live with God's name. So when rich people die, they don't have anything. But poor people, when they die, they have God. But we are all equal because anytime we can die. I've been here at Pashupati Temple for nine or 10 years. I have seen thousands and thousands of bodies burn.

"When a king burns, it is different. When royal people die, a lot of army people come here and they make music. When normal people burn, undertakers just put them on some wood and make a fire. Everybody has to go, even we sadhus have to go. We don't have to stay here on earth."

Asked if he would like to be a king instead of a sadhu, Das grinned, exposing a few missing teeth.

"I do not want to live like a king. I like to live this kind of sadhu life. A king is a king and he is a god in Nepal, but he also dies. I am a sadhu without money, but I don't worry about getting food. God takes care of everything, if I do good karma. I have been reincarnated many times, as many things, as animals and so on, and had many, many different lives. I cannot remember my past lives, but in the Hindu religion there are many powerful books and we have learnt about this. Earth is the place to do karma. We are coming naked into this world and going out naked.

"But it is better to be born a sadhu than a king, because a king is only a king of the public world. A sadhu is a king of kings, because when a king goes to learn about God, the king comes to the sadhu."

During the past few hundred years, Nepal's various monarchs, prime ministers and other rulers often turned away from the deadly intrigue of Kathmandu's treacherous politics and consulted sadhus and other holymen to find wisdom and bliss.

While the sadhus spoke, another holy man, Raday Das Biraghee, 42, quietly adorned his forehead with a thick splat of bright yellow powdered dye. Biraghee also covered his nearly naked body in white ash from the sadhus' camp fire, in keeping with ancient Hindu tradition which regards all ash as auspicious because it comes from fire, which is sacred.

Stroking his powder-speckled, bushy black beard, Biraghee

said:

"I agree with Bogindra Das, I also don't want to be a king in my next life, because a king has to take care of everyone, and has to look after rich people and poor people. A sadhu's life is better. A sadhu is carefree. A sadhu can go everywhere. When a king visits another place, he has to take bodyguards and look everywhere and worry. When a sadhu visits, he doesn't have to worry at all. If a sadhu wants to go to another country, such as India, and stay a long time, no problem. But if a king wants to go and stay a long time, it is a big problem."

Soon, the group of sadhus rose to look for food, which they got by begging from visitors at the Pashupati Temple complex. The sadhus strolled past the charred ghats where several people had been cremated earlier that day. Nearby, a few urchins sifted through the shallow Bagmati River's silt and water, looking for gold-filled teeth from cremated corpses, or perhaps a piece of jewelry. All the corpses' ashes, burnt bones, and other debris are shoved into the river after the flames of each cremation fire dies down.

As the sadhus disappeared behind a shrine, a group of casually dressed men arrived, carrying a dead person wrapped in bright orange cloth atop a stretcher. They carefully lifted the body off the stretcher and placed it on the cement steps which descend into the river next to the cremation site.

They began building a fresh wooden pyre.

Upriver from Pashupati, a sadhu named Jagannath Das lived in a tiny cave. Das told me why he liked his cave.

"I have small body. This place I live. I make meditation here. Many, many mantra. Very old mantra. Many gods. Sun, moon, earth is power. Sun, moon, earth is big power, no? Marijuana smoking is good. One chillum, two chillum, three chillum, four chillum. No matter how many marijuana, meditation good. Alcohol is fighting. Many, many people died. Marijuana is no fighting."

Das took off his white seashell bead necklace and held it up. He pointed at the necklace's elephant-headed Hindu god, carved from a small pink stone.

"This Ganesh. Elephant is big power. This is also mantra. It is very long story. Shiva and Shiva's son fighting. Shiva cutting Shiva's son, but no understand. Big fighting. Big power inside. After cut..."

Das gestured as if slashing his own throat.

"Cutting. After this, 'Oh cutting my son!' After this, elephant head come. Shiva story is very long story. Hindus have many, many stories.

This..."

He held up a big, old, brown hardcover book.

"This book. People read. Aum mani shanti. This book Sanskrit."

He pointed at a small green wooden door near the back of his cave.

"Kali inside. Want to see Kali?"

But before he could open the cabinet and display his statue of the Hindu goddess, two other sadhus entered the cave, changing the mood. One asked for tea.

Das said, "He can take tea with me anytime."

The sadhu then told Das, "It would be so much better with milk."

Das ignored the veiled request and silently poured two cups of plain tea, offering it to his guests.

The other sadhu began singing:

"Once when I was hungry / all I asked for was a rupee. / Once when I was hungry / all I asked was a rupee."

Das shook his head and said, "I am not the same as these other holy men. Today is good. Tomorrow is god's choice."

One famous sadhu who pushed his physical body to the extreme was Bhagwan Gopinath, born in 1898 in northern India's mountainous Kashmir.

He became a drug-ingesting visionary, revered by countless followers. Affectionately called Bhagwan Ji or Bhagwan Gopinath Ji, he achieved strange mystical states and national fame as a jivanmukta or "liberated soul" during the mid-20th century, resulting in his posthumous appearance on a three-rupee Indian postage stamp 100 years after his birth.

Starting in the 1930s, Bhagwan Ji often plunged into a deep hallucinatory stupor, which he and others interpreted as transcendental.

"The room and Bhagwan Ji's bed were covered with layers of dust which he would not allow to be swept," wrote his biographer Shri Shanker Nath Fotedar.

"Cob webs and spiders were also present in this room. During this period, a rat had bored a hole in one of the heels of his foot which had been there for a long time.

"He would sometimes take handfuls of datura, opium, panak and other intoxicants in this period of intense sadhana.

"At times, Bhagwan Ji would vomit basinfuls of blood, and his body was wholly swollen and he looked like a ghoul. On one occasion during this period, his sister reminded him of the intense suffering which they were undergoing and suggested to him to take up a worldly life. His reply, firm and direct was, 'Our boat is in the midst of an ocean, either both of us will land safely or get drowned'."

After seven years, "he came out of this great ordeal, clairvoyant and clairaudient, with full vision of the past, present and future. A siddha with a badly mauled body but a radiant soul."

Unlike some sadhus, he was not into sex.

"At 20, Bhagwan Ji's ways were becoming visibly godly," Fotedar wrote. "Some of his classmate companions, in order to test him, took him to a house of ill fame, which they visited to satisfy their carnal desires. They went to the woman's room by turns. Bhagwan Ji's turn came last of all.

"He went into her room and found her lying in a compromising position. Addressing her as a witch, he bade her stand up, administered her a rebuke and advised her to give up her sinful ways. Then he flung a rupee coin at her and left the room.

"He felt that it was all bliss. His companions had found bliss in illicit sex indulgence while he had found it in abstinence."

Bhagwan Ji also advised devotees to be celibate.

"Once, another man fell for the shapely legs of a lady, began to follow her, and stated that he tried to meet her. When he went to see Bhagwan Ji, the latter told him, 'What is the charm in fine legs? The whole body is food for Mahakala, the God of Death'."

A poem sung by devotees in Bhagwan Ji's honor emphasized his drug-filled chillum:

"Denying food for days and nights / He only kept his chillum live / And his mind got stamped with Om."

Bhagwan Ji's devotees insisted he ultimately realized "undecaying super bliss."

In a collection of scribbled "oracles," Bhagwan Ji explained his secret recipe for spiritual enlightenment:

"Throw your 'self' in the simmering cauldron of incessant mental discipline, and bake it fully as that of the 'super self.' With the fire of self-scrutiny from below, and the non-leaking lid above it, make the self fool-proof from any norm whatsoever. This delicacy of the 'self' needs to be prepared with the fragrant spicy salt of self-education. Be vigilant that nothing leaks out of it. This fully fried 'self' should be tasted by himself only. Otherwise, O my Sentience, what have you attained on coming into this world?"

Professor J. N. Sharma also wrote about Bhagwan Ji's legendary powers:

"He brought the dead back to life temporarily or permanently, as the situation demanded. Once he asked someone -- probably Mahakala, the God of Death -- to wait till the next day," so a man who had just then died could be brought back to life and attend his daughter's wedding.

"The man came back to life, blessed the newlywed couple, and died for good at about noon the next day.

"Once, two cooked fish, chewed and swallowed by Bhagwan Ji himself, were vomited by him in their original form, that is, as two live fish."

Another devotee wrote:

"In the last 30 years of his earthly existence, Bhagwan Ji would keep talking to invisible forces while he would be smoking his chillum. At times, he would not even respond to people around him. None dared disturb him while puffing his chillum with his eye turned skyward, emitting and receiving vibrations.

"In such planes of mystic exhilaration, natural propensities of human organs are said to reverse the roles, where the eyes can speak, the ears can see and the mouth can feel."

CALCUTTA'S DOM CASTE UNDERTAKERS

India's spiritual rituals also have a miserable downside for those who cannot escape Hinduism's traditions.

When Hindus die in India, regardless of how wealthy or high caste they are, only impoverished and scorned Untouchable caste Doms can prepare the cremation fire and prod the smoldering corpse to ensure it burns.

Doms are even allowed to facilitate the last rites of Hinduism's highest Brahmin caste members, but Doms have been forced for generations to remain trapped into being India's undertakers. They are widely despised and discriminated against.

Except at the gates of death.

"We think Doms are lowly because the work they do is unsophisticated," Rajiv Prakash, a middle-class Hindu told me in his Calcutta shop where he sold home appliances.

"I would not marry a Dom. I cannot go against society like that. I think it is wrong, there should not be Untouchables, and they should not be treated like that. But if I marry a Dom, I would suffer and be rejected by my society. Even if I love the girl, if I came to know she is a Dom, I would break it off," Prakash said.

Madhab Ghosh, a Toshiba salesman from Bangladesh visiting Prakash's shop agreed and said Hindus can identify a Dom even if the person lies about their caste.

"A Dom would not be able to conceal their caste. You would know from the way they dress that they are a low caste. Or the way they talk would not be so intellectual."

The Indian government meanwhile has officially tried to end "caste discrimination" but the problem remains widespread.

"The president of India was an Untouchable," Ghosh said. He was referring to the 1997 election of 76-year-old K. R. Narayanan to the largely ceremonial role. Narayanan was India's first Untouchable caste president.

"I could marry his daughter, but that's because it would be different. Because if it were the president's daughter, people would forget that she was an Untouchable," Ghosh said.

"But I cannot be a rebel against millions of Hindus in India. If I wanted to be like that, it is better I go to America or Germany or some place. Even I know it is wrong, it is already inside my brain. It is like with computers. There is ROM and RAM inside. I would not accept a glass of water from a Dom. I would say, 'I am not thirsty' so as not to hurt their heart. If I were alone, OK, I might take it. But not if someone could see me. Because then my circle would reject me. I can't help it. You cannot go against your society."

Foreigners who happen to die while holidaying or working in India are often given by their embassies to the Doms, who see that the corpse is neatly stacked atop wooden logs of a funeral ghat in whatever city the foreigner happens to die in, or placed in a modern "electric crematorium" if one is available nearby.

Foreigners' relatives who oppose cremations, or want the body sent back to their country of origin, can pay airlines expensive fees to ship the corpse home in a sealed coffin. Less costly is to send an urn of ashes by air freight.

"I am a Dom, my work is dead bodies," Sham Sharma, 22, told me while a funeral began in Calcutta's squalid cremation zone at Kali Ghat.

"I burn bodies every day. In one day, maybe five bodies. My uncle, father and my grandfather are Doms and they also burn bodies. I don't know how many bodies I've burnt. In my life, maybe 2,000 bodies?

"I'm working here six years. My only one problem is money. I like working here. No money, then it's not good. Money, it is then alright. I collect the bodies and put here. And do everything. People say, 'He is Dom. Very, very good. Here is a dead body, come here.'"

As he spoke, a relatively rich group of men arrived. Twelve of them carried a bamboo stretcher which supported the body of an elderly woman.

She had been tied to the stretcher's green bamboo slats, so she would not slide off when the small procession walked to the ghat.

A Brahmin priest offered instructions to the men on how they should perform age-old Hindu funeral rituals.

The eldest son, bare-chested and head freshly shaved as required by the rites, picked up a red clay pot of nearby Hooghly River water and poured it over his mother's corpse.

The son's "thread" -- a white string worn throughout life and slung diagonally across his chest and back, from shoulder to waist -- showed he was a Brahmin.

The woman on the stretcher had been wrapped in a blue sari, concealing all but her wrinkled face.

Her dead mouth was open.

The family quietly fussed over her. They removed a bright marigold cloth which was emblazoned Hare Krishna, Hare Ram repeatedly printed in red ink.

The son sprinkled flower petals upon her. He watched as nearby Doms built a rectangular pyre from heavy logs on a outdoor platform, topped by brown coconuts.

"She was 90 years old," one of the mourners whispered to me.

"She is Mrs. Singh. She died a natural death. From old age."

Mourners then hoisted her atop the pyre. Someone moved

the green bamboo stretcher away, so it could be used again.

Someone else poured clarified butter, known as ghee, over her body as a combustible fluid.

The priest invoked prayers. Someone lit incense sticks and stuck them nearby into the dirt.

One Dom handed the eldest son a cluster of long reeds, which the son lit.

Under verbal coaching from the Dom, the son used the flaming sticks to ignite the pyre, starting at the base of the logs near the woman's feet.

If the corpse had been male, the son would light the pyre near its head.

The Dom then gathered a big cluster of reeds, lit them, and randomly stabbed them in among the pyre's logs to ensure the fire would spread.

He directed the eldest son to raise his hands and pray.

The mourners, all male, walked around the pyre seven times while praying and then quickly moved away as thick coils of smoke emerged.

Other Doms stuffed more brown coconuts into the stack of logs, to help it burn. Unlike the well-dressed mourners, the Doms were clad in filthy, ripped, patched clothing.

They picked up more reeds, broke them into shorter pieces, and jabbed them into the pyre as kindling. As the flames rose, Doms poked at the pyre with long poles to increase the heat.

Mourners retreated to the shade of the ghat's mildew-covered pavilions.

"We give the Doms 500 or 300 rupees to do all this. It is from our satisfaction," one of the mourners, Soumen Bose, told me.

"Like when you tip a bearer [waiter] in a restaurant."

Five Doms now concentrated on ensuring the fire burned with intensity. They squatted on their haunches in the dirt, feeding more reeds into the flames.

Meanwhile, an argument erupted among some Dom women near another pavilion.

A policeman guarding the ghat began shouting at them and menacingly waved his bamboo lathi stick. A frightened male Dom appeared from inside the pavilion, yelling at the angry women.

"The Doms are having a fight," said Sankar Mitra, another mourner.

"Some monetary matter, I think. These Doms are paid by the government's Municipal Corporation. But the women are saying to that Dom, 'You are coming here to work, but this is our ghat.' The man is denying."

The man, now intimidated by the pack of aggressively shrieking female Doms dressed in dirty saris, fled past Mrs. Singh's cremation fire and disappeared.

Another mourner, V. K. Bansal, introduced himself to me.

"I am a general manager of Hindustan Motors. It is a Birla company. This dead woman is also my boss's mother.

"The Doms are expert in burning the bodies, where to place the wood, and how to fill the gaps. They make sure the body is burnt. How long it will take depends on the weight of the body. Normally, two to three hours. The bulky man takes longer. Lean or thin men and women, less time.

"The Doms are granting service to us. Their ancestral people were doing the same work."

According to Hinduism's ancient discriminatory caste system, Doms are so low they are considered "outcastes" and are among the members of other "Untouchables," collectively also known as Harijans or Dalits.

Hinduism professes a person's place in society is determined by their karma, a force Hindus and Buddhists believe is generated by a person's behavior -- transmigrating with the person after death to determine their reincarnation.

Devout Hindus believe they are unable to escape their fate no matter how much money they earn or where in India they live or even if you disguise your caste, become an atheist, or convert to a different religion.

Hindu fundamentalists often complain that Christians,

Muslims and others lure Untouchables and low-caste Hindus to convert by promising a life free from such discrimination.

Internationally acclaimed Indian author M. J. Akbar wrote:

"Every Untouchable is, consciously or unconsciously, reviled, but why is the Dom hated with a particular venom? The accusations are endless: he is permanently drunk, he gambles while the dead are still burning, he haggles and extorts over the price of lighting the fire, he sells blood.

"What can the Dom do? Death is his business, and if he had another he would gladly go to it. He too survives by the laws of supply and demand. And if he can bargain his way towards a better price, if he can pressurize you when you are secretly anxious to get over this unpleasant business of last rites, he will do it.

"The Dom, however, has learnt that he has a certain power which he can wield for a few minutes at each man's death, and he is not afraid to use that power, and to drink his money and die of that drink if he wants to."

Some Doms also allegedly profit from illegally selling skeletons to medical students and others in the United States, Japan and Europe, according to exporters in Calcutta.

They claim some Doms illegally purchase bodies who no one claims, bury the corpses in limestone to remove the flesh, and then dig them up a couple of weeks later to boil and bleach the bones. The skeleton of a fetus fetches a higher price than the intact bones of an adult.

After most funerals, Doms give the deceased's ashes to relatives. Devout Hindus usually try to have the ashes poured into the Ganges River where it flows past the holy city of Varanasi near where two tributaries, the Varana and Asi rivers, join the Ganges at the city's northern and southern edges.

Varanasi is also known as Benares or Kashi the City of Light, symbolizing Hindus' belief that it has the ability to bestow enlightenment.

More than 70 fabled ghats are available for funeral pyres along the Ganges at Varanasi. Despite partly-burnt corpses and other gruesome debris constantly being shoved into the river, countless Hindus descend the ghats' stone stairways which lead into the Ganges, wade fully clothed and perform a sanctifying bath. With cupped hands, they gather the river's water and slowly pour it out through their fingers, symbolically offering the sacred fluid to their ancestors.

The Ganges is revered as a living "mother goddess," spiritually cleansing anyone who soaks in its waters. This includes the ashes of the dead.

Many Hindus yearn to be cremated in Varanasi because they believe the location's holiness will free them from samsara, the repetitious cycle of life and death. That promise of transcendence and freedom after death, known as moksha, attracts diseased and elderly pilgrims who move to the crowded ancient city to die.

Those devotees are jivan muktas, who are "liberated while still alive." No matter how many days, weeks, months or years they linger without dying, they must resist leaving Varanasi on holiday or business. If they die elsewhere, it would deprive them of the maximum spiritual benefits they would have accrued if they had died in Varanasi.

Hindus who are not cremated in Varanasi, often try to arrange for Doms to burn them somewhere else along the Ganges to attain some of its spiritual cleansing. Failing that, their relatives or friends can bring a dead person's ashes to the river.

If no other alternative is possible, some people send ashes to Varanasi by parcel post to be scattered in the Ganges.

CHAPTER 2 ~ KILLERS

JAMPA PHUNTSOK & TIBET'S ARMED REBELLION

The Tibetans' enthusiasm for the lifestyle and freedom they enjoyed through Buddhism sometimes erupted into violence, often in unpredictable ways.

When Chinese communist troops began crushing a Tibetan uprising in the streets of Lhasa in 1959, one of the Dalai Lama's devoted lamas, Jampa Phuntsok, decided to defy his Buddhist vows and do the unthinkable.

He intentionally became a killer.

With the sounds of gunfire echoing in Lhasa's streets below, Jampa knelt in prayer in the Dalai Lama's throne room deep inside the Potala Palace. The young monk vowed he would try to stop the Chinese. Then he stripped off his monk's robes.

Jampa picked up an old rifle and started his new role as a horse-riding guerrilla, fighting in bloody ambushes across Tibet's harsh mountainous countryside. Virtually unknown to the outside world, the story of Jampa's spiritual and political revolution is, in some ways, a vivid portrait of Tibet's current struggle. In the eyes of the Dalai Lama and other Tibetans, Jampa became one of the greatest leaders in their quest to regain independence.

Born in 1927 into a wealthy family, Jampa was often rebellious and chafed at his parents' decision to send him to a Buddhist monastery to become a monk.

"I'd rather stay home with my parents and help farm our

land," he told his closest friends. Jampa was proud of their 100-acre estate on Lhasa's outskirts and the legacy of his great-grandfather Phuyul Damdul, a brave politician who had helped loosen eastern Tibet from Chinese control.

"My great-grandfather, who was my mother's mother's father, was Phuyul Damdul. He fought against the Chinese during the time of the previous Dalai Lama, the 13th Dalai Lama," Jampa told me with the help of a Tibetan-English translator at the Dalai Lama's Namgyal Monastery in McLeod Ganj where Jampa was sheltering since his release from prison in Tibet.

"A Tibetan general named Trimon sought the help of my great-grandfather, who was one of the top ministers of Nagrong district, to help fight against the Chinese. But the Chinese received help from [Tibetan] Khampa traitors who were bandits willing to assist the Chinese, because the Khampas wanted to rob Khanze and Dhargyal monasteries.

"Great-grandfather Phuyul was also a Khampa. He was in charge of Nagrong's defense. He organized the local soldiers, and joined General Trimon's army. Phuyul led his forces on horseback. His soldiers were also on horseback or on foot and armed with Chinese-made single-shot rifles. Together with General Trimon's army, they fought for three days and defeated the Chinese.

"Because of Phuyul's bravery, the government of Tibet, at that time, gave my great-grandfather's family a large tract of land. In Phenpo. Near Lhasa. As a reward for his bravery and service to the nation. They also gave him a certificate about his bravery which says whenever Tibet's independence is threatened, the sons of this family should render their services. I have four brothers. Our parents always told us it is our duty to give up our lives in the service of the nation against its enemies."

The certificate was to become prophetic.

During those long ago years, China's Manchu emperors enforced their influence over much of Tibet, at least until the

Qing Dynasty in Beijing was overthrown in 1911.

"As a child, I would imagine Phuyul on horse-back with the other warriors, and think of him having super courage, a sort of superman whose bravery no one could match. I thought of him riding with his hat on, handsome on horseback and fighting.

"My relatives admired his warrior tradition and the use of guns more than I did, because when I was eight years old, in 1935, I joined the monastery at the Dalai Lama's Potala Palace in Lhasa. Phenpo is just north of Lhasa, four hours by bus along a winding road. I didn't have much time anymore to daydream about Phuyul. And it is very out of the ordinary for a monk to daydream about using rifles.

"Actually, I simply wanted to stay with my mother on the land and did not want to join the monastery. All five of us brothers were made to be monks by our parents. My father had a relative in the Potala Palace who was a monk, so I was sent there under the Dalai Lama's care because I was the eldest. All five of us boys were sent to various monasteries because Tibet's tradition teaches that it is good to send your sons to monasteries and devote them to religious life.

"My one sister stayed home with our parents. She later spent 10 years in jail. Today she lives in our home, on our land in Phenpo. My parents were farmers and also traveled to nomadic camps looking after the animals. My father would bring firewood home or to our relatives. We were the richest of the 23 families in our area. We were a wealthy family.

"I was not very happy to go to the monastery. But one thing that forced me to go is when my mother told us that our ancestors, including Phuyul Damdul, committed a lot of sins so we must go and read the scriptures to serve the spiritual welfare of our parents and ancestors. Phuyul killed a lot of people, which is a sin in Buddhism. My mother was deeply religious and she believed Phuyul had sinned even though he was fighting for Tibet. Today, however, I no longer agree and I think he led a glorious life and did the right things.

"At the age of eight I went into the Potala Palace as a

student. But I did not have a desire to join the monastery and lead a religious life. I even ran away many times, beginning when I was 13 years old. My teacher eventually handed me to the monastery's disciplinarian who, when I was 16, gave me the first whipping of my life.

"He gave me 25 lashes with a thin, black, braided leather whip. We call the person who whips children in the monastery a gaygur. The word gay means teacher and the word gur means discipline. They are much feared in all monasteries, even today. Even the 6th Dalai Lama was whipped by his own special teacher.

"Our gaygur, who was named Tseten, was appointed by the Dalai Lama and he was a gigantic figure with a special robe that had padded shoulders which made him look even more ferocious. He had a dark face, and was tall and slim. We children in the monastery liked to prove our courage by not crying during a whipping.

"The disciplinarian only wanted to give me five lashes to make me cry. But because I didn't cry, he whipped me 25 times. Still I didn't cry. But he stopped at 25. My parents had never whipped me. So then I went to my relative, who was also my teacher in the monastery, and said, 'I don't want to stay in the monastery because of the whipping'. I showed him the sores on my buttocks. He ignored my pleas.

"But soon, I suddenly began studying very well and in one year I was able to learn the whole course of scriptures by rote and to recite the prayers. I think it was because I realized there was no possibility that I would be able to go home, because I would just be returned to the monastery. So I thought I might as well study. Also I was becoming older."

Jampa's defiance, even in pain, had started. He grew more religious as he matured and practiced Tibet's unusual form of scholastic debate.

"When I was 17, I started becoming deeply religious. This was because I was studying lamrin, which is the way, or purpose, of Buddhism. My teacher was the [14th] Dalai Lama's junior tutor, Trijang Rinpoche.

"Lamrin teaches you how to train the mind. Actually, I began understanding the true meaning of religion when I was in [a Chinese] prison and suffering. When I was being tortured, starved and forced to do physical labor, then I understood what my great teachers meant.

"At the monastery, I was a good student but one of the naughtiest monks in the monastery. The naughtiest thing I did was gamble with cards and dice, which is not allowed. It is very rare for a monk to do this.

"I was a monk, but did not become a lama. A lama has the power to reincarnate himself as he wishes. Everyone else, including monks and even non-Buddhists, is reincarnated according to our deeds. A monk can become a lama by dedication to religion and gain this power."

In 1950, China began enforcing its claim on Tibet. In 1957, a popular revolt in eastern Tibet against China's rule was crushed amid reports of Chinese atrocities. Jampa worried his life as a monk in the Potala might soon be disrupted. He heard news that Chinese forces were relentlessly crushing any Tibetan resistance and, after the Chinese military secured outposts and supply lines, were moving westward towards Lhasa.

"By 1959, when the Tibetan uprising against the Chinese began, I was 32 and deeply devoted. I had been taught to play the long Tibetan horn, called a gyaling, and to create the sacred sand mandala. In 1959, my attitude about the Dalai Lama was the same as it is today -- the Dalai Lama is the ultimate savior and leader for this life and for future lives. He is the gonkep. The word gon means something you place above your head. The word kep means the person who saves you from crisis, trouble and all problems.

"I also have a special attachment to the Dalai Lama because since I was a small child I saw him in the Potala Palace and talked with him. During my meditations, I studied the teachings of all 14 dalai lamas and their history. I feel he is unique and different from all other people."

Tibetans staged an armed revolt against the Chinese in Lhasa in 1959. Jampa looked out over the 17th century Potala's fortress-like walls and saw Tibetans armed with knives, sticks and stones assault communist Chinese military positions while Chinese troops rushed through Lhasa's narrow lanes and gunned them down.

Suddenly, the Chinese fired artillery at the Potala, at nearby Sera Monastery and other holy buildings. Chinese forces seized Lhasa's government ministries, factories, shops, schools and offices. Armed with rocket launchers, assault rifles, grenades, bandoleers of bullets and anything else designed to kill, the Chinese soon turned Lhasa into an armed camp.

When Tibetans dared to go outside their stone hovels and farm houses, they were greeted by green-uniformed Peoples Liberation Army troops ready for war, lined up with loaded weapons slung across their backs. Sounds of occasional gunfire and radios blasting Chinese music and propaganda echoed in the rock-walled streets.

This 1959 Lhasa uprising was apparently sparked by the Chinese authorities' request for the Dalai Lama to attend a cultural show. Ominously, they told the Dalai Lama to arrive without his bodyguards. Fear swept the Potala Palace. The invitation was interpreted as a plot to kidnap and possible execute the Dalai Lama. Suspecting the Chinese could seize him even if he did not attend, the Dalai Lama prepared to flee his homeland.

Terrified monks rushed to Jampa and told him the Dalai Lama was soon going to escape to India disguised as a commoner. They begged Jampa to escape with them, even though amid the snowy peaks along their exit route, Chinese troops continued to slaughter Tibetans.

Jampa, despite being a Buddhist monk grounded in non-violence, wanted to stay and fight the Chinese.

He considered a shocking scenario. Should he break his Buddhist vows?

Kill as many Chinese as he could?

Jampa knew he would suffer inevitable punishments in Hell as described in Tibetan Buddhist scripture for having committed such deadly sins, in spite of his intention to save Tibet and the Dalai Lama.

Jampa could not foresee an estimated one million Tibetans would eventually perish in the long years after China's takeover. But he predicted Chinese communists would enforce their ban on religion by imprisoning and executing lamas and monks, and Beijing would force all Tibetans to pledge allegiance not to Buddha but to Mao.

"In 1950, before Chinese troops reached Lhasa, they began invading from eastern Tibet. So the government of Tibet sent monks from Sera, Drepung and Ganden monasteries, about 30 or 40 monks from each monastery, to Chamdo, capital of eastern Tibet to join the Tibetan government's army and fight the Chinese," Jampa said.

"I was hoping they would also send monks from the Potala Palace's monastery because I wanted to volunteer to fight. The feeling I had was that I heard the Chinese were against religion and they would kill the Tibetan monks, destroy the monasteries and kill the religious teachers.

"So I had no anguished doubts about my decision to give up my vows and take up arms even though in my future lives I would be reborn among the lower levels of life, such as animals, or in the world of suffering creatures or in Hell. But I thought this would mean only one person's life, my life, would be destroyed and if I did sacrifice myself, I would be able to save countless monks' lives and they would be able to continue teaching Buddhism for generations and generations.

"I felt that even though I would be reborn among the lower levels of life, my action would amount to saving an entire religion. I did not have many mental problems about my decision. My only thought was to face the Chinese and stop them so the purpose of my being a Tibetan would be served. I thought I must get a gun and kill the Chinese invaders and this would serve the purpose of my being a Tibetan."

He knew by heart the texts in The Tibetan Book of the Dead, which describe how the Lord of Death will grab such a sinner and "cut off his head, extract his heart, pull out his intestines, eat his brain, drink his blood, devour his flesh and gnaw his bones".

"The Dalai Lama had already left the palace and was traveling to India, so I did not have a special conversation with him about my decision to pick up a gun. Instead, I went and prostrated three times before the Dalai Lama's empty throne and I spoke my heart for the cause of Buddhism and Tibet's independence. Then I asked the Dalai Lama to please kindly forgive me for giving up my vows."

In the dim firelight of the Potala's butter lamps, Jampa then took off his maroon woolen robe and changed into civilian clothes.

Jampa told other monks about an armory of ancient weapons stored in the Potala Palace's basement. But most of the monks withdrew to follow the Dalai Lama's caravan. Only a small group accompanied Jampa into the dark, musty cellars. They removed dirt-encrusted rifles, swords and other outdated weaponry.

Jampa knew they were no match for China's well-organized People's Liberation Army. But he distributed the inadequate weapons to rouse the monks to fight, and he hoped to get better weapons very soon. Grasping a rifle for the first time, the monks were unsure how to shoot.

Through the palace's windows they could see Chinese troops storming the Potala's walls and entrances, hunting for the Dalai Lama. Some monks were so frightened by the loud explosions and falling masonry that they dropped their guns and fled. Even Jampa was alarmed when he watched the Chinese troops advance.

"I thought the Chinese were cowards and we could kill them easily. But the Chinese troops were attacking. Never retreating. They were courageous. Tibetans were forced to retreat by the sheer number of Chinese soldiers. We weren't able to defend the Potala for very long."

A messenger told the monks the Dalai Lama had safely escaped Lhasa. Elated, Jampa decided their tiny group should leave the Potala before it was completely cut off. They would regroup later and attack Chinese convoys and outlying camps. To engage the Chinese army in the capital now would be suicidal.

Several weeks later, Jampa was no longer recognizable. He traded his clothes for a traditional horseman's outfit. He would now wear a brown woolen knee-length chuba coat, fur hat, and tall leather riding boots.

Like many Tibetan warriors, he protected himself from bullets by wearing a gau amulet box, slung on a leather strap across the left side of his body. Inside the box, two small statues of protector deities included a traditional blessing from the Dalai Lama, written in gold ink.

Jampa now saw himself as a guerrilla. He brandished a rifle and galloped alongside other Tibetans across the rugged moonscapes and forests of Tibet.

"There was a highway robber called Samphal and he collected a large gang. Together we rode our horses across the countryside fighting the Chinese. We had tents and all the utensils and extra horses to carry our rations and equipment. There were 150 in my group. They were 100 monks from various monasteries, plus some lay Tibetans and soldiers. Also included were five or six bandits. Many in my band died."

Jampa and the other rebels used hit-and-run tactics. He believed the Dalai Lama protected him through supernatural powers. Jampa said he never suffered major injury in any fighting. And he felt he was also fulfilling his great-grandfather's tradition to defend their homeland.

"I fought the Chinese until 1960. I killed about 30 Chinese. But I'm not sure the total number, because I don't know how many I killed in battle. I'm very sorry to tell you now that I felt satisfaction when I was killing Chinese. I know as a monk I should not tell you, but honestly, I feel I achieved something and I wished I could kill more Chinese.

"We divided ourselves into units of 100. I was appointed the gyapon, or leader, of one unit."

The duty of the gyapon was to carry out decisions arrived at the guerrillas' secret meetings in consultation with other gyapons. They planned which units should attack, how many rebels should be there, where they should fight, and other things. A gyapon also had to "inspire those under him, maintain discipline, and lead them on."

America was opposed to the spread of Chinese communism into Tibet and supported some Tibetan guerrillas from 1957 to 1971. The secret CIA program also helped Tibetan insurgents launch raids from camps in Nepal. US-trained Tibetan guerrillas never won much territory. Lhasa was never vulnerable to their attacks which hit scattered Chinese targets in the countryside. Jampa said he heard about those CIA-backed insurgents at the time, but insisted he never met them.

Meanwhile, the Dalai Lama and 80,000 refugees had fled on foot and horseback across the Himalayas and gained sanctuary in India. But part of the blame for why the outside world soon abandoned Tibet's cause may be because of India's then-Prime Minister Jawaharlal Nehru.

During the 1950s, Nehru was said to have warned America and other Western governments not to condemn China's invasion of Tibet. Nehru may have feared Washington's support for any anti-Chinese Tibetans would tar Tibet's independence struggle as an artificial US-orchestrated effort.

Nehru's increasingly confused policy of mutual coexistence failed abysmally when India, in embarrassing disgrace, lost a brief war against China in 1962. Beijing claimed the Himalayan territory it seized -- along Tibet's east and west -- had been wrongly mapped as part of India by British colonialists.

Meanwhile during March 1960, Jampa surrendered and was jailed.

"I went to surrender because the Chinese caught my family and were going to torture them if I didn't. I thought it was better that I suffer, rather than they.

"Anyway, I was almost out of ammunition, and my rebel group of 100 fighters was now reduced to me and four friends. The others had been killed or seriously wounded. So I explained to the other four why I was going to surrender. I said to them, 'You don't have to surrender with me if you don't want to'.

"But the four others also agreed to surrender. So we and the Chinese arranged it. The Chinese were waiting for us in a building in Lhasa. As we approached, a Chinese officer shouted, 'Give up your guns.'

"We dropped our guns immediately.

"The Chinese officer then shook our hands and said, 'It will be better if you now also give us all the information about your past activities, and about all the other rebels fighting against the Chinese in Tibet.'

"I replied: 'I am just a cook for these rebels, I don't know anything. No one really knows much about the other rebels because they are fighting in different locations without much communication.'

"The Chinese officer then threw a big party for me, my four friends who surrendered, and all of my relatives who were released. But after that night, the Chinese would come to my home every day and force me to undergo long, hard interrogations.

"Actually, I didn't give up all my weapons when I surrendered. I hid more than I gave them. I hid the weapons with the family of my younger brother.

"While the daily interrogation sessions at my home continued, I also heard there was fresh fighting by Tibetans against the Chinese in the north, in Ata Zolma, about 10 days' horse ride from Lhasa. So I secretly planned to join the rebels with some other Tibetans in Lhasa and get my hidden weapons. But this plan was leaked to the Chinese and they arrested me and nine other people, including my three brothers.

"I think the leak happened because one of my friends who was going north with me happened to tell his relatives, and one of his relatives leaked the plan to the Chinese. So they threw us all in jail.

"Before the Chinese invasion, mine was a large and very prosperous family. But after I involved myself in the independence struggle, everything was lost.

"In my family of six brothers and sisters, the eldest, a sister, spent 10 years in jail. The Chinese starved my two younger brothers to death in labor camps in Kongpo in 1961. Another brother spent eight years in prison. My youngest brother spent 18 years in prison.

"My own tortures were beyond any human imagination. Beatings, forced starvation, and shocked with electric cattle prods on my hands and electric shocks inside my mouth. And slave labor."

Jampa said one of his most daring exploits occurred during the start of his long years of imprisonment in Lhundup Prison. Four Tibetans in the prison had been sentenced to die for fighting the Chinese. They were depressed and frightened. Jampa told some of the other Tibetan political prisoners in Lhundup, those he could really trust, of his plan. When they all lined up to go to the toilet later that day, Jampa would jump one of the guards and grab his gun.

That would signal all the other political prisoners to do the same and fight the Chinese inside the jail.

"I told my friends, 'I don't mind dying for this.' But when the four Tibetans who were scheduled to die heard of my plan, they vetoed it saying, 'Don't do it. You can't win. It will cause not only your death, but also the death of countless other prisoners. And we four will also be executed afterwards anyway. It won't be any kind of a success'."

So instead, Jampa secretly taught inmates in Lhundup Prison the ways of Buddhism whenever he could. But they had to be careful. Usually, the Chinese forbade all prisoners from talking. If a prisoner spoke a few words to another prisoner, the guards would demand to know what was spoken.

"The most embarrassing torture I suffered is when we male

prisoners were made to stand naked and the women prisoners were also made to stand naked opposite us. The feeling of shame for me as a monk was worse than the beatings.

"The guards ordered us all to undress and to stand with our hands at our side and not cover ourselves up. We had to stand like that for one hour. Never in my life as a monk did I imagine such shameful things would be done to people. There were 100 male prisoners and 30 female prisoners. The shyness we felt was too much."

In 1976, Beijing broadcast an announcement:

Mao is dead.

Mao's fanatic Red Guard then began to fight among themselves, jealous of each other and greedy to show their own superior adherence and adoration of "Mao Zedong Thought."

Jampa, still behind bars, became hopeful when told of Mao's death, and the subsequent correcting of some of the communists' leftist extremes. Those extremes had been enforced by Mao's widow, the fanatical Jiang Qing, who was reviled among Chinese as The White-Boned Demon. She and her three top associates were being denounced by the post-Mao regime as the Gang of Four.

Some of the evils of Mao's Cultural Revolution, which began in 1966, ended with his death.

China then came under the influence of Deng Xiaoping, praised by the West as a "human sparkplug" who ignited the economy by allowing Chinese to profit and foreigners to do business. Deng claimed he wanted better relations with the West.

In Tibet, some of Mao's harshest policies slowly eased. Food became more plentiful. Some animals were returned to farmers and, after many years of restrictions, Tibetan farmers were allowed to let them graze and privately sell some of their produce. But under Deng, families still labored to meet quotas on the amount of goods they had to produce, before being allowed to sell the excess for personal profit. Quota failures resulted in fines.

Many Tibetan women, who could afford it, traditionally had braided their thick, black hair with precious turquoise, coral and silver jewelry. Under Mao's rule, they barely had money for cheap plastic buttons or tin for decoration. After Mao died, Tibetans became slightly more prosperous but still restricted to communist "work units" which controlled what jobs they could have, where they could live, who they could befriend, and a myriad of other restrictions.

Thousands of Tibetans continued to escape across the border to freedom in Nepal and India.

During his imprisonment in the 1970s, Jampa spent much of his time secretly arranging an underground network of activists. Most of his informants were inside Tibet's jails.

They reported the identities of arrested Tibetans to him, as well as their alleged crimes, incidents of torture and whether they had been executed. Jampa helped smuggle this news from his prison cell to the Dalai Lama who was now settled in self-exile in northern India.

As Jampa's experience grew, so did his reputation among inmates. They trusted him with more names and details. Jampa and other prisoners compiled lists of inmates throughout Tibet each week. Jampa had been a cook in several jails for many years, and much of this information was passed through his secret network of other prison cooks.

"After I was jailed, I was tortured many, many times. But one of my tortures occurred because of a funny misunderstanding. In 1971 or 1972, I was working in the jail as a cook for the prisoners. I had to make a fire. To get wood, I went to get the wood shavings left over by the jail's carpenters. I asked permission from the Chinese guards to let me go to get the wood. The guards ignored me and did not respond, so I went anyway and got the wood shavings and started a fire.

"Suddenly, the guards started yelling at me and beating me with a long stick. One guard said to me in Chinese, 'You went to get wood? Are you trying to defy me?' But I misunderstood his Chinese language and thought he said, 'You were trying to run away.' So I repeated some of the words which he was yelling because I was trying to say that I wasn't trying to run away. But actually what I was repeating meant, 'Yes, I am defying you.' So he kept beating me and yelling at me!

"And every time he yelled, 'Are you trying to defy me?' I would repeat it back to him, not knowing what it really meant. So he kept on beating me! This went on and on until another guard stopped him and cleared up the problem.

"One of the worst tortures came two or three months after I was first caught. After I surrendered, I was tied by my hands from the ceiling in Lhundup Prison on the outskirts of Lhasa, and the Chinese guards beat me while demanding I confess to killing soldiers from the Peoples Liberation Army.

"I feared I would be killed by these Chinese and my biggest worry was that I would die and, even though I believed Tibet would one day become independent again, I would never get to see the Dalai Lama again. So I didn't give up.

"The guards beating me said, 'You committed a crime.' But I told them, 'We fought the Chinese in our own land because you came to enslave our people.' After beating me with sticks and kicking me with their boots for 20 minutes, they stopped and untied me.

"The lowest, darkest moment in my life in jail came not when I was being tortured but when the Chinese instigated my fellow Tibetan prisoners against me. When I was a cook, I hated the Chinese so much that when I discovered that the Chinese prisoners had hidden some pork in a kitchen cabinet, I went and quarreled with the Chinese prisoners about hiding it from the rest of us hungry prisoners. Then I put the pork in the food and served it to the Tibetan prisoners.

"Afterwards, the Chinese guards abused me and got the Tibetan prisoners angry at me also, and some Tibetan prisoners even spoke against me, complaining that I was serving food stolen from the Chinese. I felt I was doing it for the welfare of the Tibetan prisoners, but when my fellow Tibetans spoke against me after being instigated by the Chinese, I felt miserable.

"But in all my years of jail and torture, I never thought about committing suicide because the many years of study I had as a monk helped me face my problems."

In 1978, after 18 years in prison, the authorities released Jampa.

Freed, he began working more extensively with the network of political prisoners and activists he had helped set up over the years. They met in groups of two or three at a time. They feared raising suspicion. A year earlier, China boasted to the world that Buddhism was allowed to return to Tibet.

Jampa and others smuggled word out that the Chinese permitted only a token, skeletal staff of lamas carefully screened by communists. Genuine religious teaching and practice were still considered subversive.

A few monks and nuns sometimes went on pilgrimage to various parts of Tibet. From there, they sneaked across the border to Nepal and India. During those years, they often carried Jampa's messages with them. If his reports were especially sensitive, they memorized the news to prevent discovery along their route.

Tibetan activists used his reports to counter China's international propaganda which claimed no one in Tibet was being tortured or unfairly imprisoned.

In 1979, one year after his release from prison, security forces re-arrested Jampa.

He had "shown affection" for the Dalai Lama, because Jampa offered a few apples to the Dalai Lama's brother, Lobsang Samten, who was visiting Tibet on an official fact-finding mission.

After the delegates departed, the Chinese ordered Jampa to attend one of their political group thamdzin "struggle meetings" where people were publicly denounced and humiliated. They labeled him an incorrigible "black hat" and sent him back to prison.

In 1988, Jampa was again released.

He was still in a revolutionary mood. On March 3, wearing

the maroon robe of a Buddhist monk, he joined a huge crowd in front of Lhasa's Jokhang Temple. He listened to Chinese officials proclaim no Tibetans opposed China's ownership of Tibet. Jampa figured this annual Monlam Festival was a perfect opportunity to prove to the attending international guests that he and other Tibetans still wanted to kick the Chinese out.

Monlam or "Great Prayer" was a week-long festival, enjoyed since ancient times. It begins just after the Tibetan New Year in February or March. Before 1950, the festival in Lhasa included an invocation to the Bodhisattva Maitreya, the future Buddha. This was acted out by Tibetans carrying a statue of Buddha through the streets, circling the Jokhang Temple.

Tibet's official State Oracle would then enter a trance and predict the country's future. The Oracle also chanted prayers for the Dalai Lama's long life. After 1950, all those activities were banned.

Jampa said he thought at the time, "We can't have an Oracle tell the future of Tibet anymore. The Oracle was banned. So, I will be like an oracle. I will tell the future by shouting for Tibet's independence, and shouting for a long life for the Dalai Lama."

Jampa quietly blended in with the large gathering of monks and others attending the official program. Proud Chinese sat alongside compliant Tibetans and curious foreign delegations. In the center of this stately gathering, Jampa suddenly stood up. Alone. He raised his fist in the air and shouted:

"Long live Tibet's independence!"

"Long live the Dalai Lama!

"Remove the Chinese from Tibet!"

Stunned foreign correspondents temporarily permitted to be in Tibet for the festival, focused cameras on the Tibetan monk and scribbled his words.

Chinese officials were enraged. But they did not want to grab and drag him away in front of international guests. A public scuffle would make the situation worse for the authorities.

They let him run away. Police decided to wait until after the festivities were finished before arresting him.

But two days after his solitary voice rang out, many Tibetans in Lhasa, partly inspired by Jampa, staged one of the largest independence demonstrations in recent Tibetan history. Their fury attracted more than 10,000 Tibetans who participated in three days of demonstrations and street clashes against the Chinese, according to Western eyewitnesses.

The Tibetan Center for Human Rights and Democracy described Jampa's activities. Headquartered in Dharamsala, India and staffed by self-exiled Tibetans, one of the center's Prisoners of Tibet reports said:

"On March 3, 1988, the third Monlam Festival was held in Lhasa since the Liberalization Policy was introduced. Due to the earlier demonstrations and the subsequent killings, arrests and detention of monks and nuns, religious institutions were reluctant to attend the festival, as it was not a true representation of 'Freedom of Religion.'

"Finally, the PRC (People's Republic of China) got the high lamas to come, thereby getting the monks from the three seats: Sera, Drepung and Ganden and other smaller monasteries to join in as well. Although the number was much less than usual, Monlam was organized. However, fearing threat of demonstration during such a large gathering, hundreds of Chinese armed police and PSB (Public Security Bureau) officers were prepared to suppress a possible protest.

"On March 3, Jampa Phuntsok, a monk from Tashichoeling Monastery, stood up amongst the crowd and shouting, 'Tibet is an independent country,' 'Tibet belongs to Tibetans; and 'Chinese must go back to China.' Jampa was not arrested that day, as it would have provoked other monks to join him. The monks did not participate because they did not want Monlam to be disrupted mid-way," Prisoners of Tibet said.

During subsequent street clashes, at least 20 Tibetans and three Chinese were killed. More than 2,500 Tibetans were arrested.

When frantic police finally found and seized Jampa on March 17, he told them:

"I know the worst that can come to me now will be my death. But I don't care. Because that would be better than the tortures of imprisonment. And actually, I'm not afraid of either, so do whatever you want with me."

Jampa again joined an incarcerated population which in 1988 had swollen to 10,000 Tibetans including 3,000 to 4,000 political prisoners, according to Amnesty International in London and New York-based Asia Watch [which spelt his name "Jampa Phuntsog" in its 1994 report titled, Detained in China and Tibet: Directory of Political and Religious Prisoners].

When I asked Amnesty International about Jampa, they replied:

"Jampa Phuntsok is known to Amnesty International, and during his detention was considered by our organization to be a Prisoner of Conscience held solely for the peaceful exercise of the right to freedom of conscience and expression."

Jampa's third stint behind bars lasted from March 1988 to March 1991. When he was released once again, Jampa's fellow prisoners and other Tibetans implored him to flee to India. They told him to make contact with the Dalai Lama and others, and speak about the suffering inflicted by the Chinese.

Jampa was reluctant to leave Tibet. He told his friends he wanted to stay and continue to demonstrate -- even though he knew it would again result in a prison sentence. His friends warned him the Chinese had run out of patience. Beijing knew he was a ringleader, organizing political dissidents inside jails. His friends predicted the Chinese would probably not imprison him.

Instead, they would probably find some pretext to kill him and make his death appear as an accident. Jampa's friends convinced him he could now do much more for the independence struggle from outside his homeland.

After languishing a total of more than 26 years in wretched prisons, Jampa fled Tibet. He arrived at the headquarters of Tibet's government-in-exile in McLeod Ganj where the Dalai Lama publicly hailed him for his "strength of spirit and determination."

The Dalai Lama provided Jampa with a small room in mountaintop Namgyal Monastery, a short stroll from the Dalai Lama's residence. Jampa asked for work and was allowed to take care of the monastery's Dhukhor Lhakhang Prayer Hall.

As a koh nyer, or caretaker, he cleaned the prayer hall, waxed the wooden floor, and watched over visitors who came to view the hall's gorgeous Tibetan religious tanka paintings. The hall also displayed a raised throne for the Dalai Lama who taught the monastery's monks and lamas. They sat on the floor on six rows of flat, maroon cloth cushions.

The now-elderly Jampa often fingered brown prayer beads during our interviews while wearing a maroon sweater and maroon pants. When Jampa became cold in the evenings, he draped himself with a patched, dark maroon, quilted cape, occasionally coughing.

His face -- wrinkled, ruddy and browned by the sun -- appeared sparky and energetic. His large protruding ears, slightly sunken cheeks and eyes with diagonally drooping lids gave him the appearance of being sad and happy at the same time.

His bleak one-room living quarters in the monastery offered pale yellow walls and a cement floor. Quilts and blankets covered two single beds. The ceiling's bare light bulb was the only illumination.

On the shelves, a framed photograph of the Dalai Lama, plastic flowers, an alarm clock, some prayer books wrapped in saffron-colored cotton cloth, a few aluminum cooking pots, small boxes of food, a black portable radio and two flashlights competed for space. A small dish filled with glowing chunks of coal provided heat. Keys dangled on a red string hanging from a nail in the wall.

From the shelf, Jampa took a bundle of papers, letters and documents wrapped in a cheap yellow nylon scarf.

He kept a simple, hardcover notebook in which he sometimes wrote about his life. He looked up a detail in this book during one of our interviews. The room's one door, painted orange and with a padlock, was usually kept open and a large rectangular cloth hung over the entrance.

His wall adjoined the prayer hall. Pilgrims who walked a clockwise ambulation around a nearby shrine had to pass by Jampa's door and his corner windows. They sometimes offered him prayers of thanks.

Worried about his friends still in jail, Jampa continued his political work. His stream of visitors from Tibet included monks, nuns, businessmen and rural folk. They had arrived with instructions to seek out Jampa and relay the latest news about Tibet's gulag and the political situation. In return, he updated them about the Dalai Lama and the latest statements by foreign governments, human rights groups, international media and others who focused on Tibet's political prisoners. Jampa asked his visitors to pass on messages to activists inside Tibet, enabling prisoners, their families and the public to stay informed.

Jampa advised them:

"The best way for you to help Tibet is by following the Dalai Lama's teachings and continue working for Tibet's freedom. If we Tibetans don't raise our voices, if Tibetans don't stand and shout, the attitude of the outside world will be that all things are well under the Chinese. We have learned, the hard way, that we must struggle."

Jampa's secret prison network provided valuable insight. He filed his reports to international human rights groups, including Amnesty International.

In letters he arranged to be smuggled back into Tibet, Jampa wrote:

"To you freedom fighters in prison whose courage and determination equals that of the Lord Buddha, and whose sacrifices will be recorded by the Tibetan people, I express my solidarity. To those freedom fighters who are in hospitals and incapacitated by the Chinese, look upon your sacrifices as the highest contribution to your motherland. And to all people in Tibet, pray for the reunion of the Tibetans in exile with the

Tibetans in Tibet. Do not get discouraged by the torture and long imprisonment. Keep your spirits up."

And to Tibet's population he wrote: "Keep staging peaceful demonstrations against the Chinese."

During our interviews conducted in 1993, Jampa said:

"Tibetans are still coming out of Tibet and when they come here to the Dalai Lama's monastery, many of them also visit me. I tell them about the struggle being waged by the Dalai Lama and how he is saving our culture and seeking international help for the cause of Tibet, because not many of the people coming from Tibet are aware of everything that is being done. Whenever people come visit me from Lhasa, I personally try to do them all kinds of favors -- which in reality hardly amounts to anything -- in the hope that they will feel indebted to follow what I tell them, once they go back to Tibet.

"My staying here at this monastery is also an inspiration to the many political prisoners and activists inside Tibet. Most Tibetans in Lhasa know about me, and when they find out that the Dalai Lama is taking care of me, it is an inspiration for other political prisoners in Tibet who then realize their sacrifices and struggles will not go unnoticed. I still keep in touch with my fellow political prisoners who are jailed in Tibet.

"I also send my fellow political prisoners the blessings of the Dalai Lama in the form of 'blessing pills' and 'blessing threads.' The 'blessing pills' are made of herbs and are tiny. If they are not blessed by the Dalai Lama, they have no medical value."

Jampa then displayed a vial of tiny BB-sized, brownish pills.

"After they have been blessed by the Dalai Lama, they can help you. When you feel bad, you eat them and you will have peace of mind. 'Blessing threads' are woven threads which the Dalai Lama has blessed and they also help you and protect you. I send thousands of 'blessing pills' to Tibet every year.

"I have joined with other former political prisoners who are here in India and we stay in contact with about 100 political prisoners inside Tibet.

"To sustain myself during the worst times of my

imprisonment, I told myself, 'At least I know the Dalai Lama is alive and if he is alive, everything is fine. Ultimately the Chinese will have to give up Tibet and leave. I must stay alive in this prison so one day I can meet my surviving relatives. When I am free, it will be wonderful. I will go on a meditation retreat, live like a hermit and practice Buddhism.'

"By coming here to McLeod Ganj in India, I have met the Dalai Lama and got his blessing, which is the most important thing in my life.

"Many Tibetans were inspired by me, especially by my standing up and shouting in 1988. Because I am an old monk and I stand up, it inspires younger monks. And if the Chinese want to launch a crackdown, they will go for the ringleaders, so I want to save the younger monks from punishment. The monks from Ganden Monastery near Lhasa staged a demonstration against the Chinese the day after I did. I didn't call on them to do so, but by my standing up, I staged a precedent."

Later, Jampa became gloomy and told me:

"I have lost my faith in violence. China is a nation of millions and no matter how many people you kill, there will be more. They don't care how many people they sacrifice to achieve their goals.

"I feel useless here with the Dalai Lama feeding me. I often have the feeling I should go back to Tibet so I can contribute. I nurture a feeling to go back to Tibet and stage a demonstration again with some of my friends and monks. I'm willing to die. I always feel my dead body should come out of their prison. I've told this to the Chinese to their face. I told them I'm not satisfied, because Deng Xiaoping said, 'Tibetans are useless and worthless people.' I told them, 'I'll prove what is our worth'."

Among Jampa's visitors at the Dalai Lama's monastery was fellow prison inmate Lhakpa Tsering, a shy young Tibetan man with a pimply, ruddy face.

After saying thanks to Jampa, Lhakpa told me in Tibetan language during an interview:

"I am 22 years old now. I am originally from Toelung, near Lhasa, about half an hour away by bus. Jampa and I were together in Sangyip Prison in Lhasa in 1990.

"I was in jail for two years, from March 7, 1988 to March 7, 1990 because I took part in a demonstration during March 5, 6 and 7, 1988 in Lhasa. That was when the Chinese imposed martial law. The worst torture I suffered was the Chinese system of beating the joints of your limbs so there's no outward sign of blood or anything, but it incapacitates you for your entire life. I can't sit like you, cross-legged.

"I was a student at a middle school. I wanted to be a civil servant. My parents are farmers. Poor. I heard of Jampa for the first time after I came to prison. He was in the Central Prison in 1988 and before he was transferred to Sangyip Prison, I heard he was the one who started the 1988 demonstrations.

"I was curious what kind of a man he was and I wanted to meet him. My first impression of him was that he was very lean and in ragged clothes, but I admired him because I thought he was not an ordinary man and he had the strength to work hard. I never saw Jampa beaten or heard him being beaten, but I heard him challenging the Chinese officials and I admired what Jampa told them.

"For example, the chief guard of Sangyip Prison happened to be a Tibetan working for the Chinese who knew Jampa from a previous prison.

This chief guard said to Jampa, 'Why can't you lead a happy life at the Tashi Choeling Monastery [behind Sera Monastery] in Lhasa? Why did you come here to suffer?' Jampa replied, 'It is true I was very happy at Tashi Choeling Monastery with all the provisions given to me by the Tibetan people. But the reason I'm in prison is because the Tibetan people, including the Tibetans working for the Chinese, don't enjoy equal rights with the Chinese and it makes me very sad. That's why I left Tashi Choeling Monastery and demanded that right. You shouldn't think you are the ultimate boss. You are just like a puppet and there are Chinese officials who give you orders. So, in fact, you are like us, a servant to the Chinese. And don't feel proud to be a servant.'

"The chief guard couldn't answer, and from then on he let Jampa do his prayers and didn't force him to line up for food, and let Jampa request the other prisoners to bring him food because Jampa's physical condition was poor. The other Tibetan guards also avoided Jampa because they didn't want to face his argument.

"In Sangyip Prison, Jampa and I were in the same block. I was assigned by the prison as a Tibetan teacher to the other prisoners and I often passed Jampa's cell. Jampa asked me if I could read and write.

"I told him I was a teacher, and Jampa said, 'Come into my cell.' Jampa closed the door and told me, 'List the prisoners names, age, duration of imprisonment and places they come from.'

"Jampa told me he planned to send the list to the Dalai Lama because the Chinese may be lying about the number of political prisoners, or other Tibetans might say they were in this prison and tell lies about us. We made a list of Sangyip and other prisons which we knew about such as Drapchi, Seitru, and Gutsa. We prepared the list together and I left it with Jampa.

"Another time, on the birthday of the Dalai Lama, we prisoners couldn't celebrate. So Jampa told all the prisoners who were literate to compose poems praising the Dalai Lama. Jampa collected them and sent them through his sources to the Dalai Lama. Jampa knew the Chinese were going to celebrate May 23, 1991 as the 40th anniversary of their so-called 'liberation' of Tibet.

"Jampa told the prisoners they should demonstrate on that day in the prisons and mark it as 40 years of slavery by China. Jampa told me to prepare many postcard-sized leaflets with that message, for public distribution. I did, using four carbon papers layered together.

"I remember once, when a prisoner's father died, Jampa told the prisoner to use it as an excuse to put a prayer flag on a hill where prisoners in Sangyip and two other prisons could see it. Usually, prayer flags -- which are like the tree of life for us -- were banned," Lhakpa said.

"Jampa also told the prisoner to explain to the Chinese that six prisoners were needed to put up the flag, according to tradition. Jampa then told the six to use the occasion as an excuse to make little religious statues. So they made 600 statues of Buddha and of the goddess Tara and distributed them to the prisoners in Sangyip and other prisons."

TONY "POE" POSHEPNY, CIA IN LAOS

America's Central Intelligence Agency actively supported the failed guerrilla war in Tibet against the Chinese, and the defeated Dalai Lama's escape to India, with training, weapons and cash. Years later, the CIA moved into Laos, Cambodia and Vietnam during the US wars in those three countries, all of which also ended in failure. But unlike Tibet, the regional Vietnam War included direct, deadly roles by Americans on the ground.

In Laos, the macabre CIA paramilitary officer Anthony A. Poshepny became infamous because he demanded -- and paid for -- dead Lao communists' ears and their chopped-off heads.

Poshepny, popularly known as Tony Poe, said he dropped some of those human heads onto America's enemies while flying over his targets. He also boasted about impaling communists' heads on spikes in the jungles of Laos and joining his tribal fighters in celebratory tribal dances around the dead heads of the vanquished.

"I threw two heads from an airplane, it was a Dornier plane. The heads landed right in that [Lao] bastard's front door. We were flying at 100 feet," Poe, laughing, told me in his loud, tough, gravelly voice in the living room of his San Francisco home in May 2001.

Whose heads?

"Any [communist] Pathet Lao or someone else we didn't like. I had a bunch of heads in my hut and the blood was seeping through the floor. It was sticky. And [CIA officer] Bill Lair said, 'Get rid of those goddamn heads'."

Poe gleefully described how he also let his ethnic minority Hmong guerrillas celebrate in their stronghold deep in the jungle of northern Laos.

"These people are animists. After fighting, they had to have a ceremony. They'd put the heads on bamboo stakes and did a traditional dance around the heads, and throw pebbles at the heads. To show they were victorious."

Poe would also explain why he personally executed Vietnamese doctors who he imprisoned in a hole in the jungle even though they begged to defect from the communists.

The loquacious Poe said he rewarded his Hmong guerrillas when they brought in, as he demanded, the sliced-off ears of communists killed by the Hmong. It was Poe's way to confirm his Hmong fighters were not lying.

He paid them for each ear. But Poe soon demanded the hacked-off head of each enemy, as much more reliable proof.

After several years based in the rugged highlands of Laos where he was seriously wounded three times, Poe grew angry at attempts by senior CIA and American Embassy officers to control his activities. In response to US officials' complaints that Poe's gruesome behavior was counterproductive, he sent a bag filled with his Lao enemies' ears to the CIA station in Vientiane, capital of Laos. Poe wanted to prove his Hmong guerrillas were successfully killing communists.

The unopened bag arrived on a Friday and sat in the CIA's office over the weekend, he said.

"The ears were putrid. I shouldn't have done it because the secretary opened it up and she went crazy. The ears were in cellophane. They dried right up. You know, ears are mostly water. The human body is 80 percent water. And those cellophane-wrapped ears, they dried right up and were small."

Poe said he cut off the ears of enemy Japanese years earlier on the island of Iwo Jima. Throughout the world's history, some troops have collected body parts as grotesque souvenirs or weird talismans.

"We cut the ears off in World War II with a K-bar [knife] at Iwo."

Poe insisted during our interview that his motive in Laos was to kill communists by any means possible while relying on his more than 20,000 Hmong fighters.

Poe wasn't shy about describing how he ordered the amputation of ears and decapitations in Laos. When asked, he readily admitted committing those horrific acts.

"I used to collect ears," a cheerful Poe was quoted telling Roger Warner. Warner's book about Laos titled, Shooting at the Moon, won Washington's Overseas Press Club award.

"I had a big, green, reinforced cellophane bag as you walked up my steps. I'd tell my [Hmong] people to put them [ears] in, and then I'd staple them to this 5,000 kip [Lao currency] notice that this [ear] was paid for already, and put them in the bag and send them to Vientiane with the report.

"Sent them only once or twice, and then the goddamn office girls were sick for a week. Putrid when they opened up the envelope.

"Some guy in the office, he told me, 'Jeez, don't ever do that again. These goddamn women don't know anything about this shit, and they throw up all over the place.'

"I still collected them, until one day I went out on an inspection trip...and I saw this little [Hmong] kid out there, he's only about 12, and he had no ears. And I asked, 'What the hell happened to this guy?'

"Somebody said, 'Tony, he heard you were paying for ears. His daddy cut his ears off. For the 5,000 kip'," Poe said.

"Oh, that pissed me off," Poe told Warner.

In his 2007 book, Legacy of Ashes: The History of the CIA, Pulitzer Prize-winner Tim Weiner wrote:

"Poe told his [Hmong] grunts to cut off the ears of the men they killed as proof of their victories in battle.

"In the summer of 1965, he brought them to the CIA station in Vientiane and dumped them on the deputy chief's desk.

"Jim Lilley was the unfortunate recipient. If Tony Poe wanted to shock the new Ivy League big shot, he succeeded.

"Lilley had signed up with the CIA fresh out of Yale in 1951. He joined the Far East division and spent the Korean War dropping agents into China and being swindled by Chinese Nationalists. He would go on to serve in Beijing, first as the station chief, then as the American ambassador," Weiner wrote.

Lilley, the 1965-1967 deputy CIA station chief in Laos, was based in the capital Vientiane under US Embassy cover and said about Poe:

"People questioned whether he was killing as many Pathet Lao as he said. And so he did this thing with cutting off their ears and sending us a bag with their ears," Lilley said, laughing nervously during an interview in the documentary film, The Most Secret Place on Earth, written by Tom Vater and Marc Eberle.

"There was a move to accelerate the CIA involvement [in Laos], and they pulled in some of their best paramilitary officers. Bill Lair is the man who started the program, [also] Pat Landry, Tony Poe, Vint Lawrence. They were very good at this kind of work. And they came in, and they were the core of building up the CIA presence," Lilley said.

Air America pilot Charlie Weitz said in the documentary that he liked Poe.

"Uh, he had a couple of heads, yeah. Had a couple of heads," Weitz said.

"But when I was in Indonesia, I worked in Kalimantan, and there were headhunters there. We used to go up to their huts, and they would show us how they had the shrunken heads. But yeah, Tony did, he had a couple. But he was an ears man," Weitz said, laughing.

According to The Wall Street Journal, Poe said:

"As for dropping human heads on enemy villages, I only did it twice in my career -- including once on a Lao ally who had been flirting with the communists. I caught hell for that."

When Poe worked for the CIA, some people considered him mentally unsound.

"Obnoxious."

"A drunk."

An insubordinate "knuckle-dragger."

But the heavy-drinking, stocky Poe inspired strong loyalty and admiration among other Americans and Hmong who knew him.

"The posting of decapitated heads obviously sent a powerful message -- especially to North Vietnamese troops seeking to invade the homelands of the Hmong and Laotian people," Philip Smith, executive director of the Washington-based Center for Public Policy Analysis said in an email to me shortly after Poe died on June 27, 2003 aged 78 in the San Francisco Veterans Medical Center following a long illness.

Poe had suffered shrapnel and other wounds, diabetes and circulatory problems. His funeral was held in nearby Sonoma, California. He was survived by his Lao-American wife Sheng Ly, and their children Usanee, Domrongsin, Maria and Catherine.

Poe had twice won a CIA Star -- the agency's highest award -- from directors Allen Dulles in 1959 and William Colby in 1975.

"He successfully fought terror with terror," Smith said.

"He strove to instill courage and respect in the tribal and indigenous forces that he recruited and trained, as well as fear in the enemy. In the post-September 11th security environment, fearless men like Tony Poe are what America needs to combat and counter terrorism and the new unconventional threat that America faces from abroad in exotic and uncharted lands.

"Over the years, I have worked closely -- in various capacities -- with many senior American military and clandestine leaders involved in Laos during the Vietnam War including William

Colby, former DCI [Director of Central Intelligence]; Theodore Shackley, former CIA Station Chief, Laos; Douglas Blaufarb, former CIA Station Chief, Laos; Larry Devlin, former CIA Station Chief, Laos; and others.

"Tony Poe epitomized what the late Theodore Shackley, former CIA Station Chief in Laos, called the 'Third Option'. America -- to avoid the potential twin options of using nuclear or conventional forces to defend its interests -- should instead rely on special, elite clandestine forces to recruit, train and arm indigenous, or tribal forces, to project power, protect its interests and counter guerrilla movements, terrorism or other attacks.

"Clearly, Tony Poe symbolized America's decision to exercise its 'Third Option' in Laos," Smith said.

Born on September 18, 1924 in Long Beach, California, much of Poe's legacy would be deposited in unmarked graves half a world away, in Asia.

Poe joined the Marines in 1942. He was wounded fighting against Japanese on Iwo Jima and received two Purple Hearts. An argumentative, intense, short-tempered patriot, he joined the CIA as a paramilitary officer in 1951.

"Within weeks, he was running sabotage teams behind enemy lines in Korea. He and former CIA colleagues say Poe went on to train anti-communists in Thailand, to foment a failed coup in Indonesia and to help organize the escape of the Dalai Lama from Tibet in 1959," The Wall Street Journal reported in 2000.

During the 1950-1953 Korean War, Poe went to Korea with the CIA and "worked with the Chondogyo church group, a sort of animist-Christian sect that had fled North Korea and were being trained to be sent back across the 38th parallel," according to University of Georgia history professor William M. Leary.

"At the end of the Korean War, Tony was one of eight [CIA] case officers who were sent to Thailand. He remained there for five years, serving under Walt Kuzmak who ran the CIA cover company, Sea Supply," said Leary in a message posted on a condolence website honoring Poe.

In 1958, Poe said he and fellow CIA operative Pat Landry tried and failed to spark a coup by Indonesia's dissident colonels against leftist then-President Sukarno.

Outgunned and trapped on Indonesia's Sumatra island, Poe and Landry fled by a fishing trawler which took them to a waiting US submarine, according to the book titled, Feet to the Fire, by Kenneth Conboy and James Morrison.

Poe and the CIA also trained Tibet's tall, tough, minority ethnic Khampas and Ambos at Camp Hale in Colorado's Rocky Mountains in 1959 to help the nonviolent Dalai Lama escape, and then to fight against the Chinese People's Liberation Army.

"The Khampas and the Ambos came into Lhasa to the Dalai Lama, and the Dalai Lama didn't know who they were and couldn't speak the same language," Poe said, according to Conboy and Morrison.

"And the Khampas and Ambos told the Dalai Lama, 'You have to leave.'

"And the Dalai Lama didn't believe them. And they told the Dalai Lama, 'The Chinese are right behind us. Right outside the city'."

Soon, "using a hand-cranked Morse radio, Athar, a member of the US-trained Tibetan resistance, sent a message to Washington asking for political asylum in India for the Dalai Lama," Patrick French reported in The Daily Telegraph in 1998.

"Four hours later, the CIA's man in New Delhi sent a wire back to Washington saying that the Indian Prime Minister Jawaharlal Nehru had granted asylum to the Dalai Lama and his entourage."

In July 1959, four months after the Dalai Lama escaped, "the CIA began using C-130s, flying from a secret CIA base in Takhli, Thailand, to airdrop arms, ammunition and US-trained Tibetans into their occupied homeland," Newsweek reported in 1999.

Nine out of every 10 guerrillas who parachuted into Tibet were killed by the Chinese or committed suicide to evade capture, according to the Smithsonian Institution's Air & Space Magazine.

"The Tibetans loved their guns. They slept with them at night, right beside them. So I taught the Tibetans to sleep with their guns pointed at the door, so if someone came in, they could wake up and shoot them," Poe said according to Conboy and Morrison.

"In Camp Hale, we trained the Tibetans with two mules. And those goddamn mules kept kicking me and biting me. So I smacked them with a board, not on the bone, only on the flesh. And that subdued them.

"We showed the Tibetans the Viva Zapata film. Anthony Quinn played Zapata's brother. And he said he could look someone right in the eye and tell right away if he was a bastard. I took that as my own personal leadership style. And the Tibetans loved that movie. They adapted it to their own situation. Here was a person fighting," for their own way of life, Poe said.

"One of the Tibetans, after seeing the Zapata movie, made a hat just like Zapata, out of newspaper and he wore it," while at Camp Hale.

"The Tibetans are lazy. They are spineless, like the Lao. It was the Khampas and the Ambo who did the fighting.

"We had trained the Tibetans to pick locks. During an ambush, they found a guy who had a briefcase attached to his hand," Poe said, gesturing as if something was manacled to his wrist.

"They got the papers out and when we looked at them, we realized they were the Chinese plans for the invasion of India. We told the Indians. This was 1960. But they didn't believe us. The Indians thought we were trying to turn India against China for our own purposes."

The documents revealed Chinese troops would invade India overland along the Himalayan border.

"There was a cliff. It was straight up, and the Indians said it was impossible for the Chinese to come that way. But the

Chinese did it. They built ladders up the cliff and attacked and captured" a large number of Indian troops, Poe said according to the book.

The India-China border war lasted one month in 1962, ending with a Chinese victory.

The CIA's training and parachuting Tibetans into Tibet during secret flights was "like throwing meat into the mouth of a tiger," said Bapa Legshay who, in 1998, was the only known surviving Tibetan member of the first mission.

"We had made up our minds to die. We had been given cyanide capsules so that we wouldn't be caught alive by the Chinese," French quoted him as saying.

Some confidential CIA documents from the 1950s indicated the Tibetans previously expected America and China to fight against each other in a World War III.

"The Tibetans believe that their only hope lies in a policy of delay and playing for time until a world war or a major conflict between the United States and Communist China develops," said a declassified confidential CIA document written before the Dalai Lama fled.

"They have hesitated to send the Dalai Lama to India for fear that the Indian Government would turn him over to the Chinese."

Another document indicated some American analysts also perceived China was preparing for communism's international expansion through warfare. It said:

"The objective of the [Chinese] invasion is to occupy the area bordering Nepal and India for the purpose of infiltrating Communist agents into these states in preparation for an eventual people's revolution in conjunction with overall Communist plans for the third world war.

"During his stay in Moscow in late 1949 and early 1950, MAO Tse-tung was persuaded to accept the leadership in the liberation of Asia. He is following preliminary plans made in Yenan in 1946 with the USSR.

"The Communists intend to occupy all Tibet and use it as a

base for attacks against India and the Middle East in the third world war," the redacted document said.

A 1952 New York Times report from Kalimpong -- "this Indian border town which is the listening post and, in some respects, the nerve center of Himalayan politics -- said "intelligent Tibetans" were chafing under "unwanted" Chinese "masters" but hopeful an international war would free their homeland.

"One such possible break that bitter Tibetans hope for is a major war involving Communist China. In such a case, they would immediately offer themselves as guerrilla forces to Red China's enemy," Times' correspondent Robert Trumbull reported.

"At present, however, Chinese Reds have firm control in Lhasa, the capital. As long as they conduct themselves with their present rectitude and continue to defer to Tibetan sensitivities in certain important respects, such as the sanctity and authority of the Dalai Lama, a change in the political situation must await some occurrence or circumstance beyond the Chinese power to contain.

"Any Communist program to strip the monks of their great hoarded wealth and authority, backed by the country's united religious feeling, has been stayed, at least temporarily, since the Reds became aware that the larger monasteries were thoroughly armed fortresses manned by many thousands of formidable 'fighting monks' capable of engaging a larger force than the Chinese could now hurl against them."

The CIA soon got involved.

"The purpose of the [CIA] program...is to keep the political concept of an autonomous Tibet alive within Tibet and among foreign nations, principally India, and to build a capability for resistance against possible political developments inside Communist China," said a memo written during the 1960s to top American intelligence officials, according to US intelligence documents released in 1998 by the State Department and excerpted by the Los Angeles Times.

"The US government committee that approved the Tibetan operations also authorized the disastrous Bay of Pigs invasion of Cuba," the Times reported.

During the 1960s, the CIA also established a Tibetan rebel base inside northern Nepal's Mustang region along the two countries' Himalayan border.

"Groups of Tibetans would be armed with mortars, carbines and 55mm recoilless rifles and from [Mustang] there, would set up guerrilla units and conduct raids inside Tibet," French reported.

"During the '60s, the Mustang guerrillas were organized along the lines of a proper army, and conducted repeated raids into Tibet. The most successful raid, on the Xinjiang-Lhasa highway in 1961, resulted in the capture of a significant haul of documents.

"Recently declassified US intelligence documents show that the CIA was spending more than $1.7 million annually on this operation," he wrote.

The CIA's $1.7 million a year included "an annual subsidy of some $180,000 directly to the Dalai Lama, and it created Tibet Houses in New York and Geneva to serve as his unofficial embassies," Weiner wrote in Legacy of Ashes: The History of the CIA.

In 1972, President Nixon abruptly stopped the CIA's assistance to Tibetan guerrillas when he visited Beijing and shook hands with then-Chinese Chairman Mao Zedong, paving the way to normalizing relations in 1979.

Poe meanwhile paused several times during our interview to drink from a big bottle of Jim Beam. One of his cats was named Whiskey.

Poe veered into scattered curses, including against the late president of Indonesia.

"That asshole Sukarno."

Poe also told me he wanted to shoot San Francisco's then-Mayor Willie Brown for allowing transgender civil servants to undergo sex change operations financed by taxpayers.

"We'll shoot the bastard. We'll freckle his face, see how he likes that."

Poe wanted to attend a recent reunion of his buddies in Las Vegas, but he needed assistance to walk for any length of time. He was 76 years old.

"I don't want people to see me like this. I can't walk. I have a big ego, you know. I used to run up and down mountains. I'd be ahead of all the locals and I was carrying a full pack. I'd be up there and have to wait for them."

During the US war in Laos, Washington laid down strict rules that he was loathe to obey.

"They told us, 'You can't shoot the Russians. They are our allies.'

"Bullshit! Our allies? They were manning the anti-aircraft guns in Laos and in Hanoi where that bitch Jane Fonda was."

Poe revealed some of his signature methods of killing.

"I was a demolition expert. I would put hand grenades in glass jars. I'd pull the pin out, and put the grenade in the jar so the lever doesn't open. Then I'd drop it from the Porter [airplane] and it would fall, but it wouldn't explode until it hit the ground and the glass would break."

The CIA slipped into impoverished landlocked Laos in 1954 after hapless French colonialists surrendered and retreated from Laos, Vietnam and Cambodia -- a prized region they called Indochina.

Laos then became America's focus to stop nationalist North Vietnamese communists dominating the vacuum created by the departing colonialists. Hanoi's military wanted to use lightly populated Laos as a backdoor into South Vietnam so Vietnam could be reunited.

Poe's CIA work in Laos started in 1961, when the agency began giving weapons and cash to tough, indigenous Hmong tribesmen -- who were former allies of the French.

But the Hmong were reluctant to kill because they were animists and believed in spirits, ghosts and the afterworld, Poe said.

"In Nam Yu, I lived like a goddamn pig," in muddy squalor in the jungles of northern Laos during the late 1960s, Poe told Britain's Sunday Times magazine.

"I made a little prison there, a hole in the ground. I caught some Viet Minh doctors, who I put in there. I felt sorry for them. They asked to defect and I shot them. What was I going to do with a bunch of doctors? I never left, because I had no need."

In military author and historian Richard Gough's book titled, Tony Poe, Paramilitary, CIA's Secret Wars in South East Asia, a pilot named Bob Hamlin shared his impressions of meeting Poe for the first time. Hamlin wrote:

"I had been in Vientiane about two weeks when I had my first flight with Tony. Tony said he had a mission to accomplish that was really important to him. He showed me a spot on the local aeronautical chart and said he needed to drop something in the small village there. He had been in a fire-fight with Pathet Lao troops the night before and he showed me a leather pouch with his 'battle score' in it. The pouch contained six human ears that Tony had cut off the enemy he had killed.

"The Baron [airplane] has what is called a 'storm window' in the pilot's side window, that can be opened in-flight. Tony asked if I could pass over the village and drop the pouch out the storm window. I looked at the pouch and it was small enough, so I told him, 'Yes'. Being new in-country, I still did not know the area, so Tony guided me to the village. The village turned out to be the current home base for the enemy troops Tony fought the night before.

"We arrived in the area, and the village was at 4,500 feet elevation on the north side of a mountain and south of the Plaine des Jars. I lowered the landing gear and descended to about 100 feet above the village and, as we passed over, we could hear gunfire. I tossed the pouch out, raised the gear and dove down the side of the mountain to get away from the ground fire. That night in Vientiane, Tony and I had a couple of Scotch and sodas and he thanked me for the ride.

"Tony had a super-great background as a fighter and I respected him for his heroism and fearlessness. Tony was a great friend," Hamlin wrote according to Gough.

"I arrived in the country in February 1962," said Lawrence, a 1962-1966 CIA case officer in Long Tieng (aka Long Cheng, LS-20A, Lima Site 20 Alternate), a secret airstrip in northern Laos.

"My first impression was that I was extremely lucky. It was exotic. It was all that a young man, who had some cloudy images of what the Far East was like, should be. It was hot. The women were beautiful. I thought I'd died and gone to heaven," Lawrence said in The Most Secret Place on Earth.

Lawrence, Poe and other CIA officers soon trained nearly 30,000 inexperienced Hmong how to fight a guerrilla war.

To ensure secrecy while training them at a newly built, isolated, aerial landing strip at Long Tieng, the CIA employed Thais to lead the hands-on paramilitary lessons.

"We were using Thais. There was just so many Thais you could use as a surrogate for bringing in a lot of Americans. That had great value. It allowed the American effort to work with a very small footprint," said Lawrence.

The Americans aimed their Hmong mercenaries at communist Pathet Lao soldiers and their new allies, war-hardened North Vietnamese communist fighters who were successfully encroaching across Laos.

Hanoi's military was using porous Laos as a zigzag short-cut from North Vietnam to attack the corrupt US-backed regime in South Vietnam. Hanoi's leader Ho Chi Minh wanted Vietnam to be reunited, Marxist, and no longer dominated by Paris or Washington. North Vietnam's cross-Laos route was dubbed the Ho Chi Minh Trail.

While obediently fighting and dying as guerrillas for the CIA, the Hmong's fragile culture was nearly obliterated. Thousands perished. Thousands more Hmong fled across the Mekong River into refugee camps in Thailand. Some were resettled in America after the war.

"It was a much cheaper and better way to fight a war in Southeast Asia than to commit American troops," former CIA Director Richard Helms said.

To unleash a war in Laos, the US secretly violated the 1962 Declaration on the Neutrality of Laos, which Washington signed in Geneva along with other nations.

Kham Phat was a communist Pathet Lao soldier and "team leader" who fought against the Americans and their Hmong and Thai forces. During 1997 in Xieng Khouang province where the Plain of Jars is located in northeast Laos, he told me about the war, based on what he was taught and experienced at ground level.

"Normally we used an AK-47 [Kalashnikov assault rifle] and pistol. Or an RPG [rocket-propelled grenade], Chinese and Soviet model. Our enemies were mostly Thais and Hmong under the control of the US Army. In some places and some camps, I fought against American soldiers, to release Lao people [villages] from their control," Kham Phat said.

"I don't know how many Americans I killed because it was night time and I would fire and then we would go away. I never was injured because of my experience and the methods of the military that I was trained to do. And also because of our strategy plan of war. We saw where the enemy could escape from the locations.

"Our strategy was just to kill and just to destroy. I blame the American government and the leaders of that country. I never blamed the soldiers or the people. Nixon, Johnson, because at the war time they were the presidents. Johnson was the first man and Nixon came later.

"The US wanted to expand their colonies in the world, and also the US wanted to try their weapons that they made. The main reason was to use new ammunition for a world war [against the Soviet Union]. Not only in Laos, Vietnam and Cambodia. Because those three countries were part of Soviet communism. If they [Americans] can win in those three countries, they can win the world war.

"But America lost their war [in Southeast Asia]. It was very good for Laos, because we can have the independence. I will never forget that war and the US. Especially those presidents. Because Laos is a very small country in the world and American is a very big country with big food. Laos just has cultivation."

When the US lost its wars in Vietnam, Laos and Cambodia in 1975, Poe retired. He and his Hmong wife lived in northern Thailand until 1992 when they moved to the United States. He remained close to the Hmong community in the San Francisco Bay area, advising many of their sons to join the Marines, financing Hmong in need, and petitioning Washington for aid to Hmong veterans.

When I first met Poe in 1990 in Bangkok, Thailand, he said he was then helping desperate remnants of his Hmong guerrillas against the communist regime in Laos which had established control after winning in 1975.

"I buy the weapons for these guys. There are 10,000 guys, willing to fight," Poe told me at the time. "They'll be in Vientiane by the end of the year."

Those post-war Hmong staged only tiny ambushes and assaults. They never seriously threatened Vientiane or any other major towns.

"Ah, Tony Poe. He's like the crazy aunt down in the basement everyone has, who worked the Lao program. How do you explain Tony Poe?" said James Parker, who was a CIA paramilitary case officer fighting alongside Hmong guerrillas in Laos during 1971 to 1973.

Parker first met Poe in 1972 in Thailand, Parker told me in 2017.

"Had a month or two months with Tony then. I think every single day, he would arrive in the training camp from his home on the edge of the nearby town, and seem more or less alert until about noon, when he would be roaring drunk -- to stay loudly drunk until late in the afternoon when his daughter would arrive in a jeep driven by some Thai member of the camp staff.

"They would load Tony in the back of a jeep, usually in a stupor, to head for home, not to be seen until the following morning. Day after day and day.

"That particular story you referred to, of the kid with his two ears cut off, was a case in point. He [Poe] told it to me, but I just didn't believe it. And I think I told him so, which got him all riled up and he put on a front as if he wanted to fight or something like that. These get-drunk-every-day habits went back a long way.

"Vint Lawrence [a CIA paramilitary officer in Laos 1962-1964] told me, when he and Tony lived in a shed on the southeast side of the karst [limestone rock formations] next to what would be the [aircraft runway] ramp, that when Tony was back in the valley from trips out to far distant Hmong hill top positions, that he would get drunk every night and Vint would have to haul him around the shed to his bed. And you know Tony wasn't small," Parker said.

During the 1960s, Poe "did fly out to those god-forsaken Hmong hill top positions close to the North Vietnamese border and would spend time with the [Hmong] troops, once or twice getting into firefights with the North Vietnamese Army or the Pathet Lao, and acquit himself, by all accounts, admirably. It was very meaningful that Tony the American was out there, and put resolve in the locals to hang in and not flee.

"So maybe that was Tony's purpose. To let the common old Hmong grunt know that they were not alone. Tony and his Hmong wife were there to ensure the Hmong were represented and well treated."

Parker worked for the CIA for 32 years, starting in 1970.

During 1971-1973, he was a CIA paramilitary case officer fighting alongside an anti-communist Hmong general, Vang Pao who commanded the CIA's 30,000 Hmong guerrillas. In 1960, the CIA had found Vang Pao, and together they persuaded illiterate, impoverished, medieval Hmong tribesman in mountainous northern Laos to become mercenaries for the US in exchange for rice and money.

After too many Hmong had been killed, the CIA and Vang Pao were reduced to including 14-year-old Hmong boys to fight. To augment those dwindling mercenaries, the CIA brought in 4,000 US Special Forces-trained Tahan Sua Pran Tiger Soldiers from Thailand.

"I joined the CIA as a contract Special Operations Group paramilitary case officer in August 1970, and in November 1971 was assigned to the Lao program, initially working as a desk officer in Udorn," in northern Thailand.

"I transferred up to Long Tieng, Laos in early 1972 where I worked as a paramilitary case officer with the Hmong guerrillas. My call sign was 'Mule'."

JAMES "MULE" PARKER, CIA IN VIETNAM

In 1974, Parker was promoted to be a CIA intelligence officer in US-backed South Vietnam handling Vietnamese agents in the Mekong River Delta and liaising with South Vietnam's military until the US abandoned the American Embassy in Saigon and lost its war in Vietnam on April 30, 1975.

The next day, on May 1, 1975, Parker became the last CIA officer to leave Vietnam.

Parker returned to headquarters in Langley, Virginia. He became a staff espionage officer in late 1975 doing "CIA Directorate of Operations work as a spy recruiter and handler...around the world," starting with two years based in West Africa before returning to Southeast Asia -- "took a job to Cambodia" -- during the 1980s where he based in the "jungle," he said.

"In the 1980s there were things happening out in the hinterland that could not be followed by the CIA from the ivory towers of the capital cities. A small base was set up near a rural intersection where a wide variety of people passed overland. Some legal and official, though most travelers were without papers. Traders, refugees, crooks and soldiers of shifting alliance. I was chief there for a couple of years.

"I had a CIA communicator, couple of case officers and a military linguist attaché, plus a local staff of maybe 30 intelligent, English speaking interpreters and intel collectors. We knew what was going on.

Because we monitored a variety of nationalities and ethnics, my staff was made up of former South Vietnamese, North Vietnamese, Cambodian, Cham, Khmer Krom, Thai, Lao, Malay, Lao Tueng, and several brands of Chinese.

"We developed our compound, which was called 'Hilton' into quite a place. We had two caged tigers, peacocks, a fish pond, a swimming pool, German shepherd dogs, a cage with maybe 10 monkeys ruled by the ill-mannered Zimbo."

Parker retired in 1992 but on September 11, 2001 returned to the CIA as a contractor to "teach tradecraft to new hires" and work inside Cambodia, Afghanistan and elsewhere before retiring again in 2011.

Parker received the CIA's Intelligence Medal of Merit, a Certificate of Distinction, and two Certificates of Exceptional Service.

He authored several books about his CIA experiences in Southeast Asia, including The Vietnam War: Its Ownself published in 2016. The 706-page book included biographical and often bloody details.

It displayed photographs of CIA officers, Hmong and Vietnamese soldiers, maps, bomb sites, dead bodies and one nude Lao bar girl. The book also detailed Parker's proudest CIA successes during the war and, what he said, were reasons the US failed.

Parker wrote in his book:

"At first light, my platoon moved out toward the area where the sound had come from. The young Vietnamese man was dead. He had taken off his watch and tried to hide it in some bushes near his outstretched hand. A bag of rice lay some distance away. The man was unarmed. The first Vietcong killed by the battalion was an unarmed porter. We had come halfway around the world to kill a laborer."

Another excerpt told how "General James F. Hollingsworth rose and picked up a pointer from the map board. 'We are going to kill gooks in this operation,' he promised."

Parker's reason for joining the military was, "I'm here to learn to kill."

He described how his "Hmong, protecting their family huts, took no sappers captive. One killed, near the ramp, had his privates cut off and stuck in his mouth. Other dead North Vietnamese sappers probably had their stomachs cut open so that the Hmong could determine what they had been eating. Vang Pao was known to do this to dead enemies after an attack. He would see if they were well fed, which probably indicated they were well rested and supplied, or if the stomach were empty, which might mean they were desperate."

By 1972, Parker's views on death were bleak. He wrote:

"The last in a steady procession of men in body bags moved through the Long Tieng valley: Hmong, Thai, Lao, Air America, US Air Force. It was part of the job, handling our dead. Early in the year, when the North Vietnamese were attacking Skyline, I would take a fixed-wing Air America plane down to Udorn, Thailand, every night. The bodies of recently killed Thai mercenaries were always the last to be loaded.

"It was a gruesome sight as the body bags were being tossed on board, often a dozen or more. And I would sit through the flights south looking at the bags, wondering about the men inside, about their families and their past and what they had planned for the future.

"But it had not taken me long to accept the body bags, in the same way an undertaker becomes accustomed to his work, and after a while I would be happy to see them loaded, because it meant we would be heading south soon.

"War forces that on a person. Makes them insensitive to the

suffering and dying of others. Searching for moral justification each time a man dies in war is futile and hurts the soul. You dwell on it and the hurt makes you crazy or turns you into a drunk. The sane alternative is to put it out of your mind, resisting introspection and grief," Parker wrote in his book.

When asked during our interviews about the CIA's Vietnamese spies who Parker and others relied on while writing CIA reports for Washington during the war, Parker replied:

"Ah, the lying spy syndrome."

For the CIA throughout the world, "it's hard to recruit spies, to find them, develop them, recruit them to steal secrets, dispatch them, and then debrief them on their return.

"To the uninitiated, it's tougher than it looks. And here's another thought: when that guy or gal you've recruited to be a spy comes back in with the secret information you sent him to get, it's only at this point where the whole process gives a return on our country's investment of time, money [and] risk.

"Not the meeting, assessing, developing, recruiting, training, dispatching and the debriefing when he returns. No. You and your agent are only of value to the intel community when you finally, finally write up the intel report. The process can take years sometimes, progressing from one case officer's development to another."

Parker recalled how in South Vietnam during the war, "you find a new [Vietnamese] guy through your own spade work or maybe by referral from the US military or South Vietnamese police, and you go on to assess and vet him and recruit him and train him and send him out. And then sometimes he just disappears, losing his nerve when it comes down to actually doing what he has been tasked to do.

"And out in the bigger world of spydom, what's the life of a productive [mercenary] spy? Five years maybe, sometimes longer, but not often. They lose their edge -- their interest in having their lives disrupted and endangered -- or they lose their access. Or, after two or three [CIA] case officer handlers, the personal attachment can become weak and the [mercenary] guy maybe just doesn't gee-haw [get along] with the new case officer.

"It's a tough business under any conditions. In Vietnam, this difficult business had to be done under combat conditions, where to be found out, meant sure death for the spy."

During the Vietnam War, the CIA's American "case officers turned over every couple of years as their tours expired, and the new [CIA] guy was often taken advantage of by the existing [Vietnamese] agents.

"For example, if these [Vietnamese] agents were what is known as 'principle' agents, they sent out other Vietnamese contacts as their intel gatherers. These sub-agents were hard to keep up with...as does accountability and chain of acquisition of their information. And, perhaps most common, these hard to verify sub-agents were often ghosts, as in not really there. Vietnamese agents were found out to be 'fabricators' time and again."

As the war dragged on, some of the CIA's Vietnamese spies became increasingly corrupt.

"We're talking the end of the war here where [Vietnamese] 'principle agents' had come to know pretty much what the CIA generally was looking for. So the good scammers would just stay in place for years -- up until the end really -- feeding marketplace mush to the CIA case officers.

"And for years, if 'principle agents' who had worked for the CIA were found out to be phony, or if they hyped low-level info into something that sounded sexy [and] were found out and terminated in one province -- since they knew the business, these slicky boys would often just move to another province and make indirect contact with Americans there with a whole new invented network of sub-sources and sell their fabricated newspaper-inspired stuff, or general ground truths, to an unsuspecting new CIA guy as 'intelligence'," Parker said.

"All that new local [Vietnamese] intel entrepreneur had to do was mix in a little truth, and he would look like he had potential. Some of the [Vietnamese] agents identified as 'fabricators' were not necessarily criminal and deceitful in their work but had, along the way, lost their access or their agents were killed or just didn't come back from missions. But [they] continued to pretend that they had sub-agents, when in fact the 'principle agent' was just making up what the [CIA] case officer wanted to hear."

Among the CIA's American staff, problems arose because their own bosses demanded more and more information.

"You gotta remember that there was pressure on us CIA case officers to produce intels," he said, referring to intelligence reports.

"So the emphasis, certainly from say 1968 to 1972, was to believe your [Vietnamese] agent over reasonable doubt sometimes, and keep him on -- to provide the necessary number of reports you need for promotion, or to keep the [CIA] base you were operating from, up to standards."

As a result, CIA case officers experienced a "lot of resistance to cleaning your stable of [Vietnamese] assets, or vetting them anew after a year or so in which they had produced five or ten reports a month to you," he said.

"It does get into sources and methods that I want to avoid. Suffice it to say that good clandestine trade craft involves constant vetting of your intel agents, and there are probably a great number of case studies that show how a lack vetting resulted in bad ops and funky 'intelligence'.

"The general feeling by most [CIA] case officers is, and was, that your [mercenary] agents will always lie to you."

Lessons needed to be learned from the CIA's lack of spying expertise in Vietnam.

"This lack of intelligence, on the plans and intentions of the communists in South Vietnam, is something the CIA must bear responsibility for," Parker said.

"Tet [North Vietnam's 1968 lunar New Year military offensive] was our biggest failure. And we certainly didn't get the end game right [in 1975], as an organization that is supposed to know what's going on.

"You cannot get intel [American intelligence] operatives to stay in a battle zone for more than a couple of years at a time, so the occupational problems of [local] fabricators was unavoidable.

"I was in Afghanistan 2010 and 2011. The best intel service there was probably the Israeli Mossad. Because they had been operating in that area for years. I give you Mossad in Afghanistan as an example.

"I think the development of the drones by the CIA has done much to deal with the problems of gathering field intelligence in hostile mountains. If we had had the drones in November 1950, the US Army's 8th Army and X corps would not have been ambushed like they were in northern North Korea."

On April 25, 1972, President Nixon, National Security Advisory Henry Kissinger, and White House Press Secretary Ron Ziegler had the following conversation, recorded on Nixon's tapes:

Nixon: We've got to be thinking in terms of an all-out bombing attack [on North Vietnam].

Kissinger: I agree with you.

Nixon: We've got to use massive force. How many did we kill in Laos?

Ziegler: Maybe ten thousand -- fifteen?

Kissinger: In the Laotian thing, we killed about ten, fifteen...

Nixon: See, the attack in the North that we have in mind...power plants, whatever's left -- POL [petroleum], the docks...And I still think we ought to take the dikes out now. Will that drown people?

Kissinger: About 200,000 people.

Nixon: No, no, no. I'd rather use the nuclear bomb. Have you got that, Henry?

Kissinger: That, I think, would just be too much.

Nixon: The nuclear bomb, does that bother you? I just want you to think big, Henry, for Chrissakes.

Parker told me his two best Vietnamese military sources committed suicide in despair when the war ended.

One week before North Vietnam's victory and the end of the war, Parker's best South Vietnamese source "and friend" General Tran Van Hai accurately predicted the US-backed regime in Saigon would be toppled at the end of April.

"On April 22 when I visited Hai, he said they [North Vietnam's army] were lining up. Saigon, he said, would fall in 7 days."

Parker said he "believed in Hai's assessment. He had always been right."

But Saigon's CIA Station Chief Tom Polgar and CIA head analyst Frank Snepp refused to believe it, Parker said.

Polgar and Snepp insisted North Vietnam would allow Saigon and the southern Delta to remain separate under US protection after a last minute cease-fire, Parker said.

"The CIA leadership in Saigon...sincerely did believe what was obviously a Soviet disinformation ploy, that the fix was in, and the North Vietnamese only planned to move to the northern gates of Saigon, and that they would allow the capital and the Delta to remain free. Hard to believe that our people bought into this, but that's what I have surmised.

"Certainly I was told by Snepp, the head analyst in Saigon, that...they knew what was happening out here, and that the North Vietnamese would not take Saigon. Period."

Parker described Snepp as a condescending, pedantic elitist who during 1974-1975 spouted trivia about North Vietnamese personalities and Saigon intrigue which did not reflect the war-torn countryside's losses.

"'There will be many future generations of CIA case officers in the Delta,' was Snepp's famous closing line to us" -- weeks before the war ended.

In April 1975, Parker reluctantly parroted the lie to his Vietnamese employees that South Vietnam would not collapse, even though he knew North Vietnam's military was about to seize Saigon.

"I remember being pelted with questions about the future when I closed down the CIA compound in My Tho [South

Vietnam]. I looked each employee in the compound directly in the eye and told them that they were safe, that the CIA information was that there would be a ceasefire. I gave them this line because I didn't want to be mobbed," by employees desperate to escape.

"There was also danger from the South Vietnamese who might think about kidnapping my sorry ass and holding me as ransom for their safe exit, or in shooting me for leading them down the primrose path in our war fighting."

On May 1, 1975, General Hai was found face down dead at his desk. Hai had not told anyone he was going to kill himself.

No note.

No farewells.

Half a glass of poisoned brandy lay next to his slumped body.

"That report Hai gave me [predicting] the day Saigon would fall to the NVA (North Vietnamese Army), that intel probably had a bearing on my receipt of the [CIA's] Intelligence Medal," Parker said.

"Hai's English was almost perfect, including his use of American profanity. He'd offer up comments that could embarrass a sailor. And he was not shy about his use of profanity in criticizing the way the US handled the war, it's policy makers, its tactics and now in the spring of '75, of its sure intention of leaving South Vietnam to its own devices."

Hai often "vented" to Parker who quoted, for example, Hai saying:

"Abandoning us on the fucking battlefield, in our darkest hour, not a word of encouragement, just political shit on top of political shit, so that it all stinks. Not a breath of honesty or honor among you guys. That includes you, you turdy American piece of shit," Hai told Parker.

Parker said his other best CIA source and also "my friend," South Vietnamese General Le Van Hung, announced after North Vietnam's victory that he too would commit an "honorable" suicide.

Hung valiantly saluted his troops and shook their hands. Then he asked them to go, and had to shove some of them out the door while ignoring his wife who begged him to not to die.

Alone in his office, Hung shot himself.

Parker blamed failures by the White House, State Department, Pentagon, US Embassy and the CIA's Saigon Station for deadly mistakes during the war.

In 1963, "when [President John] Kennedy was assassinated, [Defense Secretary Robert] McNamara and his power of persuasion rose to be the alpha animal when it came to US policies in Southeast Asia, and he didn't have a fucking clue.

"Wrong-headed McNamara was the primal idiot. [Gen. William] Westmoreland his minion. The North won the war because we were led from the Pentagon by [McNamara], a complete wacko idiot who didn't listen to [President Dwight] Eisenhower about fighting the expansion of communism in Southeast Asia by denying Laos to the North Vietnamese."

As a result, North Vietnam created the valuable Ho Chi Minh Trail through Laos and Cambodia to move troops and weapons into South Vietnam.

"The war was over with Tet [North Vietnam's lunar New Year military offensive] in 1968 when [President Lyndon] Johnson lost his will to fight. He fired Westmoreland and McNamara, and sent in [Gen. Creighton] Abrams, but the war was over when he [Johnson] said he wasn't going to run for president in the fall of '68.

"Most of the fighting and dying was yet to be done before the US military pulled out in 1973, but our commitment to win was over when Tet accomplished its mission of getting Johnson to give up."

The US wars resulted in the deaths -- on all sides -- of more than one million Vietnamese, and between 200,000 to one million people in Laos, plus at least 600,000 Cambodians and more than 58,000 Americans, according to researchers.

"US intelligence interest -- when I first got there -- was on political wrangling in Saigon, and only the barest of interest in what was happening in the field. That's why my [CIA] reporting from the [Mekong River] Delta in 1974 got such little attention."

Describing Saigon's doomed American Embassy's State Department staff during the final four months, Parker said:

"In Saigon, all that was left of the Americans were place-keepers who, for the most part, had only a distant relationship with the ARVN [South Vietnam's army]."

Those Americans had never been shot at, did not have friends die in their arms, and had no close contact with any Vietnamese except mostly girlfriends and maids, Parker said.

Earlier betrayals wrecked South Vietnam's chances of surviving on its own.

South Vietnam's President Ngo Dhin Diem, who came to power in 1954, was assassinated during a 1963 coup under the watchful eyes of President John F. Kennedy and the CIA in Saigon.

Asked during our interviews about Kennedy's role in the coup, Parker replied:

"[John] McCone was the CIA Director at the time [1961-1965], but I think this whole Diem thing was mostly something managed through the US State Department. I don't think McCone had much of a voice with the National Security Council, dominated by Kennedy cronies.

"The [South Vietnamese Buddhist] monks' self-immolations, the lack of clear progress in Diem's work to pacify the countryside, and Diem's family all contributed to Kennedy's decision that a new man in South Vietnam was needed, and when the two South Vietnamese generals in Saigon privately contacted the US Embassy with the question, 'What would be the US reaction if we just took Diem out?' well, Kennedy basically just went with the flow.

"But here's the thing from my experiences on the ground: that Kennedy didn't know the Vietnamese culture, didn't know that the light-skinned Catholics running the show in Saigon -- who knew how to effectively deal with the West -- were miles apart from the majority of the people, who were dark-skinned Buddhist farmers.

"Plus they were far down that road of involvement in a conflict they could not win -- what with the Ho Chi Minh Trail, which brought down NVA people almost to the Saigon city limits. The US military was adapting to a policy of short, one-year tours in country.

"And our military had no experience in the counter-insurgency that they were being called on to manage. The weapons they had at their disposal were developed for war in Europe, not the rice paddies and villages of Southeast Asia.

"I don't think the CIA was driving the bus on this. Kennedy said to [TV journalist] Walter Cronkite on national news that he was thinking a change of government in Saigon might be necessary. And believe me, both the South and North Vietnamese military listened very closely to US news.

"Those two South Vietnamese generals who asked about the US reaction if they were to take out Diem, were not prompted by the CIA.

"Kennedy was to die himself within three weeks of Diem's assassination.

"I don't think the CIA would have had a 'satisfied' or 'not satisfied' attitude about that [coup in South Vietnam]. I think it was something that happened beyond the realm of the CIA. I may be wrong, but I think the CIA was mainly a spectator to all this.

"Did Kennedy tell Cronkite that maybe a change of leadership in Saigon was needed, intentionally to signal that to South Vietnamese who would act on it? I don't think so. He [Kennedy] was, by all evidence, woefully under-informed about the way things worked in Southeast Asia. I think he truly believed he was just talking to the American people through Cronkite.

"You shouldn't assume the CIA was the wheeler dealer in Vietnam -- certainly in 1963 -- that it has been made out to be. It had some of the smartest people on the ground over there, and because of that got some notice, but State (Department) and NSC (National Security Council) and DOD (Department of Defense) had the largest representation and called most all the shots.

"I think our government was marching steadily headlong into a quagmire for indefensible reasons. I think McNamara had a very persuasive sophisticated personality, with a head for facts and figures, but he had no fucking idea what he was doing. No clue even. And he lied constantly.

"And he surrounded himself with 'yes' men -- I'm thinking Westmoreland here -- and when Kennedy was assassinated, he [McNamara] became the alpha dog on the top level of our government. He dominated Bundy, and [1961-1969 Secretary of State Dean] Rusk and certainly [President Lyndon] Johnson. And remember though he was a hell'va man in cabinet board rooms, he [McNamara] didn't know shit. He was absolutely wrong-headed.

"If the government had proceeded with Eisenhower's advice of denying Laos to the North Vietnamese, in a way that could bring into play the weapons we had, and the military we had...bring in all that armor and all the fighter aircraft and go after killing North Vietnamese and Viet Cong in Laos and Cambodia, the war could have been won in a year, or a year and a half.

"The war was over with Tet [a military offensive by North Vietnamese and communist Viet Cong forces during Vietnam's New Year] in 1968 when Johnson lost his will to fight. He fired Westmoreland and McNamara and sent in Abrams, but the war was over when he said he wasn't going to run for President in the fall of '68.

"Most of the fighting and dying was yet to be done before the US military pulled out in 1973, but our commitment to win was over when Tet accomplished its mission of getting Johnson to give up.

"That's why my reporting from the [Mekong] delta in 1974 got such little attention. However with communist forces moving on Saigon in the spring of '75, suddenly there was interest, not so much in how we could use good intelligence to help the ARVN, but how we could protect the American place-keepers in Saigon. And get them out.

"But also keep in mind that the CIA leadership in Saigon, and to some extent (1973-1977 Secretary of State Henry) Kissinger in Washington D.C., sincerely did believe what was obviously a Soviet misinformation ploy, that the fix was in, and the North Vietnamese only planned to move to the northern gates of Saigon and would allow the capital and the delta to remain free.

"Hard to believe that our people bought into this, but that's what I have surmised. This disinformation was fed to our COS (CIA Chief of Station in Saigon, Thomas) Polgar, by the Polish representatives with the U.N. peace-keeping lackeys, and to Kissinger in Washington by the Soviet Ambassador. Or so I have been told.

"The North won the war, because we were led from the Pentagon by a complete wacko idiot, who didn't listen to Eisenhower about fighting the expansion of communism in Southeast Asia -- by denying Laos to the North Vietnamese -- but for reasons probably known only to God, decided to go with a game plane of counter-insurgency inside South Vietnam.

"You will find no answers to reasons the North won by looking at the US presence in South Vietnam there towards the end.

"You have to wonder about the Tet Offensive that started when those 19 VC [Viet Cong] suicide sappers climbed under the wire of the US Embassy in Saigon in 1968.

"How could the [CIA] agency have been in country as long as they had, and didn't have some clue that the enemy operations that would involve thousands of their troops, and almost the entire VC network? How did they pull this off without our foreknowledge?

"Well, one explanation is that they [North Vietnamese and Viet Cong forces] could move with impunity up and down the

Ho Chi Minh Trail. Move without our knowledge.

"Plans were not made by the US military and the NSC (National Security Council) for fighting that would take years and years and years. You cannot get [CIA's] intel operatives to stay in a battle zone for more than a couple of years at a time. Hell, Special Forces troops are deployed on six-month increments, so the occupational problems of [the CIA's South Vietnamese intelligence] fabricators was unavoidable.

"The US had little experience on any level in Southeast Asia in 1965. The people who knew more in our government than anyone was the CIA, [but] its case officer corps -- with time on the ground to give them some idea of what was going on -- was not more than, I don't know, 50 case officers.

"The reason the North won the war? Here's my answer:

"The way the battlefield was drawn with the Ho Chi Minh Trail and sanctuaries inside Laos and Cambodia, and the appointment of a Secretary of Defense who didn't have a clue how to fight a war, but did have a gift for persuasion, especially with the easy-to-manipulate Johnson, were the two main reasons the North won the war.

"Also our surprise -- due to our intel failure -- at Tet 1968 and our employment of military equipment built to fight a war in Europe and not built to fight guerrillas in the jungles and in small hamlets of Southeast Asia. And the enormous stupidity of the application of counterinsurgency on the situation in South Vietnam, where it did not have a chance of success, contributed to the defeat of the mighty USA against the pissant North Vietnam."

During our interviews, Parker suggested improvements could be made within the CIA for its current and future work.

"I believe we should make every effort to hire people with native fluency in a foreign language, with the idea to put them back working intelligence operations in the country where they speak the language fluently.

"But I know how important it is in the CIA to write good reports in English. It's not a good practice for the long run to hire fluent foreign speakers who cannot write coherent reports back to Langley. I think something is to be said to hiring a younger smart and energetic applicant with language aptitude, than an older fluent foreign language speaker who obviously speaks and writes English as a second language.

"Other parts to the horror of working DO [CIA Directorate of Operations] clandestine corps HR [human resources analysts] is to keep the boy case officers from marrying the lady officers. There are many more instances this produces trouble than it works out to CIA advantage. Or in selecting qualified lady case officers for a field assignment when they have a husband who works in the US.

"Or getting middle management to take tours to shit holes when their kids are in high school. Or to keep them from quitting to go work for [Washington area] beltway bandits at a much high salary, that does not require them to go overseas to do that difficult, difficult job of recruiting and running good agents.

"And you know overseas, all clandestine case officers are deployed under cover, and some have to spend long hours in the cover job. So two jobs -- one very difficult -- one pay check."

Asked what lessons America learned from its wars in Vietnam, Laos and Cambodia, Parker replied:

"I know the Air Force wanted to take the fight to the North Vietnamese...they sure wanted to be there. I don't think many of the Army and Marine guys in position when Eisenhower left, and Kennedy came in, wanted anything to do with Southeast Asia.

"But we went about the war in Vietnam in such an asinine way, such a wrong-headed way. Vietnam was the Edsel [the worst designed American automobile] of US foreign affairs. Maybe up front, the CIA should have taken a strong, more objective position: that our analysts don't think you take the situation of South Vietnam 1965 and apply US war machines and US troops untrained in jungle warfare and/or counterinsurgency, and expect to prevail.

"We had lessons learned from a lack of good intelligence in Korea [during the 1950-1953 war] that we apparently paid no attention to. We had Eisenhower's advice that Kennedy and McNamara ignored. We had absolutely no help in fighting the war from our US State Department. The US efforts in Southeast Asia were sabotaged and were kept on a wrong course by the State Department's [US Ambassador-at-Large Averell] Harriman and [1973-1977 US Ambassador to Laos, William] Sullivan.

"Laos is different. We had the enormous advantage, the CIA did, of having good men at every level, and we were allowed to fight the impossible war there against the spread of communism by using Asians [Hmong] and the barest number of Americans.

"Also our guys on the cutting edge out there who made things happen, stayed on year after year. [CIA officer] Bill Lair's advice was that he didn't want CIA case officers in pairs out at the distant outposts because they would tend to stay to themselves -- no, he wanted one-man CIA positions because it would force the CIA singleton to develop a relationship with the local commander and learn his language and absorb his way of doing things."

Parker reflected on his experiences fighting in Vietnam and Laos.

"I went to Vietnam in [August] 1965 as a 22-year-old second lieutenant platoon leader with the US Army 1st Division. During my year tour in jungles northwest of Saigon, I chased a wounded VC [Viet Cong] down a rat hole into a labyrinth of tunnels under Cu Chi, and months later led a litter detail [stretchers carrying dead and wounded] with a dying US soldier through the ghoulish Minh Tanh counter-ambush battlefield, silently passing wounded North Vietnam who were trying to leave the same battlefield dragging their wounded. By year's end, I was awarded a Purple Heart for wounds received in combat and the Bronze Star with V for bravery.

"Leading men in combat when I was 22, was the most

responsible job I've ever had. Nothing since comes close," he told me.

"Plus I enjoyed the risk taking, the danger and the adventure involved, though the part of my combat tour [August 1965-September 1966] when I had to handle the thought of friends and members of my platoon dying in the catastrophic way men die in battle was tough, and deeply, deeply hurtful.

"I was good at my work. Shit, all things considered, I was in love with it and the idea -- the ideal -- that I answered my country's call to arms. I was a proven patriot. I liked that. But I also liked the action.

"Then after the military [in May 1967], it was recruitment by the CIA [in August 1970] which I took as a pretty proud accomplishment. It wasn't a leap for me to buy into the CIA conservative way. And I did good in training, and got a paramilitary assignment to the promised land, Laos [November 1971-November 1973]. I was one of a dozen or so case officers [in Laos], less than that maybe. There were something like eight of us. That's heady stuff, Richard. The 'glamour' of the war up there. In the same way I admit that I liked combat in Vietnam.

"Our rag-tag army of 4,000 beat the 27,000 North Vietnamese that came down to kill us [in Laos]. Our soldiers and the US fighter aircraft killed them by the thousands.

"And finally that transfer [in January 1974] to work with an equally small number of CIA people out of Can Tho base [in South Vietnam] against the wrong-headed brass in Saigon and the 'let's just get the hell out' mentality back in Washington DC. That was good. My relationship with Hang and Hai [who both committed suicide] were unique to all the relationships of all the Americans with their South Vietnamese military contacts," he said.

"I have been blessed to have experienced all this. To have had the adventures, made the friends, got the awards, lived life large and dangerously. Who had it better? No one.

"So when I answer your questions, there will be these experiences and personal feeling that I will refer to, that sustain me, even now. Define who I am, even now. I cannot find fault with my five years on Southeast Asian battlefields. I cannot ever say anything that takes away from the people I knew there. Especially those who died. I hold them in the highest regards.

"But, especially in retirement from the CIA, I have studied this war. And like many who come away from looking at war as a tool of foreign policy, I am pissed at war. What a waste of resources. And I am pissed at my country's leadership in Southeast Asia and the enormously egregious, dishonest way we got into this war, and then the way things were mismanaged.

"In that, I am anti-Vietnam war. I can agree with some of what the protestors were saying at the time. Some. Although for the longest time I believed that it is not for us to question why, it is for us to do and die.

"So anyway, two perspectives. One from my experiences which is emotionally, cocky, Southeast Asia pro-war. And two from my study which is -- the way it played out -- resoundingly anti-Vietnam war."

INTERNATIONAL "BIKINI KILLER" CHARLES SOBHRAJ

"Let me please introduce myself,
I'm a man of wealth and taste.
And I laid traps for troubadours,
Who get killed before they reached Bombay."

~ Mick Jagger & Keith Richards

The French serial murderer slid his lynx physique toward a table in the tacky Casino Royale in Kathmandu's five-star Yak and Yeti Hotel. He wanted to savor some quiet gambling.

The strangler's thick hands held freshly dealt cards as he enjoyed avoiding Nepal's police. Peasants had found, nearly 28 years earlier, burnt, smoldering remains of a woman from California and her Canadian boyfriend near Kathmandu's medieval pagodas, white-washed Buddhist stupas, hashish-smoking sadhus and crumbling red-brick hovels.

But soon after Charles Sobhraj finished his baccarat and blackjack at the casino that night in 2003, Nepal's police arrested him. Those two murders in 1975 were at the top of an international list of possibly 20 murders linked to Sobhraj ["so-BRAHJ"] in several Asian countries. No one will ever know the true number of corpses he left behind because most of the dead were naive, friendly foreign backpackers slouching through the chaos of Asia for the experiences of a lifetime. All of them were unprepared to meet their doom.

"Officially, I am denying I killed anyone," Sobhraj told me during a series of prison interviews in 1985.

No one believed him.

Victims who fell into Sobhraj's clutches included American, Canadian, Dutch, French, Australian, Israeli, Turkish and other travelers innocently wandering through Asia's elaborate cities and dramatic countryside. They became dangerously distracted by Sobhraj who sweet-talked them in his smooth way, confidently projecting that he knew more about life on the road than they could ever imagine.

During a stunning criminal career careening across Europe and Asia from 1963 to 1997, Sobhraj repeatedly robbed, drugged, and murdered tourists, escaped local police, and broke out of several prisons.

In 1972, for example, Afghan authorities seized the sinister, charming Frenchman in Herat, Afghanistan, for car theft. But when Afghan security forces moved him to Kabul, he faked an illness and got himself transferred to a prison hospital, drugged the Afghan guards, and escaped.

In 1975, Greek cops locked him up. But he successfully fled while being transported in a police van when he secretly injected gasoline into a bottle of shampoo which he carried with him into the van. While police were bundling him into the vehicle, he squirted gasoline on the van's floor and ignited the fluid. Amid the screaming police and fiery chaos, Sobhraj fled to Turkey, even though he was already wanted there for a robbery at Istanbul's Hilton hotel.

Over the years, the fast-talking con artist also eluded police in Hong Kong, Thailand, Nepal, Pakistan, Iran, and France, often bribing officials, feigning illness or changing his identity. But those escapes were just a few of the scars on his long resume of crime.

Sobhraj's hunting ground for victims was usually the vulnerable, drug-saturated cul-de-sacs along the wild and fabled "hippie trail" during the 1970s which criss-crossed Asia, attracting an often stoned parade of young Westerners including idealists, explorers, scholars, artists, writers, escapists, junkies, thieves, fugitives, hustlers, smugglers and the insane. During the often blissful daze of their exotic lifestyle, many of these foreigners sought organic, spiritual and beatific peace on a paisley pilgrimage to Kabul, Kashmir, Kulu Valley, Kathmandu, Goa and elsewhere.

They had no idea that ticking among them was a real Clockwork Orange horror show lurking in the guise of a sleazy gem salesman armed with sleep-inducing chemicals and a pushy rap offering fantastic deals on cheap jewels that travelers could resell back home for huge profits, all the while offering a knock-out drink for them to sip while thinking about buying his glistening rocks.

Sobhraj, a karate expert, used his good looks, eloquent English and French linguistic skills, and pop psychology advice to dazzle wide-eyed young travelers. Lured by his personality, he arranged for them to overdose into oblivion on free drug-laced drinks and then stole their passports, jewelry, cameras and traveler's cheques.

All of this might have remained a faded, frightening story of an escaped killer who disappeared long ago, retold by experienced travelers whenever backpackers swapped the worst stories they had ever heard.

But during a hot, dusty September in 2003, local Nepalese journalists happened to see Sobhraj in a Kathmandu street. They were stupefied. Almost 28 hazy years earlier, the infamous double murders outside Kathmandu had been blamed on Sobhraj. And here he was, back in Nepal's capital. They immediately told police who rushed to handcuff him in his hotel.

In police custody Sobhraj, 59, instinctively fell back on a story he used whenever he was caught. He denied any criminal activity, especially the 1975 murders of Bronzich and Carriére.

"Bronzich's bag was found in Sobhraj's room in the Soaltee Hotel in 1975, and his telephone number was mentioned in Bronzich's diary," reported The Himalayan Times which first published news of Sobhraj gambling in the Yak and Yeti Hotel's Casino Royale, which alerted police.

Nepalese police and investigators did suspect Sobhraj in 1975, but before they could catch him, he and his Canadian girlfriend fled to Thailand. His return in 2003 to the scene of his crimes in Nepal appeared to be inexplicable.

Sobhraj apparently and wrongly assumed he would be safe from arrest and trial in Kathmandu for the double murder because any evidence, paper files, written testimony and young witnesses would now be impossible to retrieve.

Sobhraj now told the arresting police this was his first time visiting Nepal. He said he was staying in a hotel in Thamel, Kathmandu's tourist zone of hotels, restaurants, travel agencies, old brick lanes, and souvenir shops which sold Tibetan-style art, antiques, jewelry and other items.

Sobhraj said he was scouting out locations for a documentary film he wanted to make about Nepal's attractive handicrafts and fascinating Hindu culture.

No one cared what excuses he was offering. But they also never found out why Sobhraj had returned.

News of his arrest immediately echoed hundreds of miles

southeast to Bangkok, Thailand where authorities suspected him of five unsolved murders during 1975 including:

Jennifer Bolliver of Cabrillo Beach, California -- sometimes named Teresa Knowlton from Seattle, Washington -- whose body was found washed ashore in Pattaya, a sleazy beach resort on the Gulf of Thailand near Bangkok. Her lungs were filled with sand and salt water, the result of being forcibly drowned, a Thai pathologist said.

A French woman, Charmayne Carrou, was also found dead on Pattaya's beach with her neck bones broken by a powerful strangler.

Both women were clad in bathing suits, inspiring Thai media to dub the unknown culprit The Bikini Killer.

Carrou's Turkish boyfriend, Vitali Hakim -- sometimes described as a Sephardic Jew -- was also discovered dead in Pattaya, apparently burned alive.

That same year, the bodies of Dutch students Henricus Bintanja, 29, and his fiancé Cornelia "Cocky" Hemker, 25, were found beaten, strangled and burned in a rural ditch 35 miles from Bangkok. Sobhraj and his foxy French-Canadian lover Marie-Andre Leclerc, who came from the small town of Levis, Quebec, used the dead Dutch couple's passports to flee to Nepal.

Soon after the couple arrived in Kathmandu, police discovered two charred bodies on the outskirts of Kathmandu, identified as Connie Jo Bronzich, 29, of Saratoga, California and Canadian Laurent Carriere, 26. In some published news reports they were wrongly named Annabelle Tremont and Laddie DuParr.

By the time those bodies were found in Nepal, Sobhraj and Leclerc had already fled to Bangkok where, to his dismay, his alleged murders earlier that year were now being exposed in greater detail.

Interpol and Thai police suspected Sobhraj used the French alias "Alain Gauthier" and lured victims to their deaths in Thailand by offering to sell them gems from his modest apartment which he shared with Leclerc on Soi Saladaeng off busy Silom Road in the heart of Bangkok. That neighborhood opens onto tourist-friendly hotels, travel agencies, banks, embassies, Patpong Road's bars and prostitutes, and bustles with first-time travelers gawking in culture shock.

After Sobhraj convinced potential customers to enter his apartment to view some gems, he allegedly served them drinks laced with powerful sedatives and laxatives, rendering them zonked but also, when they awoke, extremely ill -- if they awoke.

Those who could open their eyes found Sobhraj worriedly fussing over them, blaming possible food poisoning from something they ate before meeting him. He politely offered to nurse them back to health, while concocting toxic potions that would keep them quivering and helplessly sprawled in his apartment for several days until he could extract their passports, foreign exchange and other precious items from their weakening grasp.

Police were also hunting Sobhraj for allegedly attempting to murder two Australians, Russell Lapthorne and his wife Vera, after repeatedly drugging the Melbourne couple and stealing more than $2,000 worth of their belongings in 1975.

They survived.

When Sobhraj and Leclerc had fled Kathmandu and were back in Bangkok in 1976, Thai police were able to bring him in for questioning about those cases. But the Thai police neglected to closely watch Sobhraj while he was waiting to meet senior officers in a Bangkok police station. When police looked the other way, the experienced escape artist simply walked free.

Sobhraj and Leclerc immediately traveled south, overland across Thailand's border into Malaysia. They were joined by their alleged partner in crime, a mysterious never-captured citizen of India named Ajay Chowdhury.

During the early 1970s, the three of them bounced around Europe and Asia until they arrived in India. Sobhraj realized the country's tangle of corruption, red-tape and chaos created a target-rich environment for the quick-witted, flashy, homicidal maniac. But India also possesses unfathomable traps. Its wheel of life and death can turn vicious as it grinds across the ancient countryside and eventually it began to crush Sobhraj.

Charles Gurmukh Sobhraj was born on April 6, 1944 in Saigon to an unmarried Vietnamese woman and an Indian tailor when Vietnam was part of colonial France's Indochina. Sobhraj's father abandoned the family. His mother met a French army lieutenant. The mother and her young son secured French citizenship.

Sobhraj's childhood was reportedly a painful quest for love, withheld by his now squabbling mother and step-father who alternately accepted and rejected the troubled child as he shuttled back and forth between Vietnam and France. Sobhraj said alienation turned him into an outcast who dabbled in petty theft to get more attention and out of boredom with the soap opera around him.

Beginning in 1963, French authorities incarcerated the teenage burglar in brutal detention centers. When he was 24, he married French woman Chantal Compagnon who gave birth to their daughter in 1970 when Sobhraj was based in Bombay, stealing cars and smuggling valuable commercial goods.

India's police arrested him in 1973 for robbing a jewelry shop in New Delhi's then-swanky Hotel Ashok. He and a partner seized control of a room, including its flamenco dancing guest, and for three days drilled through her floor to access the jewelry shop, scarfing up thousands of dollars in loot.

After escaping while on bail, Sobhraj took his wife to Afghanistan, where he targeted hashish-smoking foreign hippies and freaks in Kabul, but was arrested, escaped, and fled to Iran.

His wife, stuck in the Kabul jail, was later released and, fed up with a life of crime on the run, grabbed their daughter and returned to Paris.

His criminal activities continued for years. His brother, who became his partner, eventually suffered an 18-year prison sentence in Istanbul.

In 1977, Sobhraj and his new girlfriend Leclerc were imprisoned in India for the madcap act of drugging an busload of French tourists during 1976 in New Delhi's Ashok Hotel and attempting to rob them. His drug-filled treats which he offered them were too strong and zapped the tourists too fast. Staggering, slumping, babbling tourists slowly passed out in the lobby, screwing up his plot to rob them upstairs after they returned to their rooms.

Some of the groggy tourists saw through the scheme and wrestled Sobhraj to the floor while shocked hotel staff called police. During interrogation, his other partners reportedly implicated Sobhraj and Leclerc for murdering French tourist Jean-Luc Solomon two years earlier.

Sobhraj and Leclerc allegedly killed Solomon in 1975 by drugging him in a different New Delhi hotel, before robbing him and leaving him for dead.

Years later in January 1981, Sobhraj and Leclerc were still languishing in New Delhi's decrepit Tihar Jail, the largest prison complex in South Asia, serving out their 12-year sentences for their Ashok Hotel mass-drugging case while awaiting the eventual acquittal of Solomon's murder.

Then one day, a young Australian woman arrived in New Delhi and declared she planned to marry Sobhraj. She said she fell in love with him while reading his gruesome life's story in a paperback expose in Australia.

"I had never heard of Charles before, until I saw his book in a shop in Australia almost a year ago. The [book] cover was staring at me," the 25-year-old Australian woman told me soon after arriving -- but before visiting him in Tihar Jail.

The frightening 1979 book she read titled, The Life and Crimes of Charles Sobhraj by Richard Neville, described gory details of Sobhraj's killings, based on extensive interviews Sobhraj had with Neville inside Tihar.

"I read it about three times and felt sorry for Charles," said the woman, who asked not to be identified because her parents might be "embarrassed" if news of her unannounced upcoming marriage appeared in her hometown newspapers.

While reading the book, she began corresponding with Sobhraj, then 36 years old. Amid their rapidly escalating romantic letters, the girl broke up with her Australian boyfriend who opposed her correspondence with Sobhraj.

"My boyfriend was afraid he would be killed by Charles. I thought Charles needed a friend. I couldn't accept that he killed people. It was just a mental block. I put it down to his past. People change. People don't have good pasts all the time."

After one week in New Delhi, she met Sobhraj for the first time inside prison.

Sobhraj proposed marriage.

She accepted.

"We're going to get married!" she told me, smiling after they became engaged.

"He first proposed to me by mail. All the time he wrote me, I wondered if it was a con. He wasn't as I pictured him. He was small, thin. He doesn't seem to be hard."

First, she had to return to Australia by the end of the week to take care of her six-year-old daughter who was vulnerable without her. That did not leave enough time to complete the paperwork required by Australia to marry in India. So she promised to return frequently, wed Sobhraj and then visit him as many times possible in Tihar until he completed his jail sentence.

When I asked for her prediction about married life with Sobhraj, she replied that if he was freed from prison, Australia probably would not let him enter the country, so they may settle in South America.

"I thought I'd send my father a copy of Charles' book for Christmas [one month earlier], with a note attached saying: 'How would you like this man as your son-in-law?'" she said, laughing.

"I'll tell my parents when I get back home. My mother was worried before I left for India. She said she hoped I wasn't getting involved in drugs or anything fishy like that."

Several days later, she appeared for another interview. This time she was distraught and downcast.

She told me how during her meetings with Sobhraj in Tihar Jail, she would recite her own poignant love poems to him, but he always replied about how to send money to him in prison, and what currency to change it into before it reached India, and what countries and banks were better than others.

Every time she read him another love poem, he began describing the complexities of yet another currency sent from some other country and what bank would be good for that money so it reached him fast and without too many banking fees.

She desperately tried to woo him. She reminded Sobhraj of her favorite poem she wrote for him, about how "the chains of a prison cannot bind our love."

But every time she recited the stanza, "the chains of a prison cannot bind our love," he would reply that if the money she was going to send was in Australian dollars, it would be better to change it into British pounds in Australia and send that instead, unless she already had US dollars to transfer to India which, in that case, a bank in Hong Kong where his friend had an account would be more efficient.

The Australian woman soon departed India.

She did not return.

In October 1981, another tearful woman -- this one from California -- said she was leaving India miserable because authorities in Varanasi would not let her marry Sobhraj while he was there, imprisoned along with Leclerc awaiting the outcome of another murder trial.

The prosecution in that case demanded Sobhraj and Leclerc be hanged because they allegedly committed the murder in Varanasi, India's holiest Hindu city.

"I'm fed up. I'm leaving India because they won't let me see him," Shereen Walker, 35, told The Hindustan Times, sobbing loudly in her hotel room.

Walker, a graduate psychology student at the University of

California Los Angeles (UCLA), wanted to wed Sobhraj in a prison ceremony but was allowed only one 20-minute visit.

After reading two books about Sobhraj, Walker had written to him six months earlier.

"I love him and he loves me. It was the urge to understand a person like him. I saved up money to visit India and eventually meet him. We like each other and decided to get married.

"But not the way the papers have described it -- that I walked in demanding to get married to him. Oh, I'm so embarrassed reading it. It was not my idea in the first place."

By March 1982, Walker was still frustrated. She now feared Indian authorities were going to kick her out of the country, or at least refuse to extend her tourist visa. So she publicly demanded in an open letter to the United Nations, then-President Ronald Reagan, India's then-Prime Minister Indira Gandhi, the American ambassador to India and other officials that they protect her from arrest and expulsion.

"I am being threatened with imminent arrest and bodily harm because I am married to, and in love with, Charles Sobhraj, facing trial in Varanasi, India," she wrote in the letter, also sent to me, from the city 400 miles southeast of New Delhi.

"I have had a nervous breakdown and am getting worse both physically and mentally. I cannot get any money, as the police wrote something in my passport and no one will cash my travelers' checks," Walker's letter said.

Walker wrote that she "married" Sobhraj in November 1981 in Varanasi's jail while she was ensconced in a nearby hotel during his trial. The California woman alternately called herself Shereen Walker or Mrs. Charles Sobhraj. She said her visa was valid until April 1982, but Indian authorities wanted her to leave immediately, threatening her with arrest.

During that trial, prosecutors accused Sobhraj and Leclerc of killing Israeli tourist Alan Aaron Jacobs in 1975 by feeding him an overdose of drugs in his hotel bed near Varanasi's human funeral pyres along the Ganges River. The couple's motive was to steal Jacobs's money and passport.

India's media dubbed the deadly lovers the Drug Killers.

The Varanasi court sentenced Sobhraj and Leclerc to life imprisonment in 1982 but spared the couple from the gallows because -- according to the judge -- they murdered with such elegant finesse that their victim did not realize he was dying, and thus suffered less than if he knew he had been poisoned.

Sparing the two killers' lives, Varanasi's Additional District Sessions Judge Dinesh Sharma ruled:

"True, the murder of an innocent Israeli national who had come to this country as a tourist was pre-planned and committed in pursuance of the criminal conspiracy with a touch of professional skill. Yet it must be said that there was no brutality or dastardliness about the crime. So abstruse was the device employed by the accused to do away with the life of the deceased, that even the victim could not suspect any foul play."

Sharma said the deceased fell asleep within half an hour of the drug overdose without suffering and died peacefully.

Years later, Sobhraj and Leclerc overturned that conviction on appeal.

When Leclerc later developed ovarian cancer while in prison for the Ashok Hotel drug-and-rob case, India's Supreme Court allowed her to "temporarily" return to Canada for medical treatment.

She died there one year later.

In July 1983, the blue-eyed, once-pretty Canadian was now 37, gray-haired and emaciated. While she waited in New Delhi International Airport's departure lounge, Leclerc told me:

"I am innocent, but nobody wants to believe it. I don't feel great joy leaving India, as if I had been freed, because the Supreme Court gave me the condition that I had to come back to India in one year. When you have third-stage cancer, you don't know if you will be living after a year. The prognosis of the doctor said I can be dead in six months."

Would she return to India if cured in Canada?

Leclerc rubbed her groin in pain, smiled and gently replied:

"I can't say what I will do, because if you are so sick, you cannot plan. In the condition I am going, it is like somebody dying, just to have a bit of pity and to let her die with her family."

Are you in love with Sobhraj?

"No. The question should be, 'Did I ever love Sobhraj?' I don't think so. I stayed with him because I had no passport, no money, and did not speak English then."

Is Sobhraj a murderer?

"I can't say. I never saw him kill anyone. I consider Sobhraj a man who is sick," Leclerc said, delicately smiling.

Indian investigators meanwhile suspected Sobhraj may have also murdered his Indian partner Chowdhury several years ago. But an Indian news photographer said to me just after Leclerc's flight departed:

"I told police I saw someone who looked like Chowdhury visiting Marie Leclerc, while she was smoking hashish in a five-star hotel during her going-away party just before her flight."

Two years later in 1985, during our interviews while Sobhraj inside Tihar Jail, he still appeared suave, muscular and excited. He moved easily among guards and other prisoners in the visitors' hall. He had been advising wealthy Indian jail mates how to present their cases to the courts and local media.

When I asked how many people he killed during his lifetime, Sobhraj replied in aggressive, French-accented English:

"Officially, I am denying I killed anyone. Of course I am denying!"

Wearing his typical gear of neatly pressed slacks, slip-on shoes, a shirt rolled up at the elbows and a big golden wristwatch, Sobhraj resembled an urbane Vietnamese salesman, with high cheekbones, giving a hard-sell to a customer in a snazzy showroom instead of a convicted prisoner in the bowels of a wretched prison.

He projected bravado while a cluster of Indian prisoners watched in awe from a respectful distance. The now-balding Sobhraj told me his priority was to block extradition from India to Thailand, where he feared certain execution because the statute of limitations had not yet expired for the wanted Bikini Killer.

"According to the Thai constitution, they can shoot anyone without trial. So I don't think you can get a fair trial there. There is no evidence to connect me with the crimes there. If I go free from this jail, I will try to stay in India, get residence here and do my writing," Sobhraj said, grinning.

"I have my own cell. I make it like an office, with an electric typewriter. I find pleasure in writing short stories. I will try to get married. I don't know yet. I want to settle. Kids is what I want. There is no question of my going back into crime. I've been trying to legalize my situation. I fought my cases patiently. Years ago, I said I would win. Now I want to live quietly."

Sobhraj tried to project a woeful image of innocence and repentance during our interviews -- a performance he repeated since childhood to everyone close to him.

"My advice to a young person is, it will not be worth getting into crime. As far as possible, a young criminal should try to get out of crime. Society will have to play a role in that. But the most important role is yourself, the psychological changes, your thinking and instincts. Accept the advice of specialized people."

Then came Sobhraj's classic, ghoulish cliché:

"Here," he said, handing me a bottle of soda. "Have something to drink."

For several years, he lorded over Tihar Jail's miserable universe including the prison's superintendent who Sobhraj blackmailed. Whenever Sobhraj went to the superintendent's office, their conversation inevitably turned to ways that the superintendent could profit from Sobhraj, who generously offered to cut him in on a slew of devious business deals which would easily profit the delighted jailer.

But Sobhraj also planted eavesdropping devices which recorded the superintendent's illegal rackets. When Sobhraj later played a few sound bites, the frantic superintendent had no choice but to agree to share power with the usurping inmate or else suffer exposure. That scam worked for a while but eventually leaked and hit India's media. The government investigated the superintendent's activities, and transferred him elsewhere.

Despite denying that he ever killed anyone, Sobhraj wrote descriptions of himself promoting his never-published memoirs, shamelessly hyping that he was a "master jail breaker," "master criminal" and "master murderer."

He showed me short stories he wrote while in prison, including his version of Prime Minister Indira Gandhi's 1984 assassination. Sobhraj's written description of her two Sikh bodyguards shooting her dead in the garden of her New Delhi residence was filled with his own fantasies and macabre, bloody imagery rendered in graphic slow motion detail with her splattered blood reverently depicted in words.

When I asked about various charges against him in seven other countries, Sobhraj smiled and replied:

"Nobody has applied for my extradition except the Thais."

Sobhraj said he enjoyed sharpening his wits by reading German philosopher Friedrich Nietzsche and Swiss psychiatrist Carl Jung.

"I believe the childhood I had played a lot in my development. Certain traumatic things in my psychological setup."

He enjoyed respect among Tihar's staff.

"He is a good man," a policeman guarding the main gate told me. "I know Charles very well. Maybe he is a killer. But he is a very brave man."

In 1986, about a year after our prison interviews, Sobhraj did the thing he knew best: he escaped Tihar Jail by hosting a birthday party for the Indian guards and serving them drugged sweets. They nodded out after stuffing their faces.

Sobhraj drove out through Tihar Prison's gates in a shiny white car he arranged through a contact. When guards eventually awoke, India's authorities freaked out and, embarrassed by scathing international media coverage, searched for Sobhraj everywhere.

"I think Sobhraj is so sexy and daring," an Indian stewardess cooed while gazing at his photo and reading the news of his escape. "I'd love to meet him. He must be laughing at the prison and police," she told me.

Parliament Member and famed author Kushwant Singh wrote in his weekly satirical column in The Hindustan Times:

"I couldn't be the only one to applaud Charles Sobhraj. However despicable a drug-peddler, murderer, womanizer and thug he might be, he has panache, brains and audacity that few could match. His recent jail break puts him in the category of the Jackal and Abu Nidal. Bravo mon ami Charles. I hope the slobs never catch you."

Bombay's police soon found Sobhraj hiding in nearby Goa, India's hedonistic beach resort and a favorite sandy pillow for foreign criminals laying low.

Bombay police laid a meticulous sting. Dressed in wrap-around sarongs, they posed as waiters, cooks and other staff at Sobhraj's habitual beach cafe in Goa. They arrested him along with British accomplice David Richard Hall when the desperate duo arrived to make a long-distance telephone call.

"Is this the way you treat innocent foreigners?" Sobhraj reportedly reacted when the Bombay Police Special Squad pounced on the two men at O Coqueiro Restaurant and Bar at Purvorim in Goa on a Sunday night. Less than one month after he broke out of jail, police handcuffed Sobhraj.

Now wearing long hair and a beard so he could mingle with his favorite targets -- foreign backpackers -- Sobhraj made a mindless blunder by hiding in Goa. The former Portuguese colony had an international reputation as a haven for heroin and hashish dealers, foreign criminals on the run from their own countries and other underworld characters.

They blended in among the nude sun-bathing and carefree foreign tourists who have flocked to Goa's west coast tropical beaches ever since hippies and freaks had begun sprawling there during the libertine 1960s and 1970s.

When Sobhraj escaped, New Delhi police told me Goa was

the most obvious place for him to hide, "but Charles won't go to Goa, because he knows that is the worst place, because everyone will be looking for him there."

Baffled how to find him, one senior police officer asked me: "Where do you think he might be? Do you think he's made it across the border to Nepal or Pakistan? We think Sobhraj will hide in Bombay for a couple of months and then try to leave India after everyone has forgotten about him."

When he was brought back to Tihar Jail, some people speculated Sobhraj intentionally allowed himself to be caught so his prison sentence in India would be extended and Thailand's statute of limitations would expire, so he could avoid extradition if he was freed anytime soon.

Sobhraj was confined a total of 21 years in India before being released in 1997. Thailand's statue of limitations had expired. Sobhraj was deported from India to France where bizarrely he postured as a decadent celebrity.

In 2015 India's MidWeek News Weekly reviewed a Bollywood film titled Main Aur Charles and said:

"Main Aur Charles is a fictional docu-drama that gives an insight into the chequered life of the most notorious, psychopathic, criminal Charles Sobhraj, who rocked the 1970s with his serial killings of bikini-clad tourists.

"The opening shot, focusing only on a man's shoes with his legs outstretched on the bow of a motorboat, foretells the enigmatic subject that the tale will unravel.

"Narrated from the point of view of the then-Delhi Police Commissioner Amod Kanth (Adil Hussain), the film does not delve deep into the psyche of Charles (Randeep Hooda). It merely documents the salient incidents in his life, starting 1968 in Thailand, spanning until his final arrest in Goa in 1986.

"The tale is juxtaposed with the police's efforts to arrest him and how each time Charles eludes them, except for the final time.

"Randeep Hooda looks and portrays Charles Sobhraj, getting into the skin of the character by physical appearance, mannerisms and mindset. His lazy smile, confident persona and electrifying charm when he woos women, makes you believe this is how Charles Sobhraj must have looked and behaved," reviewer Troy Ribeiro wrote.

"Richa Chandha as a law student named Mira Sharma, essays with competence her role of an awestruck young lady, madly in love with Charles and mesmerized by his charismatic personality. She shines in some scenes but seems listless and unenergetic in many.

"Lucky Morani in a miniscule role of psychiatrist Ashima, is wasted.

"There is no unnecessary drama, no emotional moments, no convoluted plots, yet the film manages to keep you riveted to the screen by the sheer power of Charles' life and the interesting twists it takes, courtesy his razor-sharp mind and tongue. The dialogue, 'Evil is charming, attractive and difficult to resist,' or 'acchai ki jeet hoti hai par burai kabhi haarti nahin' -- whether in English or Hindi are powerful, loaded with messages and apt in the context of the film."

After he returned to Kathmandu in 2003, he was tried, convicted of Bronzich's murder and sentenced in 2004 to the maximum 20 years imprisonment.

"His 2004 conviction in Nepal was made possible because former Dutch diplomat Herman Knippenberg -- living in retirement in Wellington -- had tracked the man he called a psychopath for three decades," the New Zealand Press Association reported.

"Knippenberg, who settled in Wellington with his New Zealand wife Vanessa, a former foreign service officer, passed on through Interpol a critical statement taken from Sobhraj by Indian police in 1976. It was used by Nepalese district court to convict Sobhraj of the murder.

"Knippenberg was 31 and on his first foreign posting at the Netherlands Embassy in Bangkok in February 1976 when a Dutch couple vanished after meeting Sobhraj, a charismatic con man living near Bangkok's Patpong red-light district.

"Knippenberg carried out his own investigation, found that the couple had been drugged, strangled and bashed before both were doused in petrol and burned, and alleged that Sobhraj was linked to seven brutal murders in Thailand between August and December in 1975.

"The diplomat assembled a 200-page dossier," the report said.

When Sobhraj tried to bluff his way free after his final arrest in Kathmandu, "he had not counted on Nepalese police in 2003 still having access to evidence from nearly 30 years earlier -- material which Knippenberg had stored -- that proved Sobhraj was lying when he said he was not in Nepal in December 1975. Sobhraj had admitted, in statements [in 1976] to Indian police, traveling [with Leclerc] to Nepal on forged Dutch passports," originally belonging to Bintanja and Hemker, his alleged victims in Thailand.

During his trial in Nepal, the government's prosecutor told the court Sobhraj had signed, nearly 28 years earlier, a Kathmandu hotel registration book in 1975 using Bintanja's name. The prosecutor said Sobhraj's latest signature in his own name in his genuine French passport, which he used when arriving in Kathmandu in 2003, matched the handwriting of the 1975 signature.

Sobhraj denied that scenario and said police were unable to produce Bintanja's forged passport or immigration records proving anyone with that name entered Nepal in 1975. He said it was unacceptable to convict him based on a photocopy of a Kathmandu hotel listing a Bintanja and Hemker checking in with a signature in Bintanja's name. Sobhraj -- an expert in forgery -- also claimed those photocopies were police forgeries created in 2003 to ensure his conviction.

"I have never been to Nepal before," Sobhraj said during his trial. "If I was involved in murder cases, why would I return?"

INDIA'S "BANDIT QUEEN" PHOOLAN DEVI

Elsewhere in India there was a much different killer who was feared, or loved, as a "bandit queen," and whose name was known throughout the country.

Phoolan Devi.

Bandits such as Phoolan Devi are known as dacoits. During the 1800s, British linguists traced the Hindi word and defined a dacoit as a robber who belonged to an armed gang. British colonialists specified in their Penal Code that a crime of dacoity must involve five or more people in a gang who have committed an illegal act.

Phoolan Devi led a gang of 39 people. All of them men.

Most dacoits in India were men. But there were a handful of feisty female gangsters. Among these, Phoolan Devi was considered the deadliest. Police chased her for years through isolated, desolate ravines where even animals found it difficult to stay alive. They repeatedly failed to catch her.

Phoolan Devi grew up southeast of the fabled Taj Mahal tomb. Twisting, dusty ravines ran right by Phoolan Devi's front door at Gorhapurwa village in Uttar Pradesh state. Police said she deserved no sympathy because she allegedly ordered her gang to line up and execute 22 landowners in Behmai village in the bleak Chambal region. She allegedly had them shot them in 1981 in revenge because the farmers helped police track and kill her first bandit lover, Vikram Mallah, and raped her.

Some witnesses claimed Phoolan Devi orchestrated the executions by shouting through a bullhorn to her gang, ordering them to shoot the 22 men.

A lone survivor, Devprag Singh, said Phoolan Devi and her 39 gang members were dressed as police when they entered Behmai, 150 miles southeast of New Delhi. When the gang rounded up the village's men, Singh realized they were dacoits.

Singh said Phoolan Devi initially began shouting obscenities and she yelled, "If anybody interferes or resists, he will be shot like a dog."

Another gang member allegedly shouted, "Come out from wherever you are hiding. Today is the day when we will take our revenge."

Singh told Indian reporters:

"We started pleading with them to let us go, that there was nobody else hiding in the village. But they ordered the 23 of us to follow them.

"They took us to the edge of the river and made us kneel down with our hands raised. Then the dacoit in a police officer's uniform shouted, 'kill them,' and the firing started."

Singh survived bullet injuries to his leg and chest because he was covered under a pile of bodies.

Whatever happened that terrible day in Behmai, it branded her as an alleged mass murderer and forced her on the run.

When Phoolan Devi first began her years of murderous crimes, she would escape into the wild countryside and emerge only to attack villages to restock supplies.

Eventually, she grew exhausted from fleeing countless police hunts and negotiated a deal that would spare her from death.

Phoolan Devi gave herself up in 1983. She led her gang, including husband Man Singh, to a public mass surrender. She trusted the Indian government's offer of rehabilitation and leniency.

But she cautiously chose to surrender in neighboring Madhya Pradesh state, at Gwalior city, where she had no enemies. Thousands of villagers flocked to her surrender ceremony. Most Indian newspapers and magazines carried stories or interviews about her. Their sensational reports evoked awe, pity and dread.

In September 1985, she glumly sat in Gwalior's squalid jail fearing extradition back to her home state of Uttar Pradesh, which had a list of her alleged 22 Behmai village murders and where she faced a possible death sentence. Sitting on a bench in the bleak, sun-baked yard of Gwalior Jail, Phoolan Devi winced while denying direct involvement in the massacre.

Dark-eyed, short and dowdy, Phoolan Devi did not appear as anyone's idea of a female gangster. Barefoot, she wrapped herself in a black-and-purple sari. She wore a cheap metal stud in one nostril. A few green plastic bangles jangled on her arms. Phoolan Devi looked like a stubby village woman with a defiant expression, perpetually on the verge of tears.

"In the Behmai massacre, I didn't kill anyone. Everyone else in the gang did," she told me in a Hindi dialect at the jail.

"I searched the houses."

Later in our interview, she boasted of having "killed some people" during other escapades.

"I didn't want to become a dacoit. People misused me," she said, alternating between sarcastic, earthy remarks and genuinely frightened weeping.

When asked what she would do now that she was imprisoned, she smiled and bragged, "I'll escape and become a dacoit again."

Her advice to any young girl trying to decide whether or not to follow in her footsteps?

"Oh yes, be a dacoit," Phoolan Devi said, sneering and sassily tossing her head to the side. "If she's been harassed, she should harass."

Beneath the bravado lived a terrified woman who knew that India's justice system often twisted slowly and brutally. Suddenly bursting into tears, she said softly:

"I don't want to be released. I want to die. I want to be punished, because I don't want this burden carried over into my next life. When I am reborn, I want to be a man. It is much easier for men to live.

"They're not oppressed. And there's not so much revulsion against them. I regret surrendering because of all the problems I have now."

Authorities said her surrender was unconditional, but she insisted the government verbally promised to give her family a gun license so they could buy a weapon to protect themselves in their vulnerable village.

No license had yet been issued. And a cousin had seized her defenseless family's land, police said. Phoolan Devi also complained she was not being allowed to leave prison to visit her family, who often stayed in Gwalior just to be near her. Phoolan Devi had expected occasional day-trips as part of her rehabilitation program.

When news of Phoolan Devi's surrender appeared in American newspapers, Susie Coelho Bono, wife of former American entertainer Sonny Bono, flew to India and wooed Phoolan Devi with dreams of fame and fortune.

Susie, of Indian parentage and a model bent on becoming an actress, reportedly smuggled a tape recorder into Phoolan Devi's cell and spent four hours a day, for two weeks, taping her story with the aid of a translator.

"We became good friends," Susie was quoted as saying at the time.

"In fact, by the time I'd finished interviewing, I felt as if we were sisters. I hope one day to get her out of India and bring her to the United States."

Phoolan Devi now cursed Susie Bono.

"She told lies," Phoolan Devi said, gazing out the door at Gwalior's dusty, hot prison yard.

"Nothing ever happened. Susie said they would make a film and pay me 60,000 rupees [$5,000 at the time]. But all she did was send me some clothing and paid me 3,500 rupees. I feel used because of this."

Phoolan Devi's short-lived notoriety did attract other fans.

"Someone from France came to Gwalior wanting to marry me," she chuckled.

Bombay's giant film industry made a box-office hit about Phoolan Devi. Not amused, she filed a defamation suit against the Bollywood movie makers for $50,000 in damages. One of her objections to the film, titled Kahani Phoolwati Ki, was that dacoits do not dance around trees when they fall in love.

Though Phoolan Devi felt abandoned, she had not been forgotten by the man who risked his life to arrange her surrender.

Police Superintendent Rajendra Chaturvedi had entered alone -- unarmed -- into the Chambal ravines to establish a meeting with her.

With great difficulty, he earned Phoolan Devi's trust. He promised her she would not be executed if she gave up. Phoolan Devi believed him and agreed.

"Any woman who went through that mistreatment, I can't blame her for being a dacoit," the award-winning Chaturvedi told me at Gwalior Jail where he worked.

"I'd do the same thing if I were her. Some women take it lying down, or become suicidal. She decided to rebel. Police view dacoits as a menace. And as a problem. But it is not a problem. It is an institution with roots in tradition, and enough beneficiaries so everyone benefits.

"The lawyer benefits because he defends dacoits. Doctors benefit because they take bullets out of them. The arms suppliers sell weapons and ammunition to them. For one bullet worth less than a rupee, they sell it to a dacoit for 25 rupees."

Police often arranged secret truces with dacoits, so authorities could proudly claim there was no crime in their district.

"That way the gang can stay in the area and know they will not be arrested or shot in an encounter. And the reputation of the police goes up because there are no crimes being committed. Local politicians also benefit by never informing on dacoits. The politician gets a cut of their profits."

Chaturvedi estimated there had been about 500 known dacoits in 1981 in the six worst-affected districts of Gwalior, Bind, Morena, Shivpuri, Datia and Gunar. Now in 1985, there were only about 80.

"Their number is small, but their terror is tremendous."

The reduction in gangsters was due to the tough Anti-Dacoity Act of 1981 which allowed courts to seize the property of bandits, prevent bail for 120 days, and arrest anyone carrying an unlicensed gun.

Police said a relatively unknown woman named Kusma Nain now ruled the Chambal ravines after enduring several years as a lesser rival to Phoolan Devi.

Another female bandit, a Muslim named Munni Bai, was meanwhile stuck in jail.

Among the tales of daring female gangsters, was a quote by a famous bandit queen named Jankshri:

"When I first went with the dacoits, I was a simple girl. But later I learned to drink and kill. I had no other way out."

Bandit queens also knew what police did to another famous bandit queen, Meera Thakur. She was killed several years ago by Uttar Pradesh state police who then stripped off her clothes.

They laid her naked body out like a safari's prize tiger catch. They posed alongside her nude corpse for souvenir photos -- and as a warning to other bandits.

Phoolan Devi said she feared police would find a way to transfer her out of prison, kill her, and also display her body in such a shameful way.

Police routinely tortured suspects to force them into confessing to crimes.

"I've tortured people thousands of ways," Chaturvedi said matter-of-factly during our interview.

"Chilies stuffed into the rectum of a man. Or we tie him to the four corners of a rope bed and stretch him to limits that are unendurable. It leaves no marks or injuries.

"Also beating on the soles of the feet. Electric shock? Oh yes, I've used electric current many a time. Without all this, the police wouldn't be able to stop crime.

"You can't behave like a gentleman," he said, reflecting over nearly 20 years as a respected police officer.

Well-mannered, urbane and a family man, with a taste for classical Greek literature, the police superintendent was repeatedly cited by government officials and the nation's media as among India's best and brightest law enforcers, based on the statistical successes of his work.

None of his well-wishers publicly applauded torture, but

most were aware that police brutality is a common occurrence among India's police force.

"When I am torturing a man I know is bad, I feel revengeful," Chaturvedi said.

"You want to inflict so much pain that he licks your feet. You want abject surrender so he doesn't think of himself as a man. You want him totally impotent.

"We have a phrase in Hindi, 'aurat jaise ghigyana.' It means 'whimpering like a woman.' That's the way you want him, so he becomes totally gone."

The widespread use of torture in India was repeatedly criticized by Amnesty International. The US State Department had cited "widespread circumstantial evidence" of torture by police throughout the country.

India's courts meanwhile bemoaned how police executed whoever they choose in "fake encounters." Indian newspapers frequently reported such incidents under headlines such as:

"Torture Part of Police Culture"

"Those Frightening Men in Uniform"

"Torture Chambers of the City Police"

In the latter example, interrogation rooms allegedly used by New Delhi's police to torture suspects were said to be in the bowels of the majestic Red Fort, unbeknown to countless tourists who simultaneously marveled at its ornate exterior. India's prime ministers and visiting world leaders including Queen Elizabeth II stood upon the Red Fort's ramparts during official ceremonies.

How does a torturer feel when he discovers his victim is innocent?

"If you later find out he was innocent, you feel very remorseful," Chaturvedi said.

"Why do you feel remorseful? Not because of the torture, but because this man has no means of going to a court of appeal. He is a poor villager who can't afford to go to the court. And you've been part of it.

"Then you feel very ambivalent. You give him money, or

help him in some way. If it was really bad, you get his nephew a job or something.

"Or you tell him, 'This time you've escaped because you are innocent. But next time...' and you leave the sentence unfinished, unknown, so he remains afraid."

One New Delhi police officer working inside Rashtrapati Bhavan, the Presidential Palace, told me that he witnessed several occasions when his colleagues attacked suspects.

"Torture is not legal, so we must be careful. We don't use electric shock, or technology, or things like that because it will show on a medical report," he said.

"We tie his hands and hang him upside down, and leave him hanging. Or we tie his hands and legs together and hang him between two desks, swinging on a rod. It usually works to get information, especially from amateur criminals."

In Indian society, police were often sneered at by rich and poor alike who assumed the cops were poorly-educated, dishonest and vicious.

Many victims of rape or robbery refused to contact police for help because they fear their intrusion.

"If you call the police, that makes it worse because then they'll always be coming around asking for money and hanging around," one middle-class housewife lamented.

Police sometimes raped, hit or verbally abused women during questioning even if the victim was innocent and merely making a complaint for a petty crime, according to women's rights organizations and court testimonies.

"There are also fake encounters when police desperately want a man," Chaturvedi said.

"We use all means, fair and foul. In police parlance we say, 'sam, dam, dand, ved,' which means we use 'foul intrigue, money, punishment and knowledge' to catch suspects. To stage a fake encounter, one man or his gang is invited to a village. There's women, wine, everything. When he's under the influence, police come in and kill him. Usually he doesn't have his weapon.

"Then the police go someplace nearby on the road and fire a lot of shots in the air. They manipulate the records to say, 'this dacoit was fleeing, we were in hot pursuit, and we shot'.

"Sometimes he's tied to a tree and shot. Or tied to a bed. Or locked in a house and shot with rifles through the windows. It's very murky business. I've witnessed it. Totally disgusting."

As India modernized, so did its methods of meting out pain. More recently, police often used a Potentio Meter to zap suspects with electric shock.

"The Potentio Meter has two brass handles connected to a wheel," Chaturvedi said.

"The faster you turn, the more current. You don't have these in every police station, but four or five are available in every district with the police. You know who's got it, and you get it when you need to utilize it."

To defend their poor reputation, police complained their lives are harsh. They were forced to work 10 or more hours a day, and could barely afford to live in slums.

Their life was also dangerous. Indian police reportedly suffered an unusually high death rate -- more than 500 a year -- and almost 25 percent of active policemen in service were said to have been injured.

Disgruntled police claimed they often received miniscule annual pay raises despite risking their lives under rigorous conditions. A lack of promotions also caused morale problems. More than 75 percent of police retired at the same rank at which they joined the force many years earlier.

These grievances were exacerbated by a lack of proper training and discipline. Police complained they were misused by politicians as private armies against dissidents and to protect well-connected criminals. Police were often used by wealthy feudal land owners and businessmen against landless peasants who demanded minimum wages, or against urban union organizers and striking workers, according to news reports and labor leaders.

"In a few states, the politicization of the [police] force has become a problem of some magnitude and will need to be effectively countered," said India's Intelligence Bureau at an annual conference of inspectors-general of police.

A glaring display of police not doing their job because of confused political loyalties came immediately after Prime Minister Indira Gandhi was assassinated on October 31, 1984 by her two Sikh bodyguards.

Several days of frenzied anti-Sikh riots rocked New Delhi and elsewhere in northern India and left more than 3,000 Sikhs dead. Many police refused to stop murderous bands of thugs or actively helped them kill Sikhs, according to survivors and eyewitnesses.

In other situations, police torture also helped turn some victims into dangerous, revenge-seeking political revolutionaries.

Many Sikh youths cited police torture as one of the main reasons they joined Sikh insurgents during the 1980s, fighting in a failed attempt to carve out an independent nation called Khalistan in northern India's Punjab state.

Chaturvedi estimated from his experience "for every one person caught, or attempted to be caught, almost three to four people have to suffer."

Phoolan Devi was eventually killed, but not in the way anyone expected.

She remained in prison until 1994 when she was freed and, in a surprise move, became a member of parliament two years later. After losing her parliament seat in 1998, she was re-elected in 1999.

Her enemies meanwhile had not forgotten. They vowed to avenge her murders. In 2001, an assassin shot Phoolan Devi, 38, at her official residence in New Delhi.

Police caught a man named Sher Singh Rana and said he confessed to killing Phoolan Devi in a plot arranged with nearly a dozen accomplices. Rana was imprisoned. But while awaiting trial, he escaped in 2004 from Tihar Jail when his friends, disguised as a police escort, appeared and secured his release to attend a court appearance in Uttaranchal state.

"It is an incredible jail break. At 7 am, we handed Rana over to a policeman from Uttaranchal as he showed us a warrant saying he had come to collect Rana to produce him before the court," a jail warden told Agence-France Presse shortly after the escape.

"There were other 'policemen' waiting near a police van. We did not suspect a thing. Later we got a shock when another police party turned up at the gates of Tihar with a warrant to take Rana away."

JONATHAN "JACK" IDEMA IN KABUL

American bounty hunter Jonathan Keith "Jack" Idema was arrested, put on trial, convicted and imprisoned in Afghanistan for kidnapping and torturing Afghans after the US invasion.

There is no evidence Idema ever killed anyone. But he maniacally raved so much about wanting to murder people, that it was obvious Idema wanted to give the impression he was a military-trained killer. Idema became notorious in Kabul for threatening to assassinate American journalists, international aid workers, Afghan mujahideen and anyone else who triggered his volatile temper.

Idema arrived in Afghanistan alongside US invasion forces in 2001. During the first few years of the US-led war, Idema strutted around Kabul dressed in military fatigues and combat boots, armed with a Russian AK-47 assault rifle shouldered across his back and a holstered Glock pistol.

"That's what I love about Afghanistan, if you tell someone you are going to kill them, they fucking believe you," Idema said during our interviews in December 2001 and January 2002 in Kabul.

"If I'm in New York and I tell someone I'm going to kill

them, they say, 'Yeah motherfucker? Well, I'm going to kill you first.' But not Afghanistan. Here they believe you."

Born in Poughkeepsie, New York in 1956, the short, stocky Idema dyed his salt-and-pepper hair black and loved to show off his weapons which he occasionally fired to intimidate people.

He traveled with a handful of young, armed Afghan men who he ordered about, often shoving wads of US dollars into their hands and waving his big military knife at them while theatrically laughing with glee. His knife was the same blade he used in Kabul at home, to eat thick, grilled steak when he invited me for dinner alongside his Afghan gang.

Meanwhile, in a worrying display of intimidation, Idema also threatened to murder an American foreign correspondent representing the Stars and Stripes newspaper. The reporter remembered interviewing Idema in a federal prison during the 1990s after Idema had been sentenced to three years for defrauding dozens of US companies for a total of $260,000.

When the journalist revealed this overlooked and disgraceful biographical information to other correspondents who were gathered together during a December 2001 party in Kabul, Idema went verbally ballistic.

"I just might have to fucking kill you! Now get the fuck out of here before I do!" Idema shouted at the reporter while other worried correspondents hurriedly exited the dining room. The two men then loudly argued while I discreetly stood behind them, eavesdropping and slowly scooping frosted cake into my plate.

"You don't believe me? Test me. Just test me! But get the fuck out of here now or else," Idema ranted.

The shaken journalist was hosting the party and politely mentioned that this was his rented house.

Idema responded: "I said get the fuck out of here. Now!"

"But this is my house."

"You think this house is yours? This wasn't your house before, so shut the fuck up. If I hear another word out of you, I swear I will..."

Several days later, the correspondent told his colleagues:

"Look his name up on Internet, and the story of him in jail will come up. His name is spelt I-D-E-M-A."

Most foreign journalists avoided Idema and warned everyone else that he was an unstable trouble-maker who liked to brandish weapons and take advantage of Afghanistan's anarchy.

Idema insisted he was acting to protect innocent Afghans from being exploited and abused by all sides, so they would not suffer from the US invasion or revenge attacks by recently ousted Taliban and Osama bin Laden's al Qaeda network.

"I work for God and country," Idema, who wore military-style fatigues with a US flag shoulder patch, said.

After much coaxing, he showed me his supposed, impossible-to-confirm resume, which he kept on his laptop. It listed military badges he claimed to have earned and his experience including:

El Salvadoran Master Parachute Wings

Royal Thai Army Balloon Wings

Royal Thai Army Master Parachute Wings

Royal Laotian Combat Parachute Wings

Kuwaiti Police Commander Badge

German Senior Parachute Wings

Nicaraguan Senior Parachute Wings

11 years in the United States Army Special Forces

18 years in Special Operations

1978: Military adviser in Nicaragua and South Africa

1979: Primary SWAT instructor for New York State police Olympic SWAT team, Lake Placid

1980: Primary weapons and tactics instructor for British SAS commandos during Operation Honeygift

1982-83: Special Forces adviser El Salvador

1984: Chief instructor/adviser for the USAID Diplomatic Protection Guard during the Haitian coup attempt

1984: Chief tactics and firearms instructor for Ron Reagan, Jr., David Morrell, author of First Blood Rambo

1985: Chief instructor in tactics and hostage rescue training for SEAL Team Two, Counter-Terrorist Group Academy

1986: Director of training for United States National Park Service and Park Police for the Statue of Liberty rededication ceremonies, SWAT, counter-terrorism and explosives training

1987: Led a classified successful rescue recovery mission to the Caribbean for a Mid-Eastern prince

1991: Adviser to the Lithuanian national police, National Academy and ARAS Commandos, The Eagle, Lithuania"

Idema also named a slew of courses he completed at Fort Dix in New Jersey, Fort Benning in Georgia, Fort Bragg in North Carolina, Fort Drum in New York and Fort Devens in Massachusetts.

His biography stopped in 1991.

"For the past 10 years, I've been 'black'," Idema said, hinting at secret missions he could not divulge.

In Afghanistan, Idema dubbed himself "a civilian adviser to the Northern Alliance." The alliance was comprised of the late Ahmad Shah Masood's former mujahideen and other guerrillas who were now helping the US invade, hunt the Taliban and their al Qaeda allies.

"I am a [former] Green Beret."

Idema also boasted that armed enemy Afghans recently threatened him on a road near the eastern city of Jalalabad, until he shouted that he was an American and bluffed that if anyone hurt him, a retaliatory US air strike would obliterate the place and everyone there.

Laughing whenever he re-told the tale, Idema said the Afghans suddenly became gracious and allowed him to continue his journey.

In January 2002, he said his Northern Alliance "intelligence assets" discovered seven hours of videotapes showing al Qaeda operatives purportedly teaching foreign fighters how to kidnap, bomb and assassinate people.

The techniques used by the alleged al Qaeda soldiers and featured in the video tapes appeared to resemble US, British and

Israeli commando tactics, he said.

After Idema showed me segments of his videotapes in Kabul, he agreed to take me to what he described as the former al Qaeda training camp where bin Laden's fighters had shot the sensational film of themselves teaching others. They abandoned the camp when fleeing the US invasion, he said.

On January 7, 2002, Idema escorted me around the bomb-littered complex of partially destroyed buildings in Mir Bacheh Kowt village, 15 miles north of Kabul, amid pine trees of Shomali Valley.

The heavily damaged buildings, formerly a children's school, were littered with countless live rockets, fuses, landmines, bullets and other ammunition scattered on the floor in dangerous piles in several buildings.

Idema's videotapes showed a handful of men in this same compound, dressed as janitors and golfers, acting out surprise strategies to seize and kill foreigners anywhere in the world.

For example, a man dressed and acting like a typical janitor was filmed idly sweeping the ground in front of one of the school compound's buildings. Other men, dressed and acting like civilian office workers, entered and exited the building. After a while, the fake janitor slowly moved his broom cart into the foyer and, sweeping and keeping his head down, slowly climbed the stairs as if he was going to sweep an upper hallway.

At a key moment, the janitor dropped his broom. He pulled a hidden gun out of his broom cart, and began blasting into the air and at walls, chasing the office workers and dividing them into groups.

Other armed men, purportedly also with al Qaeda, then emerged from random unnoticed positions in the hallway and helped him hustle the groups up onto the building's rooftop.

"When this hostage thing started, he [the janitor] went and pulled out a hand gun," Idema explained during our tour of the training camp.

Idema then pulled out his own black pistol and aggressively charged forward, as if he was an al Qaeda fighter, pushing a bunch of imaginary office worker hostages.

In other scenes videotaped at the school, dozens of purported al Qaeda fighters fired AK-47 assault rifles and rocket-propelled grenades toward a group of men who were pretending to be an audience of VIPs at a mock golf tournament.

The assassins, disguised as golfers, idled about on the camp's dirt field, their weapons hidden in white golf bags. When one fake golfer signaled them by teeing off, the guerrillas opened fire with assault rifles and a rocket-propelled grenade, obliterating supposed dignitaries which were depicted in the video by a cluster of targets. The purported al Qaeda men also started firing at a fake convoy of vehicles which supposedly real VIPs would have used.

Other tapes showed nervous men in camouflage outfits being taught to leap with ropes from the roof of the compound's two-story main building and jump through open windows.

In a session on how to negotiate with authorities, the trainees threatened to shoot a hostage and throw him off the roof.

During our tour, Idema pointed at a school building he claimed al Qaeda had been training in and attacking in the video.

"They threw a grenade into the side of this wall, the right side. On the left side of that wall, the opening there, that's where the guy fired the rocket-propelled grenade, the RPG.

"This was meant to simulate something maybe like a small embassy compound or a small compound where there was someone they wanted. Because they went in there, and they didn't just kill everybody. They took one hostage out.

"And then they went back and killed everybody. The whole time, on the right side there, were two guys on a motorcycle as their back up team. Through that door over there on the right, they brought the hostage out, they brought him around, and they put him in the back of a truck. Then they sped away with him.

"Arabic interpreters and also Afghans who viewed the tapes were able to identify the different dialects, and we know for a fact there were Kuwaiti, Iranian, Iraqi and Libyan guys here," Idema said, describing the men performing the scenes.

"It just goes to prove a point. One guy, operating by himself independently with the indigenous population, can gain more intelligence than 5,000 guys in a room watching satellites."

It was impossible to confirm the veracity of the seven hours of tapes, the identities of the men, or if the scenes were even filmed by al Qaeda.

But it was easy to see while visiting the buildings that the school's heavily damaged walls matched the damaged walls seen in the videotapes which clearly had been filmed at the complex.

During our tour of the former al Qaeda base, Idema inspected the huge array of hurriedly abandoned ammunition which lay heaped in several rooms.

"Touch no bombs and no fuses and no metal objects, because there is more live ammo and live fuses here than probably anywhere else I've seen recently," Idema told me, gesturing at a large haphazard pile.

"In this building here, was where they had a bomb-making plant. They were taking Russian claymore mines, they were disassembling the claymore mines, they were taking the explosives out of them and they were using them to build frequency induction detonators. They were using them to build electronic firing devices.

"You have a whole variety of explosive devices here. These are old mortar shells. The gray ones in the tubes are all US mortars.

"You mustn't touch anything here or pick this stuff here. There is a good chance they could have mined this or booby trapped this stuff. When I was over here earlier, last time, they had a very unusual stack over here, along with a Bangalore torpedo-type mine, so probably you want to stay away from this stuff.

"One thing that is very interesting is right here. Take a look at this fuse. They are US mortar shells. Over there, it says on them clearly: '120-millimeter mortar, out of lot 9, 89'.

"So back in '89, throughout that whole time, you've got to figure we sold surplus stock and they probably went to some place like Pakistan or Saudi Arabia. There is no way of knowing where it went yet, but we've already photographed it and we are trying to trace the lot number.

"The most important thing in this entire place, the most important thing, is this right here, this fuse. It is a very, very expensive US fuse. It is an adjustable fuse. This one happens to be a 'proximity'. And what you can do is, set this fuse so when the mortar round comes in, it either detonates above, in the air, or two feet off the ground, or on the ground after impact. An aerial burst or a ground burst, depending on whether you are going after armor or you are going after personnel.

"Inside this building, we found a whole range of bomb making devices. Everything from oscilloscopes, to soldering irons, to disassembled Soviet claymore mines, to wires. Plans for frequency induction detonators, which is a device that you put on your bomb, on your explosive device, then you have a circuit board on it and a radio. And you can key your radio, to key the other radio, and send a frequency code so it explodes. So its basically a radio-controlled bomb.

"They were taking the shells, these 20-millimeter shells, incendiary, and they were snapping them off with pliers, and then they were taking the powder out of the shells and dumping it into something else. That's where they could get gun powder from. It's a very explosive powder."

Idema pointed long, fat bullets with a different colored stripe on each bullet in a "Chinese" ammunition box:

"Notice this is black, and this red? These are armor piercing tracer incendiary, and these are armor-piercing."

Before we departed the abandoned al Qaeda base, Idema patiently gave me advice about the best way to aim, while I fired a few shots with his Kalashnikov rifle at a target.

"In Afghanistan, I usually carry a Kalashnikov. It's easier to get bullets for. If you are going to operate with the indigenous guys, you ought to be carrying the same gun. They got the same magazines, the same bullets. And they appreciate that more. They don't want you showing up with one of your $10,000 high-tech M-16s. They want you carrying what they carry.

"Ain't that right?" he rhetorically asked his nearby armed Afghan squad.

Idema soon sold the videotapes and photographs from the school for thousands of dollars to US and other television networks including CBS TV'S 60 Minutes II and an international photo agency.

"Once the footage was out there, most outlets took the view they could not afford to be left behind NBC, MSNBC, BBC and ABC America all used the tapes," ABC's Mediawatch reported in a 2005 investigation into allegations that the tapes were staged.

Idema sent an email to me on February 25, 2002 -- from his jki_specops@earthlink.net address -- proudly mentioning his success in selling his video to CBS TV, and CBS News' announcement about their broadcast.

The CBS News announcement on January 17, 2002 was headlined, "Heart of Darkness: Exclusive Videotape Shows Training Drills For Terrorists Assassinations, Kidnappings and Hostage-Taking Studied. A Green Beret, talks with Dan Rather."

CBS described them as "al Qaeda tapes...the videotapes make it easier to identify the enemy; dozens of al Qaeda faces are shown uncovered, clear and close up."

"The al Qaeda cameraman who spent hours carefully recording would-be terrorists as they learned how to kill," was also shown playing with his children.

"The seven hours of videotape, which show how al Qaeda trains its recruits, were shot sometime last year at a facility about 30 minutes from downtown Kabul," CBS reported.

"In it, recruits drill relentlessly, learning the ins and outs of assassination, kidnapping and murder. With instructors looking over recruits' shoulders, al Qaeda trainees practiced working with weapons that can take dozens of lives in just seconds, learned the tricks of terrifying innocent people and were schooled in the best way to take control of a building.

"One segment shows a drive-by shooting, where recruits are trained to overtake a car and kill everyone inside. Another shows a practice attack on a building: victims are disoriented with stun grenades, guards are killed, and hostages are quickly rounded up. Recruits shout commands in English -- a sign they would like to take scenes like this to the West.

"The tapes also show that something else was part of the terrorist training at that camp, something outsiders have never seen before. It records planning sessions where recruits were briefed on complicated ways to get close to world leaders and kill them.

"In the session, the instructors and students speak Arabic as they plan an assassination, but a translator tells CBS News that 'the person to be assassinated is a writer who blasphemed against Allah and his prophet. The beginning signal of the operation is when the driver opens the trunk. Two men with Kalashnikovs come out and fire'.

"In another segment, al Qaeda works on an elaborate scheme to kill an Arab prince playing golf. One is instructed to carry weapons in his golf bag and tee off near the proposed target. Off the golf course, but close by, an accomplice waits with a rocket launcher for the leader to give the signal. 'He gives the signal to begin by dropping his hat,' says the translator," CBS reported.

Some US and foreign investigators suspected Idema created the videos with local Afghans acting as if they were terrorists.

"Deputy Police Chief Mohammed Araf told me that Arabs had indeed used the town as a military base under the Taliban, and the buildings in Mir Bacha Kot match those on the Idema supplied tapes," Peter Bergen later reported in Rolling Stone.

Idema didn't care. He was proud and delighted to cash in so profitably on the TV and photo rights.

Boosted by that success, Idema tried to rent his skills to foreign correspondents in Kabul.

"Idema offered to organize a convoy to Tora Bora, where the Taliban and al Qaeda were making what was thought to be their last stand and where, the Americans were confident, Osama bin Laden was trapped," Britain's The Independent newspaper reported.

"After making a few checks with the British military, some of us decided to decline his offer. Those who went were robbed at gunpoint a quarter of the way through the journey by their 'guards' and made their way, bedraggled, back to Kabul.

"Jack professed to be outraged. He would take the matter up immediately with his 'good friends' General Quononi the new Defense Minister, and Abdul Rashid Dostum the warlord -- and the bandits would be summarily executed.

"After that, Idema would regularly turn up at the Intercontinental Hotel, where most of the foreign journalists were staying, attempting to sell videos and photographs purporting to show Taliban and al Qaeda terrorists training for assassinations and rehearsing gas attacks using dogs."

Meanwhile, Idema's loud, angry mood swings continued.

At a late night party in Kabul's Intercontinental Hotel in December 2001, he overheard a nearby American CNN employee belittle Idema's analysis of the Afghan war and denounce Idema as "some old guy" who knew nothing.

"I will break your fucking legs! I will break your fucking arms! And then I will..." Idema suddenly raged while escalating his threats and moving closer to the CNN employee who became wide-eyed and distressed when he saw the furious Idema approaching.

After venting at the man while others in the crowded room gawked at the scene Idema had created, he received profuse, nervous apologies from the CNN man. Eventually their confrontation dissolved into stilted jokes. Idema's public performance once again proved he could -- and enjoyed -- intimidating people with threats of physical harm.

The Dallas Morning News reporter, Tod Robberson, reported in his paper:

"This reporter [Robberson] was five feet away from Mr. Idema on April 20, 2002, when he drew a pistol during an argument and fired a bullet that went through a couch and lodged in a wall behind me...missing my heart by about eight inches."

Meanwhile, others were warning the US military that Idema was a loose cannon, jeopardizing lives in Afghanistan.

"This man is a very dangerous person by virtue of his carelessness and stupidity, and before he gets someone killed...he needs to be removed from the area," Vietnam veteran and former Army medic Ed Artis wrote in a December 18, 2001 letter to the US Army Special Operations Command at Fort Bragg, North Carolina.

"I feel that given the amount of time that he has been allowed to run around telling people he has been working for the US Embassy, Pentagon, Special Ops under cover or the CIA, that he has garnered or bought enough contacts to pose a real threat to, not only me and those near me, but the over all mission of the United States and the Coalition that is fighting there."

Artis knew Idema from personal contact and their attempts to work together that ended badly. Artis headed Knightsbridge International, described as a non-governmental organization providing humanitarian assistance in foreign nations.

Meanwhile, Idema was appearing in US news stories saving lives in Afghanistan.

Idema emailed me in March 2002, forwarding a United Press International story by Martin Arostegui, datelined Gardez, Afghanistan.

"Hidden American commando teams [3rd Special Forces Group] pinpointing al Qaeda positions with laser target designators, guided in air strikes against terrorist bases in the White Mountains for three days before Afghan troops moved into the area," the story began.

"In the dusty courtyard outside, Jack, an American special adviser to the Afghan military, treated Afghan [soldiers'] injuries, stitching a fresh bullet wound in one man's lower leg. Even without anesthesia the soldier was thankful for the treatment.

As the Green Beret [Idema] wiped the blood splatters from his face, a dozen Afghan fighters looked on, they have never had this kind of support in 23 years of war," UPI reported.

In April 2002, Idema emailed me again forwarding an Associated Press story by Burt Herman datelined Nahrin, Afghanistan, headlined:

After Afghan Quake, 'Jack Does House Calls'.

It described Idema single-handedly rescuing isolated earthquake victims.

"Jack was on his own one-man mission to help those hurt in the quake that struck this area of northern Afghanistan a week ago -- and in particular find its neglected victims: women and children," AP reported.

"Jack admits only that he is a Green Beret from Fayetteville, North Carolina, who has been in Afghanistan for more than five months on a mission he won't reveal. Afghan officials said he was a civilian military adviser to the Northern Alliance, a confederation of warlords that helped the United States drive the Taliban from power."

Idema told me his long-term goal was to "build a security force [in Kabul] with a whole bunch of [US] former Special Forces guys." They would help the Afghan government train Afghans in "professional soldiers' skills" so Afghans could be bodyguards and commandos in a new, democratic Afghanistan.

"We will start with 100 [Afghan trainees] and we'll try to get it up to 500. It will be to protect journalists, protect aid workers, protect foreign dignitaries and protect their own [Afghan] dignitaries. It won't be private. It will be Afghan government. It will partially under the control of the Ministry of Defense and partly under the control of the Ministry of Interior.

"It'll bring people from all the different commands and from all the different ministries and organizations to a school that everyone can go to. It doesn't matter what commander they belong to, or what sect they belong to. It'll train them all together. It will be the first time there will be a true coalition of Afghan forces training together and working together.

"I'll invite you to the first class. The special purpose force."

Would Idema be the instructor?

"Absolutely."

What do Afghan soldiers need to know that he could teach them?

"Professionalism. Professional soldiers' skills. The second thing I think they need is shooting ability. I think the third thing they need is organizational skills, and all the rest will come with that. Tactics are easy."

Idema's fantasies ended in May 2004.

"The FBI has now put out a warrant for my arrest -- apparently for impersonation of an Army major to enter a US military base -- and is spending more resources here to get me than they are on bin Laden," Idema said in an email to his wife in America and to CBS News.

"I am told that there are wanted posters all over Afghanistan.

"The charges are a complete lie."

The wanted posters warned that Idema was "armed and dangerous" and "interfering with military ops."

No one was sure who issued the posters, but they appeared shortly after US-led ISAF's press office emailed journalists, stating:

"US citizen Jonathan, Keith, or Jack Idema has allegedly represented himself as an American government and/or military official and the public should be aware that Idema does not represent the American government and we do not employ him."

Afghan security forces arrested Idema on July 5 in Kabul along with two American colleagues -- former soldier Brett Bennett and cameraman Edward Caraballo -- and their four-man Afghan squad.

Idema and six others had "formed a group and pretended they were fighting terrorism," said Interior Minister Ali Ahmad Jalali.

They kidnapped eight Afghans and "put them in their jail" in Idema's home, Jalali said.

Idema and the two other Americans appeared at a public trial on July 21 in Kabul. They denied charges that they kidnapped and meted out "mental and physical torture" against the eight Afghans.

When police confronted Idema and his two colleagues, one of the men "said he had orders to quickly arrest a terrorist before he could blow himself up in a government building," a police official said, according to the Associated Press.

By that time, Idema and his team had twice fooled NATO's International Security Assistance Force (ISAF) into sending their bomb-detection teams, including sniffer dogs, to illegally raid buildings and vehicles and check for hidden explosives.

"Their credibility was such that with their uniforms, their approach, our people believed they were what they said they were," Commander Chris Henderson, an ISAF spokesman told reporters in July shortly after the three Americans were arrested.

"They were operating in military style, with US flags on their shoulders, and representing themselves in such a way that ISAF believed them to be who they said they were...which was a special operations agency...a legitimate security agency.

"It was a mistake."

ISAF realized Idema was duping them when he called for a third raid and senior ISAF staff were alerted.

"At that point they said, 'This is Idema, he's not legitimate,'" Henderson said.

"Does the court think that ISAF would send me 50 soldiers and 10 vehicles if they didn't know who we were?" Idema said during his trial. "ISAF knew exactly who we were."

Meanwhile, ISAF and US officials tipped off the Afghans who raided Idema's home and discovered his makeshift torture chamber.

Police discovered three blindfolded and beaten Afghan men hanging from the ceiling upside down.

Five other men were roped to chairs.

Blood-stained clothes littered the room.

Two wall clocks, inside Idema's green-colored house, displayed the time in Kabul and Fort Bragg, North Carolina -- headquarters of the US Special Forces.

One of the roped men was Afghanistan's Supreme Court Judge Maulawi Siddiqullah. Idema tried to torture Siddiqullah into confessing links to Taliban and al Qaeda.

Siddiqullah later described his experience to journalist Bergen:

"The first night, around midnight, I heard the screams of four people. They then poured very cold water on me. I tried to keep myself from screaming, but couldn't. Then they played loud, strange music. Then they prevented me from going to the bathroom. A terrible situation. I was hooded for 12 days."

Idema had kidnapped Siddiqullah at dawn by going to his home, firing a gun and shouting, "Hands up! Hands up!" Idema also took away Siddiqullah's two brothers, four other relatives and a family employee. These were the eight men rescued by Afghan authorities from Idema's house, Bergen reported.

Idema later described Siddiqullah during a telephone interview with radio station WFNC in Fayetteville, North Carolina:

"He had explosives, detonators, plans to an ISAF base, schematics for Bagram," Idema said, referring to US Bagram Air Base north of Kabul.

"Oh yeah. No, he was just a regular old Supreme Court judge?"

Another kidnap victim, a 19-year-old mechanic named Muhammad Hanif, told the court that Idema and his team attacked Hanif's workplace, shot a few bullets into the ceiling, and seized him.

For 10 days, Idema kept a bag over Hanif's head and his hands tied, he said.

"You are terrorists. Why do you pray, and what do you pray for?" one of the Americans demanded of Hanif, according to The New York Times.

Idema told the court he was hunting bin Laden, Taliban and other Afghan terrorists.

"Bin Laden has half a million dollars on my head," Idema shouted.

"He [Idema] was operating by himself there, with the delusion that he was able to do great things for the world," a US military spokesman in Kabul, Major Scott Nelson, said.

Embarrassingly, the US military said it did receive on May 3 -- and held -- a kidnapped man from Idema.

"We did receive a detainee from Mr. Idema or his party," said US spokesman Major Jon Siepmann.

"The reason we received this person was that we believed that he was someone that we had identified as a potential terrorist and we wanted him for questioning."

The person turned out not to be a senior Taliban operative as Idema had claimed. As a result, the Afghan was freed after more than a month in US military custody at Bagram Air Base.

Bagram, 42 miles north of Kabul, was built by the Soviets during their war. When US troops invaded, they slept in Bagram's beds which displayed Cyrillic graffiti scrawled on the walls of the barracks next to wrecked Soviet MiG-21 warplanes which lay abandoned on the bomb-gouged runway.

Idema told WFNC radio that he had contacted the US military at Bagram and said to them:

"'I got a Taliban chief of intelligence in custody, I need Black Hawks and a security team to pick him up. Send a force, send force protection, get together a group, get together the MPs [military police], come out here and pick this guy up, because I can't get him to you.'

"They come out in the middle of the night, they leave Bagram. The complete force protection detail. And they pick up this guy and they take him into US custody."

Asked why US authorities released the suspect after more

than one month of questioning, Idema replied:

"Oh yeah, we had the wrong guy, sure we did.

"The only reason they released him afterwards, they didn't want to say they had prisoners that we'd given them in custody. Luckily they made a deal with this guy and he's now working for the US, which I had worked out with this guy in advance."

Meanwhile, Idema wasn't shy about promoting about how he was kidnapping people.

"In the weeks preceding his arrest, Idema was actually sending footage of himself interrogating prisoners to a major US network, hoping to sell a world exclusive," ABC's Mediawatch said.

"He sent this email to Dan Rather at American 60 Minutes: 'For Dan Rather's eyes only...we now have so many terrorists we need to a rent a jail...only money and resources has kept us from catching them all'," Idema's email said, according to ABC.

In September during the trial, Idema and his two colleagues released a videotape -- filmed by his own team -- to reporters. It showed one of the eight Afghan kidnap victims, Kabul shopkeeper Ghulam Sakhi, who Idema had seized in June for "interrogation."

In the video, Sakhi described a plot to kill Afghan politicians and attack the nearby US Bagram Air Base.

Questioned by Idema during the film, Sakhi appeared to agree that he wanted to go to America, be implanted with a bugging device, return to Afghanistan and then be tracked by satellite while meeting bin Laden.

The US government was offering a $25 million reward for bin Laden, dead or alive.

Sakhi's statement to the court however said he was innocently riding in a taxi approaching Kabul when Idema kidnapped him.

While trapped in Idema's house, his kidnappers scalded him with boiling water, severely kicked him in the chest, and repeatedly shoved Sakhi's head under water.

But Sakhi was unable to identify any of the photographs of

men who Idema said were terrorists.

Sakhi said the only way he stopped the torture was by making up a story naming someone and falsely accusing him as working for the Taliban and bin Laden.

When Sakhi named Afghan Education Ministry official Mohammed Arif Malikyar, Idema then kidnapped Malikyar who was also discovered in Idema's house during the police raid.

Another kidnap victim, Sher Jan, said, "They pulled me out of my house one morning, hooded me and broke a rib with a gun.

"They poured hot water on me too."

Idema however told the court, "None of this ever happened and there's no marks on anyone to show that it did."

Idema later told the North Carolina radio station that the men he was interrogating in his private jail were terrorists.

"They were 72 hours and 96 hours from putting together, finishing their plan, to drive fuel trucks into Bagram. Everybody listening knows how many fuel trucks and diesel trucks and food trucks come into Bagram every day. You know we called the [US intelligence officials in America], and said you've got to stop the fuel trucks right now. Immediately!

"Within one minute of the [kidnapped] guy giving us this information under interrogation, we're like, 'Stop the fuel trucks.'

"And they [the US] stopped them! So they stopped all the fuel trucks for like weeks.

"Only a month later, after this went down, they [US officials] arrested, they stopped a fuel truck in Kandahar based on our intelligence, and they were able to find the explosives and found the thing rigged to blow up.

"So I want you to imagine five fuel tankers driving into Bagram and straight towards, they were gonna drive them straight into the barracks and administration areas. You would've had about 500 dead American soldiers. Now, I was willing to kill terrorists to stop that.

"I wouldn't have hesitated one minute if I had to kill them

all. But I didn't have to do that. In fact, I didn't have to torture them at all. The judge [Siddiqullah], the only thing he complained about in uh, in court was that we didn't let him go to the bathroom for 12 hours. Well I am sorry about that dude!

"You know, he wanted a law made saying that you had to be able to go to the bathroom every three hours if you're in custody. That was his big speech in court.

"Did they tell us everything? They sure did. And why? Because we offered them money, cell phones, a job working for the US.

"We offered them Miranda soda and kebab. And anybody that's been in Afghanistan knows you can turn a guy...in about five minutes if you've got the right things to offer him. Because here you can buy anything for money. And terrorists will flip in a minute if you do it right. I mean this stuff about hanging them upside down? There's not a house in Kabul, I think, that could hold a guy from the ceiling," Idema told WFNC radio.

"But who gave you the authority to interrogate these people?" Presiding Judge Abdul Baset Bakhtyari repeatedly asked Idema during the trial.

They do not belong to Osama Bin Laden and he beat them," Bakhtyari told London's Sunday Times correspondent Christina Lamb.

"I have seen their bodies. There were red marks on their wrists and they were burned," Bakhtyari said.

"I'd like to be like Jack, because he is a very brave man. I understand he had fought terrorism and I'm sorry he has been arrested. I feel the government of Afghanistan could have done more with him.

"I see the future of Jack as very dark. I know he is a good man, but at that time he was bad and that is what is so disappointing. Until the government or the CIA says he worked for them, I don't know what to think," Bakhtyari said.

"The American authorities absolutely condoned what we did, they absolutely supported what we did," Idema told the court.

"We were in contact directly by fax and email and phone

with [Defense Secretary] Donald Rumsfeld's office, with the Deputy Secretary of Defense for Intelligence, and with [acting director of security] Heather Anderson, a four-star rank officer level at the Pentagon."

Anderson "applauded our efforts," Idema said. But nothing was signed.

"We did not want to go under contract because that would mean that we couldn't work with the access to Northern Alliance people we were working with," Idema said.

Video imagery presented by Idema during the trial also showed him arriving at Kabul International Airport in a scene he claimed proved Afghan officials knew and approved of his manhunt for bin Laden.

The director of Kabul's airport, alongside Kabul's police chief General Baba Jan, were shown hugging Idema when he and his two American colleagues landed in April.

The two Afghan officials however later claimed they were tricked into believing Idema was a US government-sponsored counter-terrorist expert.

"Perhaps everyone ended up being on trial here, not just the three Americans, but also the Afghan authorities and the US government and its policy of using so many private military contractors to carry out its policies in Afghanistan," said the BBC's Andrew North.

Before his arrest, Idema told me:

"Human intelligence is what this war is all about. Not B-52 [airplane] bombs. What is important for killing terrorists is finding the intelligence you need to hunt them down. And that's only done with personal contacts and through personal assets, human assets, men on the ground. In this war, we didn't have enough men on the ground."

The National Security Court declared Idema and his two American colleagues guilty on September 15. It sentenced Idema and Bennet to 10 years in a Kabul's brutal Pul-e-Charkhi Prison. Caraballo received eight years in jail after claiming he was simply filming a documentary of Idema's antics.

Idema's four Afghan partners were handed sentences ranging from one to five years.

"It's the same sick Taliban judges, the same sick sense of justice," a handcuffed Idema said as guards took him from the court.

"I knew that the American government wasn't going to help me. I apologize that we tried to save these people. We should have let the Taliban murder every one of them," Idema said.

"Nobody was hung upside down," he told Associated Press in an August interview during Idema's temporary imprisonment at Kabul's National Security Directorate, Afghanistan's chief intelligence agency.

"Nobody was burned with cigarette butts...nobody was beaten, nobody was tortured, nobody had boiling water poured on them.

"Did we interrogate people? Absolutely. Did we keep them up with sleep deprivation? Absolutely," Idema said.

"I gave [the FBI] bin Laden's exact address right outside Peshawar," across the Afghan border in northwest Pakistan near the Khyber Pass.

"I gave them the grid coordinates, the street and house number and everything. They got there five days after he left. It's like, what are you doing? Do you not want to catch bin Laden?"

In his WFNC radio interview, Idema described his temporary imprisonment inside the National Security Directorate:

"You are not going to believe me but I swear to you this is the truth. In my first weeks in NDS custody in Kabul, I was beaten unmercifully. The, the, the uh, US Embassy has the medical reports. They asked the doctors to tone them down. One of the doctors still gave us a medical report.

"Both eyes hemorrhaged, both rotator cuffs torn, dislocated shoulder, broken ribs, separated sternum, they poured boiling water on me. Everything that you could imagine that, anything Americans have ever been accused of, they did to me.

"I had secondary burns all the way to my knees. Do you

know what? When they did this, do you know that there were two FBI agents present? They were in the hallway at NDS. They were telling them what questions to ask me. Can you imagine the American FBI present during this kind of torture?"

After Idema was transferred to Afghanistan's dilapidated Pul-e-Charkhi Prison on the outskirts of Kabul, he lived in an apartment-sized cell, with a living room, bedroom, bathroom, kitchen, fully furnished including a satellite TV and a bar with vodka and other drinks.

In Pul-e-Charkhi, he appeared in a 2005 "Guns For Hire," a lengthy TV broadcast which investigated foreigners working as armed private security forces in Afghanistan. The interview with Idema inside Pul-e-Charkhi was directed and filmed by Claudio von Planta, with producer and reporter Sam Kiley.

Asked who paid for his comfortable lifestyle in Pul-e-Charkhi, Idema told Kiley, "The Northern Alliance did this for me."

His claim that the late Masood's Panjshir Valley-based Northern Alliance financed his stay could not be independently confirmed.

He wore khaki pants and a matching shirt adorned with a beige US flag patch on one shoulder's sleeve and, on the other sleeve, "Special Forces" and "Airborne" patches, plus army-style patches on his chest.

Idema boasted he could escape the prison anytime he liked.

"I can walk out of this prison with one snap of my fingers, and that is no bullshit. I can walk out, alright, but that means shooting a whole bunch of people. If I snap my fingers tomorrow, 1,000 Panjshir soldiers will come over these walls and they'll kill every motherfucker in this prison who isn't Panjshir."

Idema said he chose not to escape.

"I am here because I'm trying to resolve this politically," he told Kiley.

US-installed Afghan President Hamid Karzai pardoned Idema in 2007 in a general amnesty of prisoners after he served three years in Pul-e-Charkhi.

Idema soon showed up in Mexico.

"Idema did not return to the United States. Ms. Alesi, his former girlfriend, said he feared being prosecuted there for any number of things. Instead he went to Dubai and then England before moving to Mexico," the New York Times reported.

"IDEMA IS CONSIDERED VIOLENT. HE IS CURRENTLY ARMED WITH A .45 S&W PISTOL AND FREQUENTLY UNDER THE INFLUENCE OF COCAINE, HEROIN, ALCOHOL AND PAIN KILLERS," wrote Ron Barbour who ran a robosoldier.blogspot site.

In August 2010, he posted an update titled, "further-alleged-adventures-of-jack" which described Idema.

"HE USES FALSE IDENTIFICATION AS 'COUNTER TERRORISM GROUP' AND IS CURRENTLY IN MEXICO WITHOUT A VISA.

"HE CURRENTLY HAS AN M4 SEMI AUTOMATIC CARBINE, A GLOCK 9MM, A SMITH AND WESSON 45 ALONG WITH AN ORANGE FLARE GUN.

"HE IS HIV POSITIVE/AIDS VIRUS CARRIER, TYPE 1 & 2, AND MAY ALSO HAVE ADVANCED SYPHILIS," Barbour wrote.

Idema died aged 55 in January 2012 of medical complications from AIDS in the small town of Bacalar in Mexico's Yucatan Peninsula where he ran a tour boat business.

Wild unconfirmed tales immediately swirled.

"Jack Idema: Dead and Eaten by Dogs in Mexico," Barbour headlined his online Freedom Fighter's Journal blog on January 22, 2012.

"A confidential informant reports to this writer that Idema died a very painful death, and was abandoned for the last week of his life by his Mexican lackeys when the money ran out.

"The Casa Arabi resort that was owned by Idema, and where he died this morning, was said to have been looted and stripped of anything valuable, while Idema lay dying on a filthy blood stained bed vainly begging the looters for food, drink and pain killers.

"Idema weighed 98 pounds at death, covered with purple lesions [of] Kaposi's Sarcoma and had pus sores [from] herpes all over his genitals and thighs. It was his heroin supplier who found him dead in bed with vomit and feces around him.

"It is not clear what happened to the body, but there are unconfirmed reports that it has been thrown into the street and was eaten by wild dogs," Barbour wrote.

"I met this colorful character in the lobby of the Hotel Tajikistan in Dushanbe in November 2001," wrote Village Voice reporter Ted Rall shortly after Idema died.

"All he did was talk. A lot of bluster, much of it including threats about how his Special Forces buddies would track me down and murder me and my family if I ever crossed him.

"Having been bullied and beaten as a kid, I wasn't impressed," Rall said.

Some people posted their thoughts about him on an online site titled, "Keith Idema is Dead" on ComeBackAlive.com:

"Sometimes it is good to celebrate evil. MUAHAHAHAHAHAHA" gnaruki said.

"final justice for his transgressions would be to bury him in an unmarked garbage dump, and secure his obscurity," AztecDave wrote.

"He made our country look bad by becoming the face of America, leading to lord knows how many attacks against people over there," Kurt said.

"I am not saying we looked great before to the beardies, but Jack's Sodomy Upside Down Cake in Kabul sure did not help anything.

"Plus there is a limited group of people that want to turn this guy into a 'persecuted hero' and when you let someone else be in charge of a story, it will eventually become their version everyone believes. That is Idema continuing to con from the grave, and success in that will mean more little Jacks popping up in war zones getting folks killed," Kurt wrote.

"Well said, Kurt!" replied Barbour.

"Indeed, Idema was a dangerous psychopath and traitor.

"I had believed Idema to be a harmless Walter Mitty type who engaged role-playing the special ops warrior. When I read of his latest adventures, I would often laugh to myself, as I couldn't believe anyone would take him seriously.

"Yet the evidence is overwhelming that scores of people, who should have known better, were taken in by him and became his victims.

"Jack Idema was no joke. He was a highly skilled and intelligent con artist who -- fortunately for the United States -- chose to stay out of politics.

"Seriously, there are so many ominous parallels between Idema and Adolf Hitler, it's not funny! One can imagine in a parallel universe where a political 'Idema' who mastered his temper, stayed off drugs, did not engage in risky homosexual acts and served with honor in the US military, opted for a political career after discharge from the service.

"The Republican Party would have welcomed an honorable veteran soldier into its ranks, the GOP loves the soldiers. Idema could have started his political career by winning a Congressional seat in upstate New York, and from there? In his mid 50s, he could be the great presidential hope of the GOP in 2012.

"I knew Idema for over a year at FCI [Federal Correctional Institution] Butner at FCI Petersburg in 1994/95 as a political prisoner charged with the attempted assassination of President Clinton. At one point he lived in the room next to me in the Maryland Unit for several months while we both were being interrogated on a daily basis by various branches federal law enforcement.

"We often played chess in the day room, where I usually lost to Idema's more aggressive game. I can tell you that the man was highly intelligent. The prison rumor was that Idema's IQ was above 141.

"Idema's nickname by hardened federal convicts was 'Hitler' and they were afraid of him.

"I laughed at them when they told me how evil Idema was! I told them he wasn't SERIOUS about his wild tales and his threats of violence!

"I'm not laughing anymore," Barbour said.

"He was most certainly a psychopath, and trying to get inside his head was like chasing shadows," RYP posted.

"It is true to say though, he was trained in the Special Forces at Fort Bragg in Fayetteville, North Carolina and went on to indulge himself in some notorious events around the world.

"He used to come over to the UK in the early to mid-nineties and while here, he met my team at the time," RYP said.

"We were with Keith for a couple of days and while at Earls Court, he told us of many things.

"One of the accounts he gave was of one of his friends called Mr. Plum -- for the sake of anonymity.

"Mr. Plum later allegedly committed suicide, and so prior to meeting Keith at Heathrow, we all knew of Mr. Plum's untimely end, and so when Keith came over, we naturally asked him what the fuck happened with Mr. Plum.

"'He drank too much anti-freeze,' was his response.

"It was true, Mr. Plum did actually die of acute poisoning due to the anti-freeze.

"But when we asked Keith the natural question, as to why Mr. Plum would choose that way to do it, Keith's reply was chilling, not so much what he said, but how he said it.

"He told us sneeringly: 'He had no choice in the matter.'

"A subsequent conversation one of us had with him afterward revealed that 'someone' had put a gun to Mr. Plum's head and threatened to splatter his brains should he not drink the anti-freeze.

"BS? I dunno for sure either way. I do know Mr. Plum died by drinking anti-freeze and I do know he really pissed Keith off, and so connecting the two together isn't such an outrageous thing to do.

"Some years later, he calls me up from his Afghan prison cell and asks me for a favour, my stomach turned somersaults coz I knew what was coming was gonna be bad, real bad, and my ass was gonna be on the line somehow.

"He informed me that one of the guys who was in prison with him -- another American ex Special forces guy -- had been released and was stranded at Gatwick airport, and could I go and pick him up and put him up for a few days.

"I thought to myself, I'd have to drive down to Gatwick, pick up a confirmed psychopathic killer -- he was one of the guys with Keith [Jack] who did the torturing -- and let him sleep in my house.

"Now far be it from to judge anyone, but seeing as the guy had been banged up for five years and hadn't seen a woman without a black tent swirling around them, I was somewhat hesitant to allow him into my house with my wife and daughter around.

"I respectfully told Keith I was going on holiday the next day and so couldn't help him out.

"There are several people over here, in the UK, Keith did threaten to kill and I think he'd grown so used to voicing these threats as a vehicle to get what he wanted, he lost touch with the reality of it all and he paid the price dying in an obscure Mexican town with no real friends or family around him.

"He was most certainly a diagnosed psychopath and I lost count of the number of people he told me he had killed.

"It's not a nice thing to say, but you got used to it when around him, and so I didn't really take much notice, but whilst I am pretty sure he hadn't killed as many as he said, I am however damned sure he had killed a lot of people.

"If there is a hell, that's where he's undoubtedly going, but knowing Keith, he'll probably enjoy it down there, and I have zero doubt he'll inevitably threaten to kill the Devil," RYP said.

Idema's obituary in North Carolina's News & Observer described his final years in Mexico according to Penny Alessi, Idema's ex-girlfriend who was in contact with him days before he died.

"At home, he lounged in Arab robes, a cut-rate Lawrence of

Arabia. A pirate flag wafted from his house's minaret-like turret. He would often go on round-the-clock vodka-and-cocaine-fueled binges while playing Arab music, the sound track of Apocalypse Now or Louis Armstrong's What a Wonderful World nonstop."

CHAPTER 3 ~ WAR

AMERICANS, SOVIETS & MUJAHIDEEN IN AFGHANISTAN

"What has war brought them?
Grave instead of shelter.
Shroud instead of clothes.
Bullet in the stomach instead of food."

~ Marxist Afghan President Najibullah

At the dawn of the 21st century, artifacts of Afghanistan's recent wars silently lay entombed in a hulking, concrete time capsule which contained dust-caked unclassified US documents, thick spider webs, and half-smoked cigars hurriedly abandoned in forgotten ash trays.

All of this lay abandoned inside the American Embassy in Kabul after its panicked US diplomats had fled in a snowstorm 12 years earlier in January 1989. The Soviet Union was withdrawing the last of its 115,000 Red Army troops after 10 years of unwinnable warfare and an estimated one million dead on all sides.

The Americans feared their own US-armed "holy warrior" mujahideen guerrillas would soon turn the Afghan capital into a bloodbath because Moscow was leaving the vulnerable Afghan Marxist regime to its doom.

"My feeling is that it will become very unsafe in Kabul after the Soviets leave, although it appears placid at the moment," US Embassy Political Officer James Schumaker told us during his evacuation on January 30, 1989, while Marines solemnly folded the embassy's American flag in a tight triangular bundle.

The night before, the Marines had drank as much as they could of the embassy's stash.

"We are honored to have served and helped the Afghan people toward peace and freedom," Charge d'Affaires John Glassman said in a short, serious farewell speech.

"We will be back as soon as the conflict is over. God Bless the USA. We are going home."

When heavy snowfall blocked the embassy's air evacuation later that day, Glassman joked:

"Send in Rambo! Send in the Delta Force! I have a Harley Davidson parked under the US Embassy, so nothing is going to stop me from getting out of Afghanistan.

"If I can't fly out today, I'll ride right through mooj [mujahideen] territory and through the Khyber Pass to Pakistan. Every biker in America will cheer me."

It would have been an awesome sight, Glassman on a chopper hurtling down the road, riding east through Jalalabad.

But it didn't happen. The following day, their chartered Indian Airlines flight was able to arrive from New Delhi and safely ferried these last diplomats, Marines and other staff to India's capital.

The embassy abandoned a fleet of black official vehicles next to the main building, leaving the cars intentionally disabled so no one could drive them. Surrounded by a stone wall topped with barbed wire, the embassy and the nearby American Club were locked, to be guarded by Washington's enemy, Soviet-backed Afghan army troops with Kalashnikov rifles.

As the years passed, Afghans fought greedy civil wars, destroying much of Kabul. Regimes changed several times.

The tan-colored embassy eventually showed scars from repeated attempts to break into the main building. Heavy gunfire damaged the embassy's gray metal front gate along the street.

Then suddenly, US forces invaded in response to the September 11, 2001 attacks against America.

To escape heavy US air bombardments during October 2001 and the first two weeks of November, a handful of Taliban forces hid in the embassy's underground bunker, near the main building in a rose garden.

But apparently no one had gained access to the embassy during the past 12 years.

I approached the embassy's thick bullet-shattered glass front doors at the end of November. The glass doors could be opened, but the entrance was then blocked by a massive yellow metal wall, bolted from inside to stop any attempt to proceed.

Ominously, between the glass doors and the metal wall someone -- perhaps a departing Marine guard -- placed a vinyl record album attached to thick electric wires. It looked like a booby-trap.

The wires were a ruse.

The album was Rejuvenation by The Meters, a funk band. The 1974 cover was illustrated with a photograph of a black woman with a big Afro hairstyle and startled eyes, sitting on a sofa with her dress hiked up alongside a bottle of cheap red Ripple wine and a watermelon while she held up a copy of the vinyl record. On all four corners of embassy's roof meanwhile, big video cameras still pointed downward, aimed at the building's immediate perimeter.

At the back of the embassy building, frustrated Afghans had repeatedly tried in vain to smash through a metal gate and door which led to an underground garage where several vehicles lay abandoned. The gate bore rusted bullet holes, big and small.

Scattered wreckage at the building's back entrance included a toppled gasoline pump, a pulverized power lawn mower, a fire extinguisher and a label from a Chinese-made iron padlock. That lock, slashed by knife marks, held the metal back door shut.

All of the windows of the two-story embassy had been

boarded up with plywood. Some big planks had fallen off due to gunfire or the passage of time. Some air conditioners sticking out of lower windows had been dented by hammering but not dislodged. All the many windows were protected by wrought iron grills and curved decorative metal. Birds nested amid the decorative shields.

Desks, chairs and a gray metal hat rack and other office furniture were visible through some broken windows. In one office, several rectangular pieces of insulation from the ceiling poked downward.

A stone's throw away from the embassy's main building, concrete steps led down to the thick-walled bunker containing a few subterranean rooms, which were now open. The lights were on. The rooms, plus a hallway and a bathroom, were furnished with a few desks, a couple of chairs and an empty, dirty refrigerator.

"During the American bombardment, some Taliban stayed down here for about one month," embassy guard Wahid Ullah told me.

"They were hiding from the bombs. A Taliban wrote his name here," Ullah said, pointing at a signature by Mullah Ras Mohammad Ahoond near the edge of a window. Ahoond also scrawled his signature above a mirror hanging on a stone-and-brick wall.

Two copies of the Koran, Islam's holy book, had been carefully wrapped in cloth and set on top of a cabinet.

Inside a subterranean room's desk drawer lay "official business" shipping labels from the American Embassy for "unclassified" information to be sent via "air pouch" or "sea pouch" to the "US Department of State, Coordinator for Maps and Publications" in Washington.

A two-page photocopy of the Bible's Ecclesiastes rested in another drawer, including the passage, "A time to kill; A time to heal; A time to destroy; A time to rebuild."

Also near the embassy, next to some storage and maintenance rooms, two burnt US automobiles were parked, totally charred by fire. One appeared to be a Lincoln Continental or a Cadillac and most likely was used by the ambassador. The other blackened vehicle was a station wagon.

Rows of burnt filing cabinets -- now set outdoors -- contained partially burnt embassy documents. In one cabinet's drawers lay two eight-inch-by-ten-inch US flags damaged by flames. Each fried flag had a black leather strip, enabling the two flags to be fastened above the headlights on the ambassador's car and wave in the breeze whenever he cruised Kabul on diplomatic business.

An "American Embassy telephone list" dated Nov. 4, 1987 listed diplomats' office extensions and residential phone numbers, including Charge d'Affaires Glassman's, along with numbers for Marine security guards. "Useful telephone numbers" included the American Club, Snack Bar, Fire Brigade, Kabul Security, the Foreign Ministry, airport, several international embassies, United Nations offices and the US-financed Noor Eye Clinic.

On the embassy's spacious yellowing lawn amid pine trees, roses and other bushes, a gray marble headstone in memory of murdered US Ambassador Adolph Dubs had been partially smashed. The jagged memorial stone with pieces at its base no longer bore his name. Dubs was assassinated in Kabul on February 14, 1979 prompting the end to US assistance to the Afghan government 10 months before the Soviet invasion.

The post-9/11 US invasion soon brought fresh American diplomats who officially re-opened the dirt-encrusted embassy on December 17, 2001 after searching for hidden explosives.

Walking now through the spacious rooms and empty hallways felt like a stroll down a rabbit hole into a world where dial telephones, phonograph records and warnings about a Soviet threat remained where the evacuating diplomats left them.

In the American ambassador's musty office, his black, rubbery gas mask hung next to a dust-covered record player. Then-Secretary of State George Shultz's framed official portrait grinned on the ambassador's wall. Below Shultz's face on a large coffee table, a 1988 Department of State Salary Chart was open next to a colorful booklet describing how to decorate Diplomatic Reception Rooms.

The embassy's expensive Afghan carpets were gone. A forgotten coffee table book, Bactrian Gold, showed gorgeous illustrations of priceless treasures which would mysteriously disappear from Kabul's museum years later.

In the ambassador's adjoining room, his secretary's gray filing cabinet displayed metal drawers haphazardly yanked and extended after vital folders were quickly extracted. Less important files were ignored. The secretary's wooden desk drawers had all been pulled out, stacked up, and left filled only with a random jumble of office supplies.

Half-drunk cans of Coca-Cola, Fanta and 7-Up stood on tables in other empty rooms.

In the embassy's basement snack bar, a menu offered hamburgers and other American fast food. International Herald Tribunes, Time magazines and other publications matched the year on a 1989 calendar curling on the wall.

Filthy red-and-white checkered tablecloths gave a mummified but cheery look to the snack bar along with its peeling wall paper, moldy corners, warped floors, and a ceiling marred by fallen tiles.

Upstairs in the deputy chief of mission's office, his dusty desk was piled with official pamphlets. Documents included a Defense Intelligence Agency's Warsaw Pact Ground Forces Equipment Identification Guide to Armored Fighting Vehicles. A pamphlet from the Bureau of Diplomatic Security lay on a shelf near other documents stamped UNCLASSIFIED.

Walls displayed maps of Afghanistan, with red circles marking Soviet military sites during the Kremlin's 1979-1989 occupation.

"I'm told they [the Taliban] were here for about two to three weeks in October [2001], and they did get in through the back somehow, they did get into the building, they did look around," said US Embassy Public Affairs Counselor John Kincannon pointing at the rear of the building.

"We think they tossed around some papers and things like that but they didn't really seem to do any major damage, to the best of my knowledge. There are people who have periodically inventoried this building over the years, and it doesn't seem the Taliban did much of anything."

US officials said the embassy's interior appeared in such poor condition because winter weather seeped through broken windows.

Near the entrance, an old wrinkled copy of Afghanistan's Marxist government-controlled Kabul Times newspaper lay on the floor, filled with news about Soviet-installed Afghan President Najibullah who the US expected to be overthrown six months after Moscow's February 15, 1989 withdrawal.

The barrel-chested, bull-like Najibullah remained in power until 1992 when suddenly some of his army in Mazar-i-Sharif mutinied and joined the US-backed mujahideen. enabling them to seize Kabul.

Najibullah meanwhile waited too long before trying to escape. Unable to leave Afghanistan, he retreated into the Indian Embassy's compound until 1996, when victorious Taliban hung him in the street from a lamp post.

Two cigarettes dangled from Najibullah's dead nostrils.

During Afghanistan's civil wars -- 1989-2001, the years between the Soviet withdrawal and the US invasion -- the American Embassy was not the only abandoned foreign missions. Most of the others, including the Soviet Union's Embassy across town, had also shut.

Unfortunately for Moscow, their site was located in the Karte Seh sector of southwest Kabul where nearly all the official and civilian buildings were decimated during years of fighting.

By November 2001, the Soviets' heavily damaged, sprawling embassy complex was swarming with thousands of destitute squatters.

Afghan children, screaming and scrambling for alms while

shouting threats and obscenities, greeted me at the bullet-scarred compound. The easiest way to enter was through a gaping hole made by a rocket in a back wall. Here too, raucous children scampered back and forth over the wrecked wall's mangled iron support beams and fallen chunks of cement. Older boys were throwing rocks at any Afghan females who happened to be around, forcing them to hide.

After entering through the jagged hole in the wall, it was difficult to recognize Moscow's embassy. The diplomatic compound's hulking, multi-story buildings had become a slum for people who washed clothes, chopped food and did other chores as if in an Afghan village. The embassy's interior was overrun by squatters who erected makeshift brick walls, carving out a warren of hovels from the diplomats' offices.

People had stitched together filthy rags which were held up by tattered ropes in an effort to curtain off places to sleep and eat. Some girls, dressed in cotton clothes with faded purple and red floral designs, bravely peered through the ragged curtains. They darted away when a swarm of unkempt boys raised their fists and yelled. Every building on the embassy's spacious property housed men, women and children, dwelling in wretched conditions.

All the buildings' original doors and windows were either blown out or had been stolen. The Soviet embassy's main downstairs reception area was dark, squalid and littered with trash.

Many of the buildings' walls were covered with splattered stains, scrawled words and crude charcoal drawings of machine guns, tanks, people and indecipherable shapes. Every wall was smashed or pock-marked by years of machine gun or rocket fire.

"More than 23,000 people live here," Amin Nullah told me, gesturing to several of the Soviet embassy compound's tall apartment blocks which were also divided into tiny rooms and packed with people. It was impossible to confirm the total population of squatters in the embassy complex, but Nullah repeatedly insisted his numbers were correct -- 23,000 people now occupied the main embassy building and its multi-story apartment blocks and other structures.

"There is no electricity, but we have water," said Nullah, who described himself as their representative.

"They have been living here for the past two years and six months. Everyone lives here for free."

Nullah -- a fat, loud, bossy man who wore a dirty gray turban -- then got angry and insisted foreigners were not allowed to visit the embassy.

While he spoke, a nearby cluster of Afghan children amused themselves on swings and colorful, moveable metal rides which remained in the embassy's playground. A basketball court was equipped with hoops, but no nets. At the edge of the compound, a few vendors parked rickety wooden pushcarts offering vegetables and other items for sale.

During the first days of the US bombardment and invasion, the Taliban government collapsed in panic and abandoned the capital on November 13, 2001. Their Arab allies and other al Qaeda fighters fled their expensive homes and well-stocked training camps in Kabul, Kandahar and elsewhere in Afghanistan.

In Jalalabad, 88 miles east of Kabul, al Qaeda abandoned all sorts of things during their rushed escape. In their former homes and offices I found bullet-punctured targets of silhouetted heads, foreign passports, forged visas, hand-drawn bomb-making instructions, and freshly printed news clippings downloaded from the Internet reporting about the hijackers who crashed planes into the World Trade Center and Pentagon.

"Osama bin Laden spent a lot of time here in Jalalabad during his stay in Afghanistan," Nangarhar Province's Police Chief Hazrat Ali told me in November 2001.

"He knows the city well. More than 5,000 or 6,000 Arabs were living in this city and they had their own bases and training camps. Jalalabad was very much used by the Arabs during Taliban time."

Bin Laden, born in Saudi Arabia, was suspected of financing al Qaeda, an international terrorist network which attracted Arabs, Pakistanis, Chechens, Sudanese, Somalians, Europeans, Afghan Taliban and others.

They waged a worldwide Islamic holy war to oust US forces from Saudi territory and to topple its corrupt royal rulers, and to end Israeli occupation of Palestinian land.

Exploring al Qaeda's abandoned homes in Jalalabad revealed intriguing aspects of how they prepared to kill their enemies while dwelling in this otherwise dull provincial capital.

Anti-Taliban troops with Kalashnikov rifles now guarded these homes. Inside one sprawling white-walled complex, a half-filled notebook handwritten in French displayed a student's attempt to learn military lessons and how to stage attacks.

"Airplanes. Number one: Bomb with big explosive power for immediate explosion," read one entry in French.

"Protect yourself from cannons and missiles. Avoid missiles after they hit the target because they can explode later," read another entry.

A page torn from a cheap notebook listed chemical formulas including explanations written in Arabic next to the initials TNT and RDX -- shorthand for trinitrotoluene and royal demolition explosive.

Several pages were illustrated with hand-drawn schematics of large bombs and detonators, complete with "on" and "off" switches.

Another page which lay in a backyard amid debris showed someone repeatedly printed a rectangular rubber stamp which said, "Consul General, High Commission for Pakistan, London" and a circular rubber stamp for the "High Commission of Pakistan, London."

They also repeatedly printed a rubber stamp for "Islamabad International Airport, Islamabad, Pakistan" confirming an "entry" on "10 Aug 2000".

One of the inked Pakistani rubber stamps lay in the dirt. Entry and exit stamps for Istanbul, Turkey were also printed on scraps of paper.

A photographic negative, cut from a larger sheet of film, showed an official departure stamp from Jordan's international airport, with a blank space where a date could be filled in.

Half-eaten food still lay spread on dining tables and in the kitchen. Al Qaeda members and their families also left clothing, Islamic textbooks, documents, and personal letters including an address written in pencil, of Fatma Sliti in Brussels, Belgium.

Fatma's father Amor Ben Mohamed Sliti was allegedly a well-known member of al Qaeda, born in Algeria of Tunisian descent.

A small, color headshot photo of the black-bearded Sliti, sized for a typical visa application, was among abandoned papers scattered in a Jalalabad house. The man with close-cropped hair wore a dark purple shirt and was photographed in front of a white background.

A handful of similar visa-sized color photographs of other bearded men lay nearby. One image showed a young boy. A black-and-white photo portrayed an elegant unsmiling woman. Severe-looking, glaring, turbaned men appeared in similar photos.

More photos were stuffed in an Afghan Photo Studio envelope.

"I've been investigating the key role Belgian citizens played in Masood's killing," Brussels-based Belgian RTL television journalist Marie-Rose Armesto told me in February 2002.

"I'm one of the leading journalists investigating the Masood [assassination] case. Two days ago, I found the name and a picture of the second killer. The first one was already known. The two bombers were Tunisian citizens but they both lived in my city, just near my door.

"One of these guys' [accomplices] is Mohamed Sliti. He lived in Jalalabad with his Belgian wife and his children. You describe the garbage in some of the houses there, and you say that you've found the address of Fatma Sliti in Brussels.

"The father and the children have been arrested a few days

ago in Iran. They flew from Afghanistan and entered Iran illegally. This family, [and] Sliti, have been arrested in Iran with 150 other al-Qaeda members.

"The father of Fatma is a well-known terrorist. He [Sliti] was born in Algeria but flew to Tunisia before going to Brussels -- where he married a Belgian -- and then to Jalalabad. He was one of the trainers in the Darunta camp," Armesto said, referring to an al Qaeda site near Jalalabad which invading US forces repeatedly bombed from the air.

Despite the heavy US assaults, some of Darunta's mud-brick bunkers were still stocked with rockets and other ammunition at the end of November. A big rectangular sign set in white stone declared in Arabic:

"We Want to Show the Flag of Islam All Over the World."

Hundreds of thick, razor-sharp metal fragments from US bombs lay scattered all over the Darunta complex, alongside unexploded baseball-sized bomblets nestling in the earth.

Two children died from shockwaves generated by three big American bombs which hit the Darunta complex before dawn on November 23, angry villagers told me near three deep craters.

US officials reportedly identified two of the camps within the Darunta complex as part of a network run by Assadalah Abdul Rahman and Abu Khabab. Some US officials insisted "dead dogs" had been photographed at the Abu Khabab camp, amid claims that al Qaeda tested "chemical weapons" on the leashed beasts. Another camp at Darunta was reportedly run by Hezb-i-Islami. US satellite photographs of the Darunta complex showed the area riddled with "tunnel entrances," according to U.S. officials.

Thanks to the Americans, the Darunta complex was quickly seized by anti-Taliban forces.

Meanwhile, a Brussels court had convicted Sliti of being an accomplice -- alongside another Tunisian-Belgian citizen -- in the assassination of Ahmad Shah Masood in Afghanistan two days before the September 11, 2001 attacks in America.

Masood had been leading pro-US Northern Alliance insurgents against the Taliban regime.

The US government's Voice of America (VOA) news reported on March 6, 2002 that Belgian "police arrested Amor Ben Mohamed Sliti on charges of forgery and conspiracy last week in connection with the forged passports used by Masood's two killers.

"The assassins posed as Belgian journalists when they blew themselves up with Masood during a mock interview. The passports found on the bodies were stolen from the Belgian consulate in Strasbourg and the Belgian Embassy in The Hague."

Sliti had initially been "detained in Iran among a group coming from Afghanistan," fleeing the US invasion, VOA said.

"On February 27, 2002, Amor ben Mohamed Sliti, the alleged leader of an Al Qaeda assassination team, was arrested in the Netherlands after being extradited from Iran," the US government's Congressional Research Service reported.

The Belgian court sentenced Sliti to five years in prison.

The court said his accomplice was Nizar Trabelsi of Tunisia, who "admitted planning to drive a car bomb into the canteen of Kleine Brogel Air Base, a Belgian military post that is used by NATO and is the home to a US Air Force munitions support squadron," the Associated Press reported.

Trabelsi received the maximum sentence of 10 years in prison.

Sliti had previously worked as a car mechanic in Brussels. He became an Islamist in the mid-1990s after being radicalized by another Belgian-Tunisian, Tarek Maaroufi, who also became a jihadist.

"In December 2001, Tarek Maaroufi was arrested for planning to bomb the US Consulate in Milan and for his role in the assassination of Masood," the Congressional Research Service reported.

In 1999, Sliti took his Flemish wife and their five children to live in Jalalabad where he joined al Qaeda, according to Dutch journalist Guy Van Vlierden.

Here in Jalalabad, Sliti arranged his 13-year-old daughter Habiba, also known as Hafsa, to marry Muhammad Ibn Arfhan Shahin, also known as Hkimi, who was then a Tunisian guerrilla in al Qaeda.

Shahin and Sliti's cousin Hisham, also known as Hicham, were eventually imprisoned by the Americans in Guantanamo Bay. Shahin served 13 years and Hisham received a 12-year sentence.

The anti-secrecy website WikiLeaks published a November 4, 2007 US Department of Defense "Detainee Assessment" document from Guantanamo about Shahin.

His aliases included:

Abel Bin Abhmed Ibrahim Hkimi, Abdel Khalek, Abu Bilal al-Tunisi, Abu Hind al-Tunisi, and Muhammad Bin Erfane Bin Chahine.

Shahin arrived in Afghanistan in 1997 and also settled in Jalalabad in 1998, the Guantanamo document said.

"He married a woman named Habiba, the daughter of Omar Sliti, also known as Abu Nadir, and lived with his wife in the Istakhbarat -- Taliban Intelligence -- section of Jalalabad until after September 11, 2001."

Shahin "fled Afghanistan after the US bombing campaign with a group of al-Qaeda and Taliban fighters led by [an] Osama bin Laden-appointed military commander in Tora Bora. The group crossed the Afghan-Pakistan border in the Nangarhar region in mid-December 2001.

"Their Pakistani contact convinced them to surrender their weapons and gathered the group in a mosque where Pakistani forces immediately arrested them."

Among a slew of charges against Shahin, the Guantanamo document said:

"Detainee also stated that he would kill President Bush if given the chance."

Sliti's wife meanwhile divorced him, gained custody of their children, and they successfully reintegrated into Belgian society.

The Belgian government stripped Sliti of his citizenship in 2010.

Vlierden reported that Sliti then traveled to Syria in 2014, joined Islamic State (IS), and lived in its temporary capital Raqqah where he served as a tax collector, according to his daughter Habiba who spoke with French journalist Antoine Malo.

Malo interviewed Habiba, identifying her as Hafsa, in a detention camp run by Syrian Kurds holding captured IS members and their families, Vlierden reported. Kurds had captured her in 2018 when IS lost Raqqah.

Elsewhere in Jalalabad, another housing complex included its own school for boys who studied Arabic and English vocabulary plus Islamic subjects. They abandoned several rabbits in a cage.

"A gun, a girl, a glass, a goat," read a page from one illustrated English language book.

In a small backyard, a square plank of wood was painted black to depict the silhouette of a person's head and shoulders, for target practice. About 100 bullets peppered the target, hitting the face and upper body. Dozens of missed shots gouged the tan mud-and-straw wall.

In the housing complex's main yard, a brick shed protected dangerous stacks of rockets and other live ammunition.

Some anti-Taliban Afghan guards displayed piles of foreign passports they said came from these al Qaeda houses. It was impossible to determine if the passports accurately identified the people they matched, or if the documents had been stolen or forged to enable al Qaeda to sneak across borders.

A man from Yemen named Naseem Abdulqader Ahmed al-Sakkaf was listed on passport number 00345350 with a Pakistani "business visa" issued in Yemen on July 8, 1999.

An Italian passport showed a chubby-faced light-haired woman named Rafaella Palpacelli, born in 1975, who bore a Tanzania "employment visa." According to that passport, she exited Tanzania after only two weeks there in 1998.

A passport from the Soviet Union showed a heavy-jowled

Russian man who traveled from Turkey into Iran in 1993.

In the back yard of one house, scattered trash included a bra, software manuals, cookbooks, and a bunch of family photos. The pictures portrayed happy men with bushy moustaches, wearing modern clothes while posing with women, boys and girls in comfortable living rooms.

Pieces of new, carefully cut, green-and-brown camouflage cloth and tailoring instructions indicated domestic chores at al Qaeda homes included sewing military uniforms.

Color-printed documents and news reports downloaded from the Internet showed several photographic portraits released by US authorities of men suspected of crashing the passenger planes on 9/11. Apparently lacking enough blank paper, the news clippings were printed on the reverse side of paper already covered with Arabic script, including an email address of "shubeilat" in Jordan.

Laith Shubeilat was a former politician in Jordan, but it was unclear if this was his email address. In 2001, Shubeilat reportedly said he accused Jordan's King Abdullah of illegally confiscating a large amount of real estate for his own profit. Shubeilat was subsequently beaten up and allegedly harassed by police in Amman for speaking out.

In another al Qaeda home in Jalalabad, the missing occupants had earlier entertained themselves by playing an interactive computer game, Commandos Behind Enemy Lines.

The wall of their home was decorated with a postcard of Medina, a city in Saudi Arabia where Islam's prophet Mohammad lived after fleeing Mecca in the year 622. Medina is also the site of Mohammad's tomb.

Afghan civilians who lived in Jalalabad had difficult lives during the civil war years and some were crazed by the violence and poverty. The worst cases ended up as inmates of Jalalabad's Psychiatric Hospital, chained to beds or left in squalid oblivion.

"I am the son of Lenin and Indira Gandhi," a white-haired patient insisted during interviews in the hospital's dirt yard in November 2001.

Soviet leader Vladimir Lenin died in 1924 when India's future prime minister Indira Gandhi was seven years old.

"I killed Babrak Karmal," the inmate added.

Karmal was an Afghan Marxist prime minister who the Kremlin installed during their 1979-89 occupation of Afghanistan. He resigned in 1986, moved to Moscow and died there in 1996.

The patient said his name was Marshal Shah Medina -- a combination of a high military rank, Persian royalty, and the Islamic holy city in Saudi Arabia.

"I am a gift to Afghanistan. I was born in the Kremlin. I was killed and now I'm alive again. I am 100 years old."

Psychiatrists and other staff chuckled and tried to engage the old man.

One doctor said to him: "If you were born in the Kremlin, what street is the Kremlin on?"

The patient, assuming an air of superiority, waved and replied, "I am the commander of the Russians. People have punished me with the pistol."

Other inmates were more worrisome.

"I'm here for no reason," said Zadran Haiderlal who wore a dangling unlocked chain around his ankle.

"I want to leave," Haiderlal said.

"He killed his father," said Abdul Saboor, a hospital clerk carefully watching Haiderlal.

"His family brought him here. He has not had any trial and hasn't been brought to any court," Saboor said.

One of the psychiatrists, Dr. Syed Jalal, said, "Maybe this patient's family brought him here to decrease the punishment which the government was going to do against him."

"I killed my father with a pistol," Haiderlal finally muttered. "I don't know why."

A gray-bearded man wearing blue pajamas squatted on his hind legs.

"I want to stay here," Ahmed Jan said.

"I have been here for 20 years. I'm 25 years old," he laughed, stroking his gray whiskers. "My brother brought me here."

Jan squinted as if in pain and cupped his hands while gesturing like a beggar.

Saboor the clerk said, "This patient was previously in a Kabul hospital, but they sent him here because he couldn't be cured. He is a chronic schizophrenic."

Asked about his life today, Jan simply repeated the question with listless resignation.

Seventeen barefoot patients rested in the yard.

"Some patients were recently discharged," said Mohammad Noadair, another hospital clerk.

"Some were let out because we had no money for their food in October at the beginning of the US bombardment. Those patients who had relatives, we discharged."

Near the hospital's entrance, a muscular patient stretched out on a metal bed under a tree. A chain around his ankle led across the dirt and was locked around the tree's thick trunk.

"I have no name," the chained patient said.

"They lock me like this and keep me chained to a tree because if they unlock me, I will escape."

The asylum's pharmacist, Ajmal, said, "He was a boxer. He killed two people in Jalalabad. The Taliban brought him here about three months ago."

The chained man groaned.

"I didn't kill anyone."

At the far end of the yard, curled against a wall with a blanket covering much of his head, Taza Gul stared bug-eyed and mute at the madness around him.

"Sometimes the patients become crazy if they have no drugs," said the pharmacist.

"They will be very bad and noisy and attack each other and become dangerous."

The new US-installed Afghan government meanwhile was also confused about how to survive.

"I know the English words 'to kill,' 'to murder,' and 'to assassinate' someone, but what is the English when a court orders someone to be killed?" an earnest Foreign Ministry official asked during our conversation about visas.

"I know 'to hang' something and 'to suspend' something, but is there another word for 'to hang'? Such as 'to terminate a life by hanging'?

"I work here at the Foreign Ministry and I am a graduate of political science, so it is important for me to know these things."

When Russian forces first stabbed south across the Oxus River during Christmas 1979, no one in Moscow, Washington or Kabul expected rag-tag mujahideen could bring the former Red Army to its knees in a deadly stalemate. The United States, Saudi Arabia and other countries however were secretly involved in Afghanistan's politics before the Russian invasion.

Evidence of US machinations in Afghanistan's affairs were exposed when Iranian mobs seized the American Embassy in Tehran in 1979. They took staff diplomats and staff as hostages and discovered detailed State Department cables and other secret documents -- prompting Iran's new, Islamist government to describe the embassy as a "nest of spies."

Iranians retrieved a vast number of sensitive files which the American Embassy staff failed to destroy in time. Other secret documents which the embassy staff successfully fed through their shredder, were painstakingly pasted back together by the Iranian government which cleverly employed their country's fabled carpet weavers who were familiar with handling complex disjointed patterns and designs.

Piles of paper spaghetti once again became readable.

Many of the documents focused on US efforts to battle Iran's Ayatollah Khomeini. But there were plenty of communiqués from Kabul, Washington and elsewhere discussing the worsening situation in next door Afghanistan.

An August 1973 report said it had been "coordinated with CIA as appropriate and with the Department of State," and described Afghanistan's former prime minister Mohammad Daoud Khan who seized power by toppling his brother-in-law and cousin, King Mohammad Zahir.

The Biographic Report about Daoud -- "rhymes with loud," the document helpfully advised -- described the anti-monarchy coup leader's politics, education, social life, health and other details. It also relayed popular rumors:

"As Prime Minister, he was fond of inspecting shops in disguise, with the idea of ensuring the honesty of shopkeepers. As a result, he acquired the sobriquet 'demon of the bazaars.' According to bazaar gossip, Daoud punished a baker who was over-charging for bread by having him baked alive in his own oven; a more common punishment, according to rumor, was to have unscrupulous shopkeepers nailed to a wall by their ears."

The American Embassy in Kabul also weighed widespread speculation concerning whether or not the Soviet Union would invade Afghanistan to stabilize its interests amid infighting among the regime and attacks by anti-communist Islamist guerrillas and frustrated communists.

US fears deepened in 1978 when, during a pro-communist coup supported by elements in the army, Daoud and 17 others were executed inside the presidential palace. The killers buried Daoud and the other bodies in an anonymous mass grave.

The 1978 coup was officially hailed as the Saur (April) Revolution. Afghanistan's People's Democratic Party, founded in 1965, was finally on top. They had supported Daoud's 1973 coup against the king, but turned against the prime minister when he violently purged them from the government.

The revolution's slogans promised to save lives.

"Afghanistan was a backward nation: a life expectancy of about 40, infant mortality of at least 25 percent, absolutely primitive sanitation, widespread malnutrition, illiteracy of more than 90 percent, very few highways, not one mile of railway, most people living in nomadic tribes or as impoverished farmers in mud villages, identifying more with ethnic groups than with a larger political concept, a life scarcely different from many centuries earlier," wrote William Blum in his book, Afghanistan, 1979-1992: America's Jihad.

"Reform with a socialist bent was the new government's

ambition: land reform -- while still retaining private property -- controls on prices and profits, and strengthening of the public sector, as well as separation of church [mosque] and state, eradication of illiteracy, legalization of trade unions, and the emancipation of women in a land almost entirely Muslim," Blum said.

Blum meanwhile resigned from the State Department in 1967 in protest of the US-Vietnam War and became a founder and editor of the Washington Free Press newspaper. Blum also collaborated with former CIA officer Philip Agee and his colleagues in London during the mid-1970s, publicly naming CIA officials and documenting their activities.

During the 1970s, "Iran's infamous secret police, SAVAK, was busy fingering suspected communist sympathizers in the Afghan government and military," Blum said.

The US and its regional ally, the dictatorial Shah of Iran, were trying to smother the influence of Afghan communists and the Soviet Union in Afghanistan.

With Daoud dead, Moscow was hopeful its shared lengthy southern border with Afghanistan would no longer be a soft underbelly vulnerable to the US.

The 1978 April Revolution's leader was President Nur Mohammad Taraki. He tried to project a neutral, non-aligned stance. Eyeing a hostile international audience, Taraki said the coup and revolution were nationalist. But Taraki's pro-Soviet policies did little to change a growing perception that he was a communist.

A smoldering Islamic jihad against "godless communists" was now boosted by big landowners who feared their estates would be nationalized by Taraki's land-distribution programs, and by businessmen, royalists, tribal factions and others who did not want to lose influence and feudal power over a largely peasant population.

Sunni Muslim-majority Afghanistan's neighbors were turning increasingly fundamentalist. Shiite Muslims overthrew the Shah's regime in 1979 and established an Islamic republic.

Pakistan increasingly embraced Sunni Islam's traditions.

The Soviet Union and Taraki were worried that the CIA was supporting the fledgling mujahideen through Pakistan, endangering the revolution. In March 1979, Taraki traveled to Moscow, asking for military help.

"The entry of our troops into Afghanistan would outrage the international community, triggering a string of extremely negative consequences in many different areas," Soviet Prime Minister Kosygin told Taraki.

"Our common enemies are just waiting for the moment when Soviet troops appear in Afghanistan. This will give them the excuse they need to send armed bands into the country," Kosygin correctly predicted.

Suddenly in mid-1979, Afghanistan's Deputy Prime Minister Hafizullah Amin seized power from Taraki who was killed in the inter-party fight.

Amin was more hardcore than Taraki in pushing the revolution's goals. His rough tactics displeased the Soviets.

Amin's regime will result in "harsh repression and, as a reaction, the activation and consolidation of the opposition," warned Russia's KGB intelligence officers in Kabul, according to the Washington Post which in 1992 obtained some of Moscow's declassified Politburo documents.

Bruce Amstutz was US charge d'affaires in Kabul from 1977 to 1980. Amstutz wrote in an August, 1979 dispatch -- later shredded in the US Embassy in Iran -- that the emerging Afghan rebels were Islamist extremists who would probably destroy Afghanistan's economy and doom the country to remain mostly primitive.

But a mujahideen victory would be in Washington's interests, if the insurgents crushed Afghan communism and Soviet influence, he said.

"The available 'manifestos' issued by some [mujahideen] opposition groups call for a social and economic system based on the 'fundamentalist' tenets of Islam and, therefore, an opposition-led regime would probably not have social and economic reforms -- so necessary for this backward country -- high on its priority list," Amstutz's communiqué said.

"On balance, however, our larger interests -- especially given the DRA's (Democratic Republic of Afghanistan's) extremely close ties to Moscow, this regime's almost open hostility to us, and the atmosphere of fear it has created throughout this country, would probably be served by the demise of the Taraki and Amin regime, despite whatever setbacks this might mean for future social and economic reforms within Afghanistan."

Meanwhile a shredded document which originated from the American Embassy in India, dated September 29, 1979 reported:

"Islamic Association of Patriotic Afghan Students in India (IAPASI) mounted a noisy demonstration in front of the Soviet Embassy in New Delhi protesting Soviet involvement in Afghanistan. The Afghan students attempted to present Soviet Embassy officers with an 'Open Letter' to the Soviet president [Leonid Brezhnev]."

The Americans secretly arranged and paid for the demonstration.

"This demonstration was funded by New Delhi [CIA] station and organized at station behest by unilateral assent GECARRION/1, IAPASI officer," it said, giving codenames for whoever was covertly involved.

"QRMYSTIC wrote the 'Open Letter'," the shredded document said without elaborating.

America also scrutinized intriguing clues about Amin and other Afghan leaders during September 1979.

Prime Minister Amin "gained his political awareness in the United States while a student at the University of Wisconsin in the summer of 1958," Amstutz wrote.

"At that time, he took several political science and economics courses, 'used to go to the socialist professive [sic] clubs,' and 'closely watched capitalist conditions'."

Amin gained a master's degree in secondary education from Columbia in 1958, and returned to Columbia during 1963-1965 for two additional years of education. Both visits were financed by USAID grants.

"He was either 'ousted' by the United States government or 'summoned home' by the Afghan regime before he could complete the oral examinations for his PhD. at Columbia University.

"US authorities told him he had been summoned home, but upon his arrival in Kabul, he was told that the US had 'ousted' him. Although he 'demanded' the opportunity to complete his studies at his own expense, he was turned down," Amstutz said.

"Amin only obliquely blames the US for 'expelling' him because of his ostensibly political activities. On previous occasions, he has not been as polite.

"His lack of a genuine PhD. apparently still rankles, and some observers here even go so far as to assert that his premature departure from Columbia, for whatever reason, is the root source of Amin's anti-American feelings."

America's alleged clandestine activity in Afghanistan however was being turned into anti-US propaganda.

"In 1979, [George] Griffin, Charge d'Affaires of the US Embassy in Kabul, called me into his office and said that since I knew many people, participated in the parties, and walked around in the city, I should collect reports on things that I see and hear and give them to him," said Patrick Sales, according to an Afghan regime booklet, The CIA is Getting Disclosed, which displayed a cover illustration of an American flag.

"After two days, he [Griffin] called me into his office again, and gave me a form with the letterhead, 'Central Intelligence Agency.' It was written on the form that 'I, Patrick Sales, promise to collect information'."

The Kabul regime arrested Sales in April 1979, identified him as a Pakistani, and imprisoned him for eight years. It was impossible to determine if Sales had been coerced into making the statements which appeared in the booklet published in Kabul.

It quoted Sales allegedly confessing:

"The CIA members in the US Embassy paid special attention to creating subversive activities such as terror and explosions. They had given me the duty to instruct my agents to spot residential places and the working places of the party and state officials, and to study possibilities of their murder and explosions."

On Christmas 1979, Soviet troops finally invaded.

Amin was killed in yet another palace shoot-out, and a more pro-Moscow Afghan leader was installed, Babrak Karmal.

Karmal and the Kremlin presented the Soviet invasion as an "invitation" by Afghanistan to stabilize the new regime, kill the insurgency, and hopefully withdraw in six months.

Foreign correspondents were barred.

I flew into Kabul in June 1980, six months after the Soviet invasion, and claimed to be an English teacher seeking a tourist visa. The day before, mujahideen demanded all merchants in Kabul bolt their shops and go on strike in protest against the Soviet occupation.

Soviet-occupied Afghanistan was heavily patrolled. Incognito foreign correspondents were perceived as terrorists, hunted by secret police, and fingered by informants.

At the American Embassy, Griffin worriedly asked:

"How did you get into Afghanistan? American reporters aren't allowed in anymore. If they find you entered the country disguised as a tourist, they'll immediately arrest you and put you on trial as a spy. You'll be jailed. Don't you see the coincidence? You arrive on a Sunday as a so-called tourist. And the very next day there's a city-wide protest strike against the government. They'll soon start looking for who arranged it. They'll see that one day after you arrived, the strike happened, and they'll figure you're the one who instigated it.

"They don't care about proof or anything like that. Even if they know you didn't do it, they'll want to put you on a televised show trial for their own domestic propaganda and label you a CIA agent. They'll make you say you're a CIA agent if you ever want to be let out of jail.

"Last time there was trouble, the police arrested two Americans, Robert Lee and Charles Brockunier, and charged them with being CIA agents and spying. Lee was just a hippie and the other man a rug importer. They weren't doing anything at all. But the police wanted someone to blame so that they can back up their propaganda that US imperialists agents are fomenting the trouble.

"So they turned Lee into a CIA agent and kept him imprisoned for about a month. Brockunier was also held for a long time for spying. Be careful. They might pick you up and turn you into a CIA agent too," Griffin warned.

"If you do get detained, for any reason, call me at this number. It's my residence, but don't write it down. Remember it."

In The Spies, another booklet published by the Afghan regime, a photograph of a bespectacled Robert Lee appeared along with 39 other alleged secret agents -- including a handful from the United States, France and Germany.

Lee was described as "a CIA agent, who was sent to the Democratic Republic of Afghanistan (DRA) for collecting information. He was caught on July 2, 1980 by the security forces of the DRA in Khinjan district, Baghlan province, when he was committing a crime."

The booklet gave no further details.

Walking through Kabul the next day, I asked an Afghan carpet seller in a market lane called Chicken Street why so many of shopkeepers were on strike.

He replied:

"Are you a CIA agent? If you are, give me 1,000 US dollars and I will tell you everything. Other CIA agents used to give me lots of money for information."

If you explained you are a journalist, you risked being identified by the merchant who may be an informant anxious to collect a hefty reward from the government.

"If you are an English teacher, then why do you want to know about what the mujahideen are doing in Afghanistan?" a streetwise kabob seller quipped.

Hotels had government-paid informants loitering in the lobby or on the staff, according to sympathetic luggage carriers and cooks.

To dodge these traps, the handful of foreign reporters who entered Kabul frequently changed taxis during a single trip, because drivers taking them directly to embassies, trouble spots, campuses, and nearby Soviet and Afghan military bases might tell the police.

The Soviets already had announced a $5,000 reward for the capture of any Western journalist posing as an Afghan wearing a turban and traditional baggy pants. This was an attempt to also stop reporters sneaking across the Pakistan-Afghan border with the rebels.

One day, after returning to my hotel to write a news story, an Afghan in the lobby tapped my shoulder and whispered:

"The secret police came to your room twice today while you were out. They asked specifically about you, the American."

The Afghan then told me the dreaded KHAD secret police were making hotel-to-hotel searches "to find Mr. Richard."

Within a few hours, I convinced a shy, freckle-faced American Embassy secretary to let me stay with her.

She was temporarily living in the West German ambassador's home while he and his family were in Europe on vacation. She invited me into his home, decorated with huge statues of African sculpture. Now the authorities had no idea where I was staying. I spread my notebooks out, borrowed the ambassador's typewriter and wrote my next news story.

Griffin was horrified when he found out I moved out of my hotel and into the German ambassador's house.

"I wanted to warn you that I've heard the authorities are searching all the hotels looking for you. They are definitely after you. And you can't stay at the German ambassador's house, that's the worst possible place. Don't you realize if you get caught it'll be a major international incident? Not only will the Americans be involved, but now the West German government will be accused of helping you as well. You can't do it. The German ambassador doesn't even know you're staying there."

I refused to budge.

A few days later, when I started a conversation in a restaurant with an Afghan at the next table, the man quickly advised me to "talk with some kind of accent so you do not sound American. Can you speak broken English with an accent?"

Afghanistan's high rate of illiteracy could also cause problems for reporters.

In Charikar, a small town north of Kabul where I sat munching kabob and nan bread with my taxi driver in a greasy food stall, an Afghan policeman entered, put his hand out for me to shake in greeting, and then used it to pull me up out of my chair.

"To the commander," he said sternly.

He walked me to a nearby walled compound and into a room where a freshly bloodied Afghan man quivered in the corner.

The police commander mistakenly said my tourist visa was good for only one day in Afghanistan and had already expired. He asked why I was so near the Salang Pass on the day Soviet convoys were withdrawing dozens of heavy vehicles from Afghanistan.

I glanced at the bleeding man's wounded forehead and the gash on his cheek, and casually told the commander I was there as a tourist to see the spectacular mountains.

My frazzled taxi driver contorted nervously on the next chair.

An army soldier escorted me in the taxi back to Kabul. The commander gave my escort a report about my detention, which needed to be signed by the Interior Ministry, KHAD's secret police, and the Afghan army.

After a friendly chat with the young soldier during our ride, he convinced me to stop our taxi on Kabul's outskirts at the Intercontinental Hotel, and buy him a drink at the bar and a bottle of Johnny Walker for him to take home.

It helped that by the time we finished drinking at the

Intercontinental, it was already evening when our taxi reached downtown Kabul. The soldier was slurring his words, but excitedly assured me everything would be fine.

All the offices were closed for the night. Only an indifferent skeletal staff remained at each place. My report was signed by all three offices while I waited in the taxi. None of them bothered to research my case because, as the delighted army escort said, the officers on the night shift were his friends.

When I was finally released, I waved farewell to a few happy Afghan guards armed with Kalashnikov rifles slung over their shoulders. They waved back and grinned.

Behind them, posters plastered on their compound's walls showed a muscular turbaned Afghan giant smashing his bayonet down on the head of a sinewy Afghan rebel wearing sunglasses and a beret. The rebel wore a skull and crossbones. His rifle was stamped, "Made in USA."

When I said goodbye to my escort, he chuckled and said, "I know you are not only a simple tourist. I know who you really are. So tell me, please, who are you really?"

Unsure how much I could really trust him, I cautiously mirrored him and replied, "And I know you are not only a simple army soldier. I know who you really are. So tell me, please, who are you really?"

He looked at me with a bolt of amazement in his eyes and gleefully shouted, "You are my brother! You are my brother!" and hugged me in the street.

Russian troops meanwhile had learned valuable lessons after their first six months in Afghanistan, confirmed by their retreating convoy north through the Salang Pass back to the Soviet Union.

Facing problems while pursuing hit-and-run guerrillas, the Soviets decided to withdraw many of their heaviest military vehicles because Afghanistan's terrain was much too rugged and steep, requiring light-weight machines and transport. During the next few years, they also learned to parachute small teams onto mountaintops to protect their convoys against snipers whenever

Soviet tanks, fuel trucks and other vehicles rumbled through exposed valleys.

The Russians buried landmines along rebels' supply routes. Soviet officers decided it was better to secure airbases and fortify garrisons and cities instead of wasting lives chasing mujahideen into endless, stark, mountainous mazes.

Soviet army camps grew to resemble a home away from home, replete with Russian food cooked and served by buxom female Soviet volunteers. TVs showed the latest Moscow programs.

One Soviet group of singing soldiers named themselves The Blue Berets and released a record album of sad ballads about the Afghan war. Song titles included Attack and War Is No Picnic.

Younger Soviet soldiers suffered the despair, loneliness, nightmares and corruption of serving in any military's lengthy war.

Some troops turned to Afghanistan's potent hashish and heroin. Many sold their military gear to buy Japanese electronic goods and other cherished imported items.

Soviet soldiers who fought in Afghanistan were dubbed Afgantsy. Ultimately 15,000 arrived back in their homeland in sealed zinc-lined coffins.

Atrocities on both sides escalated. Witnesses said Soviet forces threw Afghan guerrillas out of helicopters and lined up innocent villagers for point-blank executions. Russians trained Kabul's KHAD secret police to torture victims with electric shock, burning cigarettes and beatings.

Russian soldiers and doctors spoke of guerrillas who castrated or impaled any Soviets captured alive, or painstakingly peeled off much of their skin and threw them squirming in agony onto the desert's hot sand.

Others told of rebels who would tie a Soviet prisoner to four camels and rip his limbs off.

Russian forces were able to project their military muscle anywhere they wanted in the country -- but at a steep price.

They often purged a region of rebels and established a garrison. Guerrillas melded into the countryside, drifting back only when the bulk of Soviet forces departed, leaving the zone under the command of the weaker Afghan army.

As the brutal years of warfare continued, the stalemate remained. All sides claimed they were winning.

"Russians? What Russians?" an Afghan communist official asked me, as our Russian jeep sped north toward the Soviet border in 1987, on the Herat-Torgundy Highway.

He grandly waved at the surrounding hilly desert of western Afghanistan near the border with Iran. The barren region was punctuated by sagebrush, a few mud brick villages, and the skeletal remains of burnt Russian military vehicles.

"There are no Russians in all of Herat province," said Sayed Abdullah, a Herat Province Committee member of the ruling Peoples Democratic Party of Afghanistan.

When I pointed at an approaching, south-bound convoy of more than 170 Russian trucks carrying fuel, supplies, ominously long rockets and mounted, double-barreled anti-aircraft guns, Abdullah said:

"Those are not Russians. They are Afghan soldiers. Our uniforms look a lot like theirs. Some Afghan people also have light hair and fair skin."

But when the soldiers on the slow-moving convoy were overhead speaking Russian while our jeep crawled past them, Abdullah grimaced and said:

"Uh, yes, I now see they are Russians. But they are only passing through Herat province. I don't know where they are going. We have no Russians here at all. We don't need them. Herat province has been declared a Zone of Peace."

The most important parts of Herat province were relatively secure thanks to the heavy military presence.

A drive north from Herat in an unarmed, unescorted jeep to the Soviet border at Torgundy revealed a safe highway, built by Russians 20 years earlier, though the asphalt was now gouged by wide cracks from Russian tank treads.

At several stops along the way, villagers chatted and expressed support for the Soviet-backed Afghan regime. They said US-armed, Afghan guerrillas staged occasional raids, but dismissed the incidents as minor.

Every once in a while along the 65-mile-long highway, small groups of relaxed Russian troops ambled in isolated military outposts.

Some worked on stalled armored personnel carriers and trucks.

Other Russians swung pickaxes to dig ditches.

A few bathed in the open desert air.

One Russian idly urinated on a huge boulder.

Herat and this highway were vital to the Soviets' ability to reinforce bases in western Afghanistan.

When the Russians invaded this landlocked nation, they poured thousands of troops down two main routes. In eastern Afghanistan, one highway led from Termez, through the Salang Pass, to Kabul.

The other highway was this one, through Torgundy to Herat. Torgundy soon became a small frontier post swamped by large container trucks guarded by barbed wire, a parked fleet of polished Russian tanks, and clusters of Russian soldiers.

Russian trains stopped on the Soviet side of the border because Afghanistan was so poor this country had no railroad tracks. Instead, huge cranes lifted loads from the trains onto waiting trucks.

The Russians had a large military camp at Torgundy and could be seen strolling about in the sunshine, often bare-chested.

"I am from Moscow," said Lev Maximov, director of AFSOTR, a big Afghan-Soviet transport company.

"I have been here in Torgundy for the past two years," Maximov told me at the border town.

"There was also peace then, and there is also peace now. No difference. On the road to Herat, we don't have any problems with security," Maximov said, tugging his corduroy cap.

Later back in Herat, as soon as night descended, the sound of persistent machine gun fire and occasional explosions echoed in the distance.

"Mujahideen gunfire? There are no mujahideen anymore in Herat province," a Peoples Democratic Party of Afghanistan member named Wiase told me, peering out the window of our government guest house and dismissing any possibility of US-backed guerrillas threatening the regime's security during the night.

"This shooting is by people celebrating the revolution," another communist Afghan official told me, referring to the April 1978 revolt even though it was now November, 1987.

When gently reminded that impoverished Afghans had little money to spend celebrating the Marxist revolution, another Afghan official said:

"Weddings. It is wedding season, and traditionally Afghans like to shoot guns to enjoy."

His remarks were drowned by several loud explosions in the darkness.

"Those are a form of communication," he said, grinning.

"One Afghan army post is telling another that it is ready and alert. Then the other post replies."

Another Afghan official quietly conceded:

"There are some bad people in Herat who still have this habit of shooting to settle arguments. But no mujahideen are here. These are personal arguments."

During the years of escalating war, the mujahideen often battled Russian and Afghan communist troops in and around Herat, and repeatedly disrupted the region. Muslim rebels sometimes escaped across the border into nearby Iran, where they had a few hidden camps.

The next day atop the ramparts of Herat's famous Bala Hissar Fort, Russian-backed Afghan Army Captain Hussain told me, "Fighting exists, but much less than before."

He said 80 Afghan officers and soldiers, armed with 82-millimeter rockets, were stationed inside this hilltop fort which was made of tan, brick walls. Several sections lay in ruin, mostly from ancient times but also an occasional rebel assault.

"We hear only occasional shots, maybe from the suburbs, but we don't know what it is. A few weeks ago, three people were killed, eight were wounded and the Princess Mosque was damaged by bandits," Hussain said, using the government's description for the US-backed mujahideen.

"When we heard the shooting at 7 p.m., we left the fort but we couldn't find anyone there. Bala Hissar Fort has been hit by rockets, but not in the past three months," the army captain said.

Gulam Azarta, another Afghan soldier atop the fort, told me:

"Against our army, the rebels are zero. The Russians left Herat province more than a year ago. The peaceful situation is improving in our country."

Life for Afghans under the regime's control in a handful of so-called Peace Zones scattered across the country, was a mix of Marxist slogans and harsh reality.

Herat had radically changed from its decadent ways before the revolution, when children stood in front of shabby, cheap hotels selling opium and hashish to international hippies and freaks traveling by highway across Asia on their romanticized "Road to Kathmandu" during the 1960s and 1970s.

Illegal opium dens, hidden in dark alleys where shriveled Afghan men lay curled on padded floors, were no longer tolerated and now closed.

Many Afghans benefited from government money and grassroots programs initiated by the Marxists. Praise for the government was often followed by the words, "...and because of the revolution, I now have a job."

Many others were still trapped in grueling poverty amid spiraling prices, shortages and other economic problems caused by war and a difficult geography, Afghan bankers told me.

Meanwhile, one week later and hundreds of miles away in the northeast town of Mazar-i-Sharif in Balkh province, an elderly man in rags shuffled from table to table in a crowded restaurant, begging for food and money.

"He is a gambler," Peoples Democratic Party of Afghanistan member Sayed Azam told me while we ate.

"Eighty percent of the beggars in Afghanistan are gamblers. They are not poor. And the other 20 percent are fond of begging.

"They have a proverb: 'By working for the government, you can get 2,000 to 3,000 Afghanis a month ($35 to $53), but we can make that by begging in a single day'," Azam said.

The following evening however, in front of Mazar-i-Sharif's famed, blue-domed mosque, a group of about 50 ragged men, women and children swarmed around a lone bread vendor and screamed, "Bread! Bread!"

The vendor whipped them with a thin branch from a tree, to force them into an orderly line so they wouldn't mob his tiny stall where he was handing out free bread as an act of piety.

"They are poor," Azam finally admitted. "But the government is very busy trying to improve the problem."

Unhappy that the noisy and chaotic spectacle of hungry people being whipped might mar the image Azam was trying to present to me of the Marxist revolution, he quickly added: "Actually, I don't know which of them is a real beggar. But if the government gives free food all the time, they will beg all the time."

Poverty was everywhere in this rugged land. Small children often did the work of adults, such as hauling heavy carts or on construction sites.

"You see children working, not because they're poor, but because their parents want them to learn how to work, because it is good for their future," Azam said.

To defuse US and mujahideen claims that the revolution was anti-Islam, the government publicized news about mosques being built with official funds, hailed Muslim clergymen who supported the Marxist constitution, and boasted of other links that might show how regime honored Islam.

While entering the blue-domed mosque however, Azam was

surprisingly critical of Mazar-i-Sharif's influential Muslim clergy.

"The Mazar clergy tell the people, 'The money you are giving is not for me, but for Ali,'" Azam told me, referring to donations supposedly directed to Ali, who was buried at the mosque and revered as a relative of Islam's Prophet Mohammad.

"The clergy tell the people, 'Imagine the money is sweet juice you are pouring in his throat during a battle'.

"But this is bad. They are keeping the money for themselves. Even now after the revolution, we cannot stop them because the people themselves want this tradition," of donating money to the mosque.

In Kabul meanwhile, Soviet Mi-24 helicopter gunships clattered across the sky, drowning out the sound of Afghans defiantly shouting Allah o Akbar in mud-walled alleys. Armored personnel carriers, full of Soviet and Afghan troops, rumbled through the streets and into the surrounding countryside where they aimed their weapons' O-shaped barrels at villagers.

In the distance, artillery, tanks and helicopters hammered out a sinister staccato of gunfire, enforcing the regime's Marxist slogans.

Mile-high Kabul rests in a wide, dry pit formed by craggy, barren mountains. Throughout the Soviet-led war, mujahideen hid in the mountains and had little chance of wresting control of Kabul from Russia's grip.

As soon as rebels ventured down toward the foothills near the capital, they ran into massive Soviet military camps built at frequent points close to Kabul's perimeter. The huge installations spread across the sand. Young, clean-shaven, mostly light-haired troops lazily sprawled atop their armored personnel carriers and alongside dug-in tanks. During summer, they went shirtless in the heat, absorbing the cloudless sky's strong sunshine. Troops watched the dry rocky mountains which stretched north toward the steep Hindu Kush, eventually flattening into desert along the Afghan-Soviet border.

Guerrillas were at a severe disadvantage. The moment they emerged from mountaintop positions, they were as visible as ants on big, barren peaks of brown sugar -- and just as easy for the Russians to pick off. As a result, much of the war was a stalemate on a chessboard strewn with destroyed villages, miserable refugees, and bleak, windswept, dead orchards. America and the West gleefully dubbed the war, "Russia's Vietnam".

Moscow couldn't win. But neither could the rebels.

American, British and other pro-mujahideen diplomats described much of the fighting throughout the 1980s as mere "pinpricks and sniping" by insurgents at the iron hide of the Red Army. The squabbling guerrillas lacked unity and extensive communication equipment and were often unable to coordinate assaults. The Kremlin eventually learned some lessons and sent in more helicopter gunships -- huge, metal behemoths feared as "flying tanks" -- because Soviet helicopters were the only weapon the rebels truly feared.

As the years rolled by in gruesome succession and the body count grew on both sides, Afghanistan's regime celebrated each anniversary of its 1978 Marxist revolution. Afghanistan possessed no sea ports. No railways. No navigable rivers. And most Afghans lived and suffered much as they had centuries ago. The revolution sought to change all that.

Many Afghan Marxists were urban idealists who said they wanted to seize big landholders' property and distribute it to landless peasants, and liberate women from Muslim laws and traditions which kept females' status on a par with their husbands' cattle. Marxists wanted to bring children into schools and try for widespread literacy, raise agricultural and industrial production, end moneylenders' exorbitant interest rates, and modernize Afghanistan in a myriad of other ways.

But most of their plans went against a timeless Afghan slogan:

"If you want to live in peace with the Afghans, do not touch zar, zan, zameen" -- gold, women, or land.

The Marxist revolution had erupted amid a series of coups. In 1973, King Zahir Shah was overthrown by his cousin, former prime minister Mohammad Daoud. Leftist-minded Daoud nationalized banks, initiated land reforms and advocated direct taxation. But he did not trust the country's deeply committed Afghan Marxists because he correctly feared Russian designs on his nation. So he clamped down against them and they retaliated by overthrowing Daoud in the nation's first Marxist coup, the glorified 1978 April Revolution.

Their pro-Russian leader Nur Mohammad Taraki seized power. But a struggle soon ended in Taraki's death in September 1979 at the hands of Hafizullah Amin. Amin, in turn, was soon killed because other Afghan Marxists and the Kremlin feared he was distancing himself from Moscow's line, and improving relations with the United States and other capitalist nations. Babrak Karmal finally emerged on top in December 1979, installed with the help of thousands of his "invited" Russian invaders.

Amid all the assassinations at the bullet-riddled Darulaman Palace, many of the Marxists' ideals also perished. Within a few months of the Soviet Union's invasion, land reform was quietly abandoned. Afghan children who attended literacy programs were fed increasingly slogan-studded political tracts written in Moscow. Russian bombardments shredded towns and villages into ruins.

Despite advances for females in scattered cities and towns, many women continued to suffer under the country's majority ethnic Pashtuns. According to author M. Ibrahim Atayee's Pashtun Tribal Customary Law, justice in Afghanistan can be served when a murderer's family gives a female from its family to relatives of the dead victim:

"When maraka decrees that the killer side shall give a woman to the heir of the killed one, and rogha is effected in this way, such a decree and rogha are called hadpa hadke -- bone fortune.

"To accept hadpa hadke does not depend only on the members of the family of the killed one, but it is discussed by all the members of the plarina and decision as to the acceptance made. It is not necessary to give only one woman in the hadpa hadke. Cases have been found in which seven women are given in hadpa hadke."

Executions however were meted out for violating a woman's corpse:

"Kafan means 'a shroud, a coffin,' a piece of cloth in which the dead corpse is wrapped up. Kafan is sacred. Nobody shall disrespect it. The taking off kafan is punishable in narkh. The punishment for the robbing of the grave to steal the cloth is different than that of committing this act to insult the dead.

"The nanawate of the one who takes off the kafan of a dead woman to insult her is not accepted and the offender shall be killed.

"The latter case rarely occurs," Atayee noted.

Forcing a man to strip also brought severe punishment, which could include execution or giving a female family member to the exposed victim.

"If having someone's waistcoat or shirt is taken off, the sharm is heavy.

"To take someone's trousers off means to disgrace him, and to restore the grace, there is no other way but to kill the offender.

"If jirga or maraka levies tawan on the offender for such an offense, it will be very heavy. In most cases the offender has to give a woman or more to the offended."

Females were not the only ones to be used as payment for other people's crimes. Among Afghanistan's minority ethnic Kuchi nomads, an innocent man would need to be decapitated if his relative was a thief:

"The Kuchi leave their surplus belongings, when they migrate, in nikano mena. Nobody will steal anything from the nikano mena. It is a belief that if anyone steals anything from the nikano mena, it will be exchanged for the head of one of his family male members."

Pashtun men could also upgrade their females by trading them for others.

"A woman given in exchange for another is called makhaiy.

Women exchanged for each other are called makhyanay. Makhaiy does not necessarily have to be as pretty and young as the one she is exchanged for."

Afghan Marxists grappling to end such traditions scrambled to display women's rights as one of the few successes they achieved in their new Afghanistan.

In 1987, Afghan women such as Roziya Zalmy, 26, were being hailed as symbols of female equality. With her black turban tied like a man's, and clutching a Russian-supplied Kalashnikov assault rifle, "Commander Roziya" was a stark contrast to the way women lived before Soviet troops arrived.

Roziya's isolated mud village, Dohab, was in western Afghanistan, 40 miles north of Herat and far from Kabul along the western border with Iran. Roziya stood five-feet, five-inches tall with shoulder-length, straight black hair and no make-up. She had three sons.

"I command 5,000 Tajik tribesmen, 1,000 of whom are armed," Roziya told me, smiling in front of her Dohab home in the undulating desert. "I usually carry my Kalashnikov, but I know how to use a pistol, rifle, hand grenades and all other weapons.

"I was a mujahideen from 1980 to 1984. But I left the mujahideen to join the government of Afghanistan. The mujahideen were deceived into thinking Islam was in danger in our country. But I realized it wasn't true. I like the Russians. They help us. When we don't need their help, their army will go back."

Her direct, challenging brown eyes scanned the horizon's low hills rippling towards Iran and peppered with deadly landmines buried by the Marxist regime to ward off cross-border rebel attacks.

Most women in Afghanistan are forced by Islamic tradition to wear a chador, covering her head and upper body. Less popular is a head-to-toe burqa sheet, which allows only hands and feet to remain exposed. While covered in a chador or burqa, females peer out through a lattice of embroidered tiny holes at eye level. Women work, shop, chat and travel while draped. A chador or burqa is enforced by most males because they fear the exposed face or bodily shape of a female can be an immoral, shameful display of tempting sexuality. As a result, Afghanistan's women spend most of their lives apart from men, secreted away in a curtained-off purdah room at home -- purdah means curtain in Persian -- or in female-only huddles at mosques, on buses, and even among friends.

After the 1978 revolution, the Marxist government shocked Afghan society by announcing women could, overnight, enjoy freedom to dress as they pleased, work in the civil service, fight in the armed forces, join institutions, and receive other equal rights.

Commander Roziya said she emerged from the revolution in a stronger position than before. Her husband sheepishly admitted that in some ways, she also had become superior to men.

"We have been married for four years. Maybe she's a better fighter than I am," Roziya's 32-year-old husband Ali Mohammad said laughing.

"She knows things better than me, that's why she's a commander. In my home, she is also my commander."

But even among the government's supporters, not everyone was pleased with communist-style feminism. In the northern city of Mazar-i-Sharif, the top Muslim clergyman inside the city's big-bubbled, blue-domed mosque said in 1987 he loved the Russians and the Afghan regime, but he never allowed women's liberation in his own home.

Moulvi Abdul Hameed, 47, was the burly imam of the ulema, or Islamic clergy, of Mazar-i-Sharif and the surrounding desert and mountains of northern Afghanistan's Balkh province which bordered the Soviet Union. He was surprisingly blunt about whether or not women should be unveiled.

"The wearing of clothes such as a chador or short skirts does not make a woman a Muslim or an infidel," Hameed told me inside the Blue Mosque.

"Women now have this freedom. But Islam says every woman who makes herself beautiful only for her husband is good. For example, I am married with two sons and two daughters. My wife is a housewife. She wears a chador when she goes outside. Why? Because it is our custom and our tradition. It doesn't show man is superior. It is for the decoration of women."

Hameed chuckled.

"For those women who are very ugly, it is better for them."

He chuckled again.

"I don't tell you if my wife is beautiful or not. But I like for her to wear a chador. She looks more beautiful with a chador than without!"

If Hameed were born a woman, would he want to wear a chador?

"That is a funny question! It is nonsense to ask me because I am a moulvi."

Elsewhere in Mazar-i-Sharif, at an all-girls' school named after Afghan female poet Fatmay Balkhi, none of the students wore veils.

Wajma Nahi, an 18-year-old student, told me in a classroom interview:

"I wore a chador until last year. I stopped because conditions here became better. Now it is peaceful. Some years ago, the counter-revolutionaries [Islamist guerrillas] said, 'You should wear the chador.' It was compulsory. I don't like wearing it because everyone likes freedom and I didn't feel free."

Back in Kabul, the Marxist regime continued to discourage chadors and burqas, but knew a mandatory ban was impossible. Most men still demanded their women's faces remained hidden by cloth, no matter what the revolution's new slogans promised.

"Usually women wear a chador," the government's All Afghanistan Women's Council General-Secretary, Nafas Jahid, 26, told me. Married with one son and three daughters, she was unveiled and wanted to liberate the nation's females. But now, almost eight years after the Russian invasion, Jahid was resigned to society's limitations.

"The chador is a tradition because the majority of our people are religious. And the chador is imposed on our women. I wore a chador from the ages of 14 to 18. I felt very bad then because we could not participate in parties and other ceremonies because of this chador. We can't see out from underneath it. But we don't advise women to wear or not wear it. We don't like to discuss with them this subject. Now they are free to wear a chador or not. Usually they wear chador. But we don't care about this.

"Our organization is a mass social organization. The main purpose is to attract women to join. To spread literacy among them, give professional training, to light their minds and create a place for women to sit together and discuss their problems. And to find jobs. The majority of women under the previous government had nothing to do.

"Many husbands were killed by counter-revolutionaries. Their families became poor. We work among them to create better conditions. There are five million women in Afghanistan today. Very few are liberated. About 160,000 are liberated, working out of their homes and in different ministries. About 15,000 women are in the Afghan army. The highest women officials in the Afghan government are four of them in the People's Democratic Party of Afghanistan's Central Committee. Now, during the revolution, the majority of university students are women or girls."

Jahid did not mention that many male students were absent from campuses because they were either forced into the military, joined the mujahideen or had fled Afghanistan.

Asked about replacing President Najibullah with a woman to rule the nation, Jahid paused and cautiously replied:

"We like to work to be in the leadership positions. But I don't want Najibullah removed because he is very active."

Changing the subject, she added:

"In America, there does not exist real freedom of women. Women there are only for men to take pleasure with, and don't have any freedom. There exists some liberated women, but very few. The conditions of freedom belong to a special strata of society, not all women. Only women who are rich and very powerful. Other women don't have freedom there."

Sayeed Karim, a senior dean in Kabul, told me his school taught females how to read, using books which explained "training children, breast feeding, and how young girls shouldn't marry at 11 or 12 like before the revolution, but at 16, 17 or 18."

In the streets of Kabul meanwhile, an anti-veil fashion scene flourished during the Russian occupation, especially in Soviet-style schools, offices and institutions. Girls and women were increasingly seen in knee-length dresses, blouses and high heels. They wore bright red lipstick and red nail polish.

Such boldness rarely appeared in smaller towns and villages.

As the war worsened, the Marxists' rhetoric became increasingly harsh. But they always tried to include Islamic-laced messages to defeat the rebels' claims that the regime was against religion. But some Marxist party members such as Sayed Azam were not happy with the way the Muslim priests were luring the public, especially when asking for donations.

"Some of the clergy tell people, 'The money you are giving is not for me, but for Allah. Imagine it is sweet juice you are pouring in His throat during battle.'

"But the bad ones are keeping the money for themselves. Even now, after the revolution, our government cannot stop this," Azam told me.

The regime's Radio Kabul however routinely blared poetic praise for Allah, mixed with updates about battlefield results and rebel bombardments. A typical broadcast during the 1980s warned:

"The scoundrel rebel bandits should not have directed the arrows of deception, cruelty, cheap ambition, and dark grudgery [sic] at our lofty president. In our nation, there is a great people who know how to color the ground with aggressors' blood and how to punish the criminal and evil aggressors. In retaliation for the rebel bandit clique's crime of shelling the capital with the missiles of traitors at 3:55 p.m. today, 16 devastating government air force planes attacked the rebel bandits' camps along the border, turning them into ruins.

"Also at the same time, scores of our planes were flying over the rebel bandits' territory, dropping lethal bombs on the heads of charlatans and turning their selected targets into ruined junk. Our planes then returned safely. Praise be to God.

"Have we not said we will turn their cities into ruins? This is our president's deed and promise. The free man's promise is his bond. O brave government pilots, this is the way to treat the enemy.

"During a meeting, plans were put forward for dispatching the third part of the president's Mohammad Corps -- may God's benediction and peace be upon Him and His scion -- which will be leaving for the battlefronts. O nation, please pay attention. On the basis of the report received, the combatants of our president, while advancing, succeeded in mopping up the filth from some sensitive regions of our great homeland which had been occupied."

In the late 1980s, Moscow became weary of its own spiraling body count and began considering with the idea of a full military withdrawal. Reflecting the worsening situation on all sides, the Afghan regime's rhetoric against America grew harsh. It published an open letter to the US Senate which said in part:

"It is the ruling circles of your country [America] who lead, organize and finance international terrorism. It is your weapons which make hundreds of people drown in blood every day in every corner of the world.

"Under the pretext that an American ship was fired at by the Vietnamese in the Tonkin Gulf, you spread blood and fire on the territory of Vietnam for several years. Under the pretext that the lives of some Americans were endangered in Lebanon, you spared no effort in massacring the Arab people in that country. Is the blood of Americans different from that of Vietnamese, Arabs and Afghans? What is the difference between you and the fascist Nazis who considered it lawful to kill in a most barbaric manner?

"But let us draw your blind eyes and filthy minds to the fact that we are always ready to shed our blood for our revolution, and proudly safeguard and strengthen it."

President Najibullah meanwhile tried to boost morale. In 1988, he told the nation the mujahideen "have claimed in propaganda that soon they will be coming to Kabul, riding on white horses. We regard this as the same as someone who divides the skin of a bear before they hunt it."

Little did Najibullah know that some of mujahideen were trying to come to Kabul -- by using imported American mules.

"Tennessee mules," a US diplomat based in Peshawar told me in January 1988. The mules were flown from Tennessee to Pakistan, given to mujahideen in Peshawar, and trotted across the border into the war zone.

"This isn't a CIA program. The mules are a legitimate aid program. Already, a couple of hundred mules have been given to the mujahideen. The program started six months ago. It is still continuing," the diplomat said.

A total of more than 2,000 mules were reportedly destined to join the rebels. The mules were only a tiny part of the estimated $715 million in military and humanitarian aid Washington gave the mujahideen the previous year, including sophisticated surface-to-air Stinger missiles and other weapons. The mules were brought in because they could be loaded with Stingers and other war material while trekking across steep mountains.

American officials said a high death rate for Afghan mules -- from landmines and other attacks -- created a mule shortage. But the Americans' mules-for-war program became highly embarrassing to the US-backed Pakistani government which liked to publicly deny any involvement in Afghanistan's affairs. Guerrillas loaded the beasts and, thrashing them with sticks or branches, moved the mule convoys west across the Pakistan-Afghan border.

"We don't talk about such cross-border programs because

the Pakistan government publicly says these programs do not exist," the diplomat said. "Pakistan does not like the publicity because that gives an appearance that Pakistan is too much in bed with the United States. It is bad for Pakistan's political health."

The mule program was especially controversial and unique because it involved American citizens directly advising the Afghan rebels on how to use US livestock against Russia's military.

"The United States brings the mules here and trains the mujahideen how to load a mule and handle a mule," the American envoy said. "Afghans traditionally abuse their mules. The United States advises them that keeping your mule healthy and happy is the key to the jihad."

How many Americans were in Pakistan directly involved in the mule seminars?

"Four."

He refused to elaborate.

Critics said it was a classic case of sending coals to Newcastle, because Pakistani mules were popular and relatively inexpensive in Peshawar and elsewhere in the country, where they are used extensively in agriculture, transport and hard labor. Buying mules in the United States and flying them halfway around the world was much more costly than haggling for mules in local markets. An audit of the mule deals was not made public. But forcing American mules into the Afghan mujahideen's forces was backed by then-Texas Congressman Charles Wilson, whom the diplomat described as a "mujahideen groupie" because of his zealous support for the guerrillas.

"Charlie Wilson came to Pakistan and said he had seen the mules, they are here, and they are beautiful," the envoy said.

Wilson, an influential member of the House of Representatives' panels on intelligence and cash flows, was also quoted as saying at the time:

"In Vietnam, we lost 58,000 men," compared to the Soviets who suffered 15,000 deaths in Afghanistan.

"That means they owe us."

The mules' impact against the 115,000 Soviet troops in Afghanistan was "impossible to measure, but it's going well," the diplomat said.

The mujahideen however were not entirely happy.

Rebel commanders complained the Tennessee mules were not as strong as Afghan mules and not accustomed to the country's blisteringly hot, dry summers, and freezing winter blizzards.

"I heard from some mujahideen that some of the mules are behaving crazily," said Dr. Sayd B. Majrooh, a former Kabul University professor who was now director of Peshawar's Afghan Information Center.

"The mules are kicking like mad and some could not be used. Also, the mules are not very good climbing down mountains. They are good going up the mountains, but not down. No one knows why."

President Najibullah was staging public celebrations to exaggerate his power, especially while marking the 10th anniversary of the 1978 Marxist revolution.

He treated Kabul to a parade of heavy weaponry and uniformed Afghan soldiers, plus Afghan women dressed in ornate tribal dresses brandishing assault rifles. Bizarrely, 1988's April parade was conducted in total silence, except for loud prerecorded canned applause broadcast over tinny speakers.

Afghan and international officials, diplomats, journalists and others sitting in the grandstand and watching the parade march by, could hear the taped clapping and cheering and quickly realized no one could see anyone actually applauding.

Meanwhile across the border in Pakistan, beyond the Khyber Pass, veiled women and bearded men clogged the bazaars of Peshawar. In 1988, Toufiq Shah's face -- topped with his ridiculous pompadour of bulbous, shiny black hair -- mischievously smiled as its tall owner strolled Peshawar's lanes.

Young and elegant, Toufiq's face had recently appeared across the border in India where it grinned in New Delhi's quasi-taboo, timidly decadent discos. The face soon blushed with pleasure when two young foreign women visiting New Delhi fell in love with the man himself.

Now, trapped alongside millions of other Afghan refugees in and around squalid camps in Pakistan, the face only occasionally displayed delight, surprise, or eagerness. In Peshawar's bleak, dusty streets, Toufiq was having problems pursuing his goddesses who he described as "girls who are too beautiful."

When a young Muslim woman passed by with her beauty partially covered, Toufiq ecstatically whispered to his buddies, "Oh please help me, I will die if I cannot know her name!"

He displayed a letter which he kept in his shirt pocket.

"It is a love letter from my Australian girl friend," he told anyone who would listen.

But now, beautiful girls were occupying less and less of Toufiq's time. A nightmare was rapidly smothering him.

His new, more serious woes, involved his sister and mother. They depended on him because their father recently "died from a disease."

After Toufiq came to Pakistan from India three years ago, they were not able to get their expected visas to escape to Europe or America. As a result, he had to remain in Peshawar to take care of them. Toufiq was now stuck.

"My brother, instead of being the momma's boy he once was when he slept with our mother in the same bed with her even when he was a teenager, now my brother has gone to America and stopped writing us. He only sends the occasional card. It is terrible. And now I cannot go back to India, because I must stay here in Peshawar to take care of my sister and mother. And this place? Can you imagine? There are no girls!"

Pakistan's harsh Islamic laws punished adultery by whippings or stonings.

As a result, men often behaved like sexually frustrated hyenas. If females walked without a veil, men crudely whistled and yelled insults. No traditional Muslim girl was ever seen dating a man, unless their relatives were in tow. Debonair

Toufiq knew he would never find romance in Peshawar.

His family's visa troubles also meant he would not be leaving Pakistan anytime soon. So he wouldn't be able to live overseas with any of his foreign girlfriends.

"Not even the American girl in Mary Land with big breasts," he dreamily lamented, while his heavy-lidded eyes pondered his future.

"My American girlfriend, oh, I have been so bad to her. I have made such a big mistake by not writing her. For nearly two years I didn't write a line. And you know what she has just written me? She said, 'Anyway, I love you, please come to America.'

"But I cannot do it. How can I leave my mother and sister here? The people here are so disgusting, I tell you. These people see I am living with my sister and mother and we are all on our own, but some people are making stupid comments. Vulgar things they are saying. Even though they know I am my sister's brother. You can imagine what foul things they are saying about me and my sister living together.

"How can I get out of here?"

With a sad sweep of his hand, almost as an afterthought, Toufiq then introduced a skinny, shy Afghan man who had been standing next to him in the bazaar.

"This is Abdul."

Abdul smiled but didn't have anything to say.

A third Afghan was also with them. He was from Kandahar, Afghanistan's second largest city. Back then, Kandahar was a bleak, southern, urban oasis decimated by years of Russian and Afghan government bombardments and anti-communist rebel attacks.

"You know the only two things Kandahar is famous for?" Toufiq laughed, causing Abdul to suddenly giggle with delight.

Kandahar Man, who heard this joke too many times before, blushed and started protesting, "No, no, no!"

"What two things is Kandahar famous for?" Toufiq teased Kandahar Man. "Desert and heat? Flies and no water?"

Toufiq leered and burst with louder laughter. "Kandahar is famous for only two things -- pomegranates and homosexuals!"

All three Afghans convulsed with laughter.

"You know pomegranates?" Toufiq asked through a doltish grin, spitting more laughs. "And, and..." another round of chortling sent them into a triangle of hysterics. Kandahar Man kept shaking his head, shouting, "No, no, no!" and laughed just as hard as Toufiq and Abdul.

"Please wait here and soon we talk everything," Toufiq told me.

"We are going to prayers now and will return. Wait here at this calendar shop."

After thanking me profusely, the three walked down a narrow pathway filled with hanging cloth, brass pots and lanterns.

An hour later, only Toufiq returned.

He said Abdul and Kandahar Man needed to catch a bus to go to their homes in one of the nearby refugee camps.

Toufiq, without his usual grin, now wanted to go to a nearby tea shop, sit upstairs and talk seriously about the war. As he pushed his way through the teeming food market, he mentioned Gulbuddin Hekmatyar.

Toufiq quietly confessed he supported Hekmatyar's rigidly fundamentalist Islamic mujahideen in their attempt to seize power in Afghanistan, pushing out other mujahideen factions. Toufiq was distressed that Hekmatyar's enemies were saying evil things about the bearded, turbaned leader who headed one of the most powerful and feared, CIA-financed Afghan rebel groups, Hezb-i-Islami, or Party of Islam.

Hekmatyar's many foes said he was a dangerous, diabolical man who would devastate Afghanistan if he came to power in Kabul. Hekmatyar was a deadly threat to innocent Afghans, they warned. They said Hekmatyar's mujahideen were also looting and killing foreign correspondents and medical workers in Afghanistan's northern mountains.

Toufiq defended Hekmatyar as a man of honor who could

do no wrong.

Toufiq insisted French medical workers who recently complained they were attacked by Hekmatyar's rebels, were not really medical workers. Toufiq said they were suspect characters because many were French communist sympathizers.

"One of them was a French girl, who was pretending to be medical worker. And you know what thing she did? This French so-called medical girl? This French girl made love with a rebel commander. Not one of Hekmatyar's, of course not. His men would not do such a thing. But with one of the other groups. They made love in the northern mountains. I swear to God, I tell the truth! And do you know where? They made love inside a mosque! Can you believe it is so? What kind of girl is this? Making love inside a mosque? So why you are telling me they are only medical workers? This is so bad. Inside a mosque!

"I know I am also not good. I am not bad like that of course, but I am a little bit bad because I am all the time going after this girl and that girl. Chasing girls too much. But don't you see? That is why I have now joined Hekmatyar's group. His mujahideen are pure mujahideen. They are fighting only for a pure Muslim land. He is a pure Muslim. There is no dirt in his heart. Not one dirt in his heart. They want a society of the Koran.

"I would have been married to a woman by now, I would have had a family, everything, and not be chasing all these girls like this, if I had obeyed the Koran. That is why Hekmatyar's Hezb-i-Islami are correct. Of course we must live according to the Koran. It was written by God. What other way can we live except what is written by God? And our mujahideen do not do those bad things.

"It is the other mujahideen groups, the ones who are saying they are pure in their heart, but really, some of them are opportunists. They are shaky Muslims. Some are just taking the money of the others who are Muslim, but not fighting for the Afghan people. Only Hekmatyar is. That is why he is my leader."

Afghanistan's Russian-backed Marxist government dubbed Hekmatyar one of "the butchers of the Afghan people."

In 1982, it published a booklet, The True Face of Afghan Counter-Revolution which portrayed the communist government as glorious, while denigrating all opponents as CIA stooges.

Hekmatyar was one of the government's worst enemies.

"He was expelled from a military school for engaging in homosexuality," the booklet claimed, without offering evidence for any of its allegations.

"In Kabul, he used his secret links to get in touch with the US Embassy and the CIA, which were recruiting renegades and professional criminals for the purpose of setting up a terrorist network. He had performed his first exercise in homicide in 1970, when he murdered a university student. He was put behind bars, but because of his secret connections, he got out in 1972. So a convicted murderer served only two years!"

Afghanistan's regime also printed little propaganda booklets packed with horrifying stories about various attacks by mujahideen and often focused especially on Hekmatyar's guerrillas.

One booklet purportedly quoted a boy:

"They put the Kalashnikov submachine gun across my eyes and said that since I wanted to study and did not want to fight in the holy war, they would make me blind. They fired, and as a result, I cannot see any more."

The little booklets said Islamist rebels, especially Hekmatyar's, threw acid into the faces of females who wanted to go to school or work.

"At present, raping of women, abduction, buying and selling women, forced marriages, murder, hanging and amputation of breasts of women are typical crimes committed by the acid-spreaders and many other similar groups," said one of the English-language tracts, issued in Kabul.

The Afghan regime also published alleged confessions from captured rebels.

"I have passed on 40 men and women various kinds of death sentences, such as execution, stoning to death, burying alive and skinning," one alleged Islamist guerrilla said.

"When I used to pass the stoning death verdict on someone, I ordered that the man should be half-buried. The method consists in digging a pit, placing the person into it in such a way that only half of his body is buried, and then throwing stones at him until he is dead. The order of skinning was executed through skinning the convict by some persons with small knives. If the convict was a woman, her breasts had to be cut off first. The victims were buried while they were half alive."

Hekmatyar denied his mujahideen committed such crimes.

Our interview in January 1988 took place in his guarded house in an upper-class Peshawar neighborhood, near the border's Khyber Pass checkpoint.

Black-bearded Hekmatyar sat while fingering a string of Islamic prayer beads.

He harshly condemned both Washington and Moscow, and denied charges that his CIA-financed mujahideen murdered and looted innocent people. Hekmatyar said he was fighting to help rule Afghanistan and turn it into a fundamentalist Islamic nation after Russia's withdrawal.

The long years of warfare, coupled with intense rivalry among mujahideen groups, had taken its toll on him. Hekmatyar said he was hunted by communist spies and Western secret agents trying to stop him from allowing the Afghan people to live under the 1,300-year-old teachings of Allah.

Did Hekmatyar direct his men to kill Andy Skrzypkoviak, a BBC television cameraman who had been murdered inside Afghanistan in rebel territory three months earlier?

If not, who did?

And why was Skrzypkoviak's wife now petitioning Washington and everyone else to stop funding Hekmatyar with US tax dollars because America shouldn't be financing such a bloodthirsty leader?

The BBC's Pakistan-based correspondent George Arney

reported when Skrzypkoviak disappeared:

"Witnesses saw him struggling with a group of Hezb-i-Islami guerrillas who were apparently trying to snatch his camera. Later they heard gunshots. No body has been found, but Andy hasn't been heard of since. Five hours later, the same group of guerrillas is alleged to have robbed a 30-horse French-funded caravan laden with clothing and money for hard-pressed villagers," Arney reported.

When asked in our interview if his Hezb-i-Islami guerrillas killed Skrzypkoviak in northern Afghanistan's Nuristan region of Paktiya province, Hekmatyar glared.

He stopped fingering his prayer beads.

He quietly set aside his tea and replied:

"It is a concocted story. Some intelligence services are involved in making up the story. Even in the story there is no eyewitnesses known, and no other proof to confirm this happening. Hearing mere gunfire in a war should not convey that Andy was kidnapped by Hezb-i-Islami. Who in Hezb-i-Islami has kidnapped him?"

Hekmatyar said the BBC cameraman was traveling near Kantiwar Pass with a rival guerrilla faction, Jamiat Islami, and it was they who should be held responsible for his disappearance.

"How is it possible that out of a group, one man is killed and his body is missing? Why isn't that group blamed for that?

"This is not the first time the BBC and other intelligence services make up such vicious stories and make up such ruthless propaganda. It is pathetic that while we are fighting the Soviets, they stab us in the back.

"As far as we know, Andy was working for intelligence services."

During the Soviet occupation, Hekmatyar's estimated 30,000 rebels received most of the CIA's covert aid to various Afghan mujahideen groups.

The CIA included highly prized, sophisticated Stinger anti-aircraft missiles.

Anxious to dispel the image of being a CIA creation, a stone-faced Hekmatyar said flatly:

"The Americans do not give us aid. We have not taken anything from the Americans."

Stingers?

"These are just rumors. We have not received a bullet from the Americans."

Among mujahideen groups, Jamiat Islami was considered the most powerful guerrilla organization and the worst enemy of 36-year-old Hekmatyar. Jamiat's crafty, seemingly unbeatable leader -- nicknamed The Lion of Panjshir Valley -- was legendary Ahmad Shah Masood.

Some guerrillas claimed Hekmatyar, an ethnic majority Pashtun, was jealous of the popularity of Masood who was a minority Tajik.

Masood was lavishly praised and exalted by most American and other Western journalists, aid workers and diplomats. The Russian-backed Afghan army begrudgingly lauded Masood as The Fox because of his skill, daring and ability to survive repeated Russian and Afghan regime offensives in the northeast.

After Soviet forces withdrew in 1989 and the delicate Afghan Marxist regime collapsed from an onslaught by rebel groups and mutinous troops, Masood became Afghanistan's defense minister in the mujahideen's first government in 1992.

A sidelined Hekmatyar then laid siege to Kabul.

Throughout the early 1990s, the shunned Hekmatyar demanded a big chunk of power over Afghanistan. As a result, at least 50,000 innocent civilians in Kabul, along with countless mujahideen on all sides, perished in rival bombardments which turned much of the capital into jagged rubble during the 1990s.

During our interview, Hekmatyar expressed suspicion of both Washington and Moscow for interfering in Afghanistan.

"We don't know what interest the West has in supporting Masood and taking special interest in him. Masood eliminated all those in his own Jamiat Islami who opposed his supremacy. Later on, Masood attacked mujahideen of other parties and these parties complained of this."

Hekmatyar's opinion of foreign involvement in Afghanistan was also expressed in his 1986 Hezb-i-Islami poster. It showed a map of Afghanistan, colored green to symbolize Islam, being attacked by a big, angry eagle which carried a bomb in its claws. The eagle was about to drop the bomb to destroy Afghanistan.

One wing of the eagle was made from a Soviet flag. The other wing was the flag of the United States. The bird's head bore the flags of Great Britain, France and other nations. The United Nations' insignia was emblazoned across its chest.

The caption sarcastically asked if this murderous eagle was "the UN role in solving the political problem in Afghanistan."

Two days after interviewing Hekmatyar, a problem arose.

Toufiq reappeared with a seemingly generous invitation for lunch at his friend's house. Toufiq led me to what looked like an abandoned building in a backstreet of Peshawar. We entered an upstairs barren room with a low ceiling. Several gloomy, bearded men sat on the floor in a semi-circle with their weapons next to them on the floor.

Toufiq looked unhappy, guilty, and afraid.

"Please, a mujahideen commander wants to meet you. He is all right. Do not be afraid of him. I told him you met our leader Hekmatyar. Uh, please, do not worry. Many people are afraid when the commander asks questions. Some people are afraid because of his forceful and strong personality. The commander wants to..."

The commander cut him off. He spoke rapidly and angrily in Pashto. Toufiq translated:

"The commander wants to know who arranges your protection here in Peshawar?"

Protection?

"Who protects you here? The commander wants to know if something happens to you, or someone captures you, or someone wants to kill you here in Peshawar, who will arrange your protection?"

The lunch invitation was a trap.

It rapidly degenerated into an interrogation.

The unidentified commander was a swarthy, brutish hulk. As a hardcore Hekmatyar loyalist, he too was obsessed with foreign spies. He demanded more answers, increasingly personal and increasingly threatening.

"Does your newspaper get money from the government to pay you? Can your government protect you here if someone tries to kill you? What about the CIA? Is the CIA protecting you? How many CIA agents are in Peshawar to watch out for you? If you are going to be killed, will the CIA come to save you?"

He didn't believe my intentionally relaxed, carefree replies about an unprotected, free press. The grilling went on and on. The only escape from the commander's increasing suspicions would be to change the subject. But he ignored every attempt to discuss a new topic.

Perhaps the commander would be interested to hear what I was recently told by an Afghan psychiatrist who personally knew President Najibullah who was leading the Afghan military's war against Hekmatyar's mujahideen and other guerrillas?

As soon as Najibullah's name was mentioned, the commander fell silent and moved closer, intrigued.

Fortunately, my story about the psychiatrist and his analysis of Najibullah made for handy, drawn out re-telling.

The psychiatrist, Dr. Mohammad Azam Dadfar, knew Najibullah in Kabul for many years before Najibullah became president and even earlier, before Najibullah ran Afghanistan's dreaded KHAD secret police and its torture chambers.

The commander listened and nodded eagerly.

Telling the story brought a respite from the commander's questions, but then what? Through tiny windows, I could see night had descended, leaving us in a darkened room without electric lights and illuminated only by a few flickering candles.

I told the commander about Dadfar's clinical diagnosis of Najibullah's subconscious. Toufiq translated each new detail.

Dadfar, 41, was currently running a newly built white-walled Psychiatry Center for Afghans, financed by London-based Amnesty International and other organizations, 40 miles east of Peshawar near the Khyber Pass.

"We want to know how people are affected by things like bombings, mass slaughter and torture," Dadfar told me a week earlier.

"Our aim is to rehabilitate victims of torture and treat post-traumatic disorders caused by the war."

His clinic's bookshelves were lined with the latest issues of Integrative Psychiatry, the New England Journal of Medicine, and black folders labeled Psychiatric History Sheets containing extensive notes.

The psychiatry center had rehabilitated 341 torture victims aged 12 to 80. About 90 percent of them had been beaten, 73 percent were jolted with electricity, and 33 percent suffered genital torture while detained by KHAD, which continued Najibullah's brutal techniques and punishments.

Dadfar said in 40 percent of the cases, Soviet officers were present during interrogations, and 10 percent of the victims were tortured directly by the Soviets.

Moscow and the Afghan government denied all allegations of torture.

Each day, about 60 patients showed up at Dadfar's clinic for treatment. Most were turbaned, bearded men wearing traditional baggy cotton clothes. They sat waiting their turn next to women who were usually veiled.

"Most of the people are severe cases. We use psychotherapy, discussions and meditation." He had treated about 15,000 patients since the clinic opened two years earlier.

Dadfar had been jailed for 14 months when the April 1978 coup brought the Soviet-backed Marxists to power in Afghanistan.

"I was active in the student movement, an anti-Russian student. I was tortured. It was mostly psychological torture."

While imprisoned, he vowed to one day help rehabilitate

other inmates. After the Soviets poured thousands of troops into Afghanistan during Christmas 1979, he was released in a general amnesty. He left his homeland in mid-1980 and came to Peshawar as a refugee.

To recover from his nightmares of prison, he conducted "self-therapy," relying on sports, meditation and his understanding of the psyche.

After he opened the Psychiatry Center, he realized psychological techniques used in modern America and Europe had limited use treating people from an ancient, impoverished land steeped in Islamic tradition and tribal rituals.

In the dim light of the room, the black eyes of the commander, his men and Toufiq stared transfixed by the story and my overly dramatic gestures which I hoped would increase their attention.

They carefully followed Toufiq's translation at the end of every sentence.

After telling the commander that Dadfar received his degree at Kabul University where he later became a junior lecturer in the psychiatric department for five years, I told the commander about "Najibullah's brain."

I loudly mimicked the psychiatrist's voice and Afghan accent and spoke in first-person, in a high pitch as if I was Dadfar.

Toufiq translated:

"Najibullah was my classmate at medical school for one year, so we know each other. Najibullah is paranoid! He is not normal!"

The commander and his guerrillas began laughing, seeming to congratulate each other on something they already knew, now being medically confirmed.

I told them what the psychiatrist had said:

Najibullah was always ready to fight. He was intolerant. When anyone had a logical criticism about Najibullah's ideology, he became aggressive. He is physically strong, but emotionally naive. He personally tortured people when he was the head of KHAD's secret police for six years. Torturers are usually psychopathic. The Russians chose Najibullah to head the country partly because of his violent personality.

"What is my medical evaluation of Najibullah? Ha! I am a psychiatrist, and I have known Najibullah many years. And I can tell you, in all honesty..."

...dramatic pause while the commander's eyes glistened with expectation...

"Najibullah should be in a mental institution! Najibullah is crazy!"

As soon as Toufiq translated, the commander burst into heavy, bellowing laughter. He shouted the anecdote to the other guerrillas in the room to make sure they understood. They also burst into laughter and the commander waved to a nearby gunman and barked a few words, still laughing with delight. Dishes of cooked food appeared. The interrogation ceased.

While we ate, Toufiq quietly told me I was now free to go back to my hotel, but the commander invited me to attend a wedding party on the outskirts of Peshawar the next morning. The commander would meet me and Toufiq here at this building after breakfast and take us there. I should come alone, only with Toufiq.

I happily told the commander I was delighted and impressed with his gracious hospitality and would love to meet him tomorrow for a party on the outskirts of Peshawar alone in the middle of nowhere.

I thanked him profusely for the dinner, shook everyone's hands, departed by taxi, packed my bags in Green's Hotel and fled Peshawar before dawn.

In January 1989, to halt growing fears among the public and regime officials in Afghanistan, the government forced more people to learn how to kill. In the fabled, heavily fortified, hilltop Bala Hissar Fort overlooking Kabul, new recruits started training.

Among them was a 17-year-old raven-haired girl, Nafizy Kareem, who held her Kalashnikov assault rifle aloft and opened fire, experiencing for the first time its power and kick.

Kareem staggered under its recoil as the nearby snow-covered mountains echoed with 20 blasts from her rifle.

"I have never fought in a war before, but if the guerrillas come, I am ready," Kareem told me. She was part of a new Special Guard to defend Kabul. Wearing lipstick, earrings, low-heeled dress shoes, maroon knee socks, and a camouflage skirt and blouse, Kareem had already become a third-lieutenant in the Special Guard.

"The difficult condition our country is in, causes us to fight side by side with our brothers," she said, before breaking into mirthful giggles along with a handful of other shy females in the mostly male contingent.

Their team was based inside the crumbling ramparts of Bala Hissar, where Afghans in 1878 famously slaughtered 556 British soldiers during London's failed attempt to dominate the country.

Dilapidated Bala Hissar was now hosting mostly males aged 16 to 50, dressed in new, brown woolen uniforms and black boots. Their Kalashnikovs appeared to be in mint condition.

Kareem and the others practiced handling their weapons, saluting, marching and other military drills. The Special Guard had not yet been tested in battle. They were scheduled to soon protect Najibullah's palace, and support the regular army, said Major-General Mohammad Azim. He had little respect for the approaching rebels.

"The Russian troops withdrew from the cities of Kandahar, Herat, Jalalabad and so many other places during the past months, but the rebels have not taken a single city. So we are not worried at all," Azim told me.

Another Afghan who worked in the Marxist party's Central Committee agreed with Azim and told me:

"The Special Guard, plus other newly formed militias who are made up from the trade unions, women's organizations, youth groups and other elements, will be called on to defend the capital," and fight alongside the Afghan army, air force and Security Ministry's dreaded tsarandoi police.

"If they [mujahideen] kill all our armed forces and all the party men and everyone else loyal to the government, who will be left for the rebels to govern? Only the trees? Fields? Buildings? It is impossible to kill so many people," Azim said.

Kareem and the other Special Guards did not know that in three years, Najibullah's reign would collapse, mujahideen would bombard Bala Hissar, seize it, and turn the army's bunkers, dormitories and other buildings into one of their own rebel base camps to rule Afghanistan under Islamic law.

Kabul remained relatively safe throughout the Soviet's war. But when the final February 1989 Soviet military withdrawal date drew near, many embassies evacuated Kabul.

Soviet journalists and Russian Embassy diplomats said they would remain in Kabul after their military withdrew, but they expressed worry about possibly being murdered by mobs or mujahideen.

Grimacing with forced smiles, some Russians in Kabul told me in February, 1989, that they had become anti-war during their long years posted in Afghanistan. They lamented how their Soviet comrades committed "genocide" against innocent Afghan civilians.

Yuri Tyssovski, Kabul bureau chief of the Russian news agency TASS, chose to change his residence. Hurriedly boxing up his belongings in his suburban Kabul home, and calling for his pet German shepherd which was trained to sniff out land mines, Tyssovski told me:

"I am only moving into the Soviet Embassy across the street for safety. My boss asked me if I wanted to leave Afghanistan, but I told him no, because I want to stay on and continue my work. It is my duty.

"I will stay one year more. It will be difficult for us. There are various predictions of how the situation will be.

"It may be awfully bad, moderately bad, not so bad, or even good. So, let us see. It is impossible to guess anything, so why be worried about it?"

Tyssovski had recently been wounded in a rebel attack during a Soviet media trip in eastern Afghanistan. Pulling down one side of his pants, he displayed horrible scars on his thigh where shrapnel ripped into him.

"I have a whole arsenal in this house, including hand grenades which I hate. But I need them for protection."

He raised his glass of vodka in a toast and, laughing in an almost painful way, said:

"One day the rebels are going to come for me. But I am ready. I have already cut off my balls and put them in the refrigerator, so I can hand them to the mujahideen when they arrive!"

Another Russian journalist based in Kabul, eyeing a convoy of wearily clanking Soviet tanks withdrawing from the capital, bluntly told me, "For the Soviet Union, this war was a waste. Nothing but a waste."

An upbeat Russian official disagreed and told me:

"It was impossible to cut off all the caravan routes used by the rebels. But it is not correct to ask if the war was a success or defeat for the Soviet Union. We did not expect to fight or beat somebody. It was not some sort of an occupational war. We came not to intervene, but to help a legal government."

Many of the Soviet forces were thrilled to leave.

Elated Soviet Air Force Commander Colonel Pavel Vinokurow poured tumblers of clear vodka and cheered as his helicopter gunships clattered into the cold February sky above the Russians' military air base at Kabul International Airport.

"Peace! Peace!" six of his blond, blue-eyed combat pilots cheered in unison and then drained their glasses.

Vinokurow generously opened a fresh unlabeled bottle of alcohol.

One of the pilots pulled out a red-handled dagger and, after wiping it clean on a rumpled front page of Pravda, began slicing a pale yellow slab of bacon fat into big cubes and offered me a shiny chunk.

"This is Ukrainian bacon fat," Vinokurow said, popping one in his mouth and handing the other cubes around the lunch table to me, New Zealand journalist Adam Kelliher and American photographer Richard Ellis.

"Ukrainian bacon fat is the best in the world!" he exclaimed.

We asked what kind of alcohol it was, because at Kabul's one-mile high elevation, the effects were pulverizing.

"This must be the de-icing fluid used in the planes," one Russian joked. The other Russians laughed, agreed, and held their glasses out for more.

"We make this vodka in the other room," a Russian pilot quipped while extracting a short, pink sausage from an open tin can.

A week later they would all be flying home, hoping they would never have to return to Afghanistan.

Some of them doubted that the 9,000-man, Soviet-trained Afghan air force would be able to keep mujahideen away from the nearby snow-capped mountains. The Russian air force officers knew Kabul's airport would soon be the insurgents' target in a rebel advance on the capital to topple Najibullah.

Vinokurow told me the Afghan government would be able to keep the airport secure. As he spoke, four Russian Mi-24 helicopter gunships, circling above us, spouted scores of reddish-yellow flares. A large, slow, departing Aeroflot plane did the same. It was an attempt to fool the mujahideen's US-supplied heat-seeking Stingers.

While flares spewed down from the sky, the Aeroflot corkscrewed higher and higher in a tight circle, rising directly above the airport. All military and civilian planes did this while flying above Kabul, arriving or departing, to ensure they would not be shot down by a Stinger.

The planes needed to attain their highest cruising altitude while directly above the relative safety of Kabul's airport before leveling off and flying over rebel-infested mountains. Arriving international passenger and commercial flights also dared not descend from their peak altitude until they were directly above Kabul. Only then did they slowly spiral their way down.

"I will probably be the last Russian out of Kabul," chuckled

Vinokurow. "We will have our farewell ceremony on February 12 or 13."

The air force commander stared at the returning helicopters as they swept in low to land after escorting the Aeroflot.

"I have been in Afghanistan two and a half years," Vinokurow said before falling silent, his face suddenly drained of joy. Nearby, a cluster of Soviet helicopter pilots photographed each other in front of a helicopter. Snapshot souvenirs.

Pointing heavenward to helicopters escorting another outgoing plane, one of the posing pilots told me, "We shield the planes with our bodies. It is better for our helicopters to be shot down instead of a plane.

"Some of the enemy have been nicely trained and can fight. During the past nine years of war, they received very good experience. But overall, they are unorganized and fight only as guerrillas."

A nearby Ukrainian paratrooper, adjusting the strap of his AK-47 on his shoulder, said:

"I'll tell my friends all about Afghanistan. I have a lot of things to say to them because this was my first trip abroad. I was stationed about 300 kilometers southwest of here. I was protecting the posts and covering the area there. How can I describe the enemy? They are people who fire rockets on civilian areas, killing women and children."

These 300 paratroopers were the last Russian forces to withdraw from Kabul.

Within days, the capital's defense would be turned over to an Afghan army, bolstered by civilian militias, paramilitary police, secret police and palace guards.

The legacy of the twisted warfare between Moscow and Washington across Afghanistan would then be written.

Swarthy, turbaned US-backed Muslim rebels, most of them illiterate and living in poverty, had fought for nine years until the Kremlin's bloodied forces called it quits. Russia retreated under military pressure for the first time since World War II.

In domed mosques, teeming bazaars and mud-walled villages, Afghans who survived would suffer the aftermath of the devastating interference by Russia and America.

More than one million died, mostly civilians.

The war created countless maimed victims on all sides, devastated towns and farms, shattered traditions, and permanently wrenched families apart. More than five million refugees had fled.

Afghanistan was now filled with enough hatred, anger and fear to fuel acrimonious civil wars for several years to come, after the Soviets' withdrawal.

Tales of how Afghans fought the Shourovi (Soviets) would be handed down from generation to generation. Their stories would be added to tales of previous foreign invaders. Alexander the Great. Genghis Khan. Babar the first Mogul emperor. Failed British colonialists. And others.

"There will be a bloodbath," a glum senior American diplomat told me.

"But just whose blood will it be? Peasants? Or politicians who already have a lot of blood on their hands? There are scores to be settled because people did a lot of evil and treacherous things.

"Sure there will be bloodshed. But I don't think a war of all against all. Unless Pakistan or Iran pour oil on the fire.

"Najibullah is young, physically frightening, and a tough talker. He is the fair, big man, as opposed to the mean, big man. He can't compare with any of Hitler's deputies. He's more a tough tribal leader. He's quite good in public. If he had a few more men who supported him, he'd be better off," the American envoy said.

"He's increasingly an alone figure. A good officer with lousy officers. Factionalism and competitiveness, and future anxiety also cause problems for him. And he's not liked by the people, because the man in street has suffered from the war, is poorer, and their sons were killed because of the Soviets.

"Najibullah's associating with the Soviets, like on TV kissing them and so on, doesn't go down well with the public."

After the Soviets departed, Najibullah's regime shivered with fear and helplessness.

Random mujahideen rocket attacks on Kabul increased, usually veering off-target and slamming into bazaars. Kabul reinforced its "porcupine defenses" with a "ring of steel" perimeter of weapons pointing outwards toward the surrounding rebel-infested mountain peaks.

Meanwhile, Najibullah's ability to stay in power, without Soviet troops in Afghanistan, was being strangled by the thick hands of his presumably loyal officer, General Abdul Rashid Dostam.

Notorious and ruthless, Dostam was secretly plotting a mutiny against Najibullah after having wearily supported his faltering regime for the past several years. By professing loyalty to the government and the Soviets, Dostam had become one of Afghanistan's most influential and strongest warlords.

Dostam, 38, had grown powerful by acquiring possession and command over Russian jets and tanks that the Marxist government had given him to defend his Mazar-i-Sharif stronghold in the north against mujahideen. Dostam also enjoyed the loyalty of the Afghan army's minority ethnic Uzbeks and some of the other tribes in and around Mazar.

The Soviet and Afghan governments armed and financed Dostam because they considered him a reliable guard, 200 miles northwest of Kabul, based in his Qala-i-Jangi fortress headquarters in a desert wasteland near Mazar-i-Sharif.

Dostam's militia of Uzbeks were widely feared because of their reputation for slaughter, torture, rape and plunder. They were not mujahideen, because they had supported Najibullah's army against the guerrillas up north.

But when the Soviet Union began having financial problems in 1991, Moscow cut off Najibullah's budget.

With no money to pay his mercenary Uzbeks, Dostam decided to lead them against Najibullah and convinced his former enemy mujahideen to help him seize Kabul.

He turned traitor against Najibullah in April 1992, three years after the Soviet military withdrew from Afghanistan. Dostam knew the mujahideen desperately needed him to help topple Najibullah, because the insurgents were too weak and fractious to oust the regime on their own.

So he allied himself with the mujahideen, emerged as a leering Jack-in-the-Box, and changed Afghanistan's fate.

In 1992, much of the world saw the bloody end to Najibullah's regime as a victory for the mujahideen and US foreign policy. But the mujahideen did not win the war against the Soviets. The Islamist guerrillas never controlled a single province. It took Dostam and other mutinous generals within Najibullah's army to topple him.

Dostam then played both sides and extended his personal protection to Marxist government officials who were terrified they would be slaughtered in a bloodbath by the victorious rebels who had vowed to slit their throats after so many terrible years of warfare.

When Dostam's stern, moustached face loomed alongside victorious mujahideen in a clumsy, post-Najibullah power-sharing arrangement in Kabul, many of Afghanistan's frightened Russian-schooled soldiers, officials, and teachers recognized their former ally and became less nervous. They decided to continue working at their jobs under the new mujahideen-led regime.

As a result, there were not many revenge killings immediately after Najibullah's government collapsed. Mujahideen became the new bosses at government ministries and institutions, but the poorly educated rebels had zero skill or experience in administrating bureaucracies.

Instead, the newly arriving mujahideen who poured into Kabul randomly trashed parts of the capital, including ministries, factories, shops, schools, and offices. They also packed themselves into every hotel, including the once-elegant Intercontinental and the now-down-at-heels Hotel Kabul.

Heavily armed with rocket launchers, Kalashnikovs,

grenades, bandoliers of bullets and anything else designed to kill, they turned the town into a chaotic armed camp.

When you exited your Hotel Kabul room, you entered a dimly lit hallway packed with enough mujahideen and weaponry to wage an insurrection. Guerrillas lined up at the toilet with loaded, ready-to-fire rocket launchers slung over their shoulders. They casually cradled AK-47 assault rifles while watching translated Tom & Jerry cartoons on the upstairs lobby's television.

Every night -- celebrating or simply bored -- they fired rockets, anti-aircraft guns, flares and anything else that could make huge, explosions in the night sky from 7 p.m. to midnight for weeks.

But many mujahideen hated their rival guerrillas. They were splintered into a dozen factions, occasionally slitting each other's throats. Traveling through Kabul meant you had to go from one faction-infested neighborhood into a competing one. The worst sections were controlled by Dostam's dreaded, hashish-smoking Uzbeks.

Recognizable by their flat turbans worn high above their ears, Uzbeks were allowed by Dostam to loot parts of Kabul. No one else could control them.

Kabul became a fascinating, deadly city laced with raw anarchy.

You could enter gutted and looted government buildings and see the Marxist regime's intestines on display in the rubble of offices, equipment, and furniture. You could witness the mujahideen's new, confused coalition government struggling to manage the administration they had seized and crippled.

When you met ousted Afghan Marxist officials who you knew from their haughty years in power, many of them now quivered in fear of execution despite the reassurances they had received.

After Najibullah was ousted, it was possible for some foreign correspondents to reach Dostam's notorious desert fortress by flying north from Kabul over glacier-covered Hindu Kush mountain peaks aboard one of his Russian-supplied, camouflaged Antonov transport planes.

At Mazar-i-Sharif's airport, now controlled solely by Dostam, more than a dozen prized Russian MiG-21 and Sukhoi warplanes waited on the tarmac for his orders. Dostam had the warplanes, but suffered an embarrassing lack of fuel.

Nearby lay the skeletal waste of dismembered MiG jets which had been wrecked in warfare and cannibalized for parts, alongside Dostam's collection of Soviet tanks, armored personnel carriers, artillery guns and other weapons.

From Mazar's airport, Dostam provided a Russian helicopter gunship to fly us across the northern desert to his thick-walled, tan mud, Qala-i-Jangi fortress.

His fort was adorned by pastel blue columns. Bright pink-colored sunlight filtered into its main rooms through tall windows draped floor-to-ceiling with day-glow pink curtains in front of white lace -- giving the fortress's interior chambers the atmosphere of a ridiculously gaudy boudoir.

The slightly pudgy Dostam was solemn yet hospitable. He wore a camouflage uniform, cap, and black leather boots. Speaking in Dari, a Persian dialect, Dostam told us he came from a "peasant family" in a village near Mazar-i-Sharif.

"I have a seventh-grade education," because economic hardship prevented further study, Dostam said.

"After 1970, my interest was to be a military officer, and I became an officer. In this very headquarters, I took my course to be an officer."

Dostam was anxious to clean up his vicious public image and appear as a devout Muslim. He denounced the US government's Voice of America radio, and complained that it lied when it "broadcast that I was drinking alcohol and using bad language."

Dostam said he was a man of peace.

"If we were war-mongers, we would have sided with Najibullah who talked of reconciliation, but he never was for reconciliation. I have never run away from any duty or any military operation."

Dostam denied consistent reports over the past several years that his Uzbek forces savagely tortured mujahideen, civilian dissidents and other suspects, raped innocent female villagers, murdered people without cause, and more recently during the past few weeks, allowed his Uzbeks to loot parts of Kabul.

"It is propaganda which was waged since a long time ago against me and my forces. It is an accusation."

Dostam said he had "a big army, so there might be some cases" of abuse, but any allegations would be investigated.

Sitting on the upper terrace of his impressive stronghold -- Qala-i-Jangi translates as Fortress of War -- Dostam said he went out of his way to unify the squabbling rebels so together they could topple Najibullah.

"During the past six-and-a-half years, we were able to unite all the guerrilla forces in the north and equip them."

During Najibullah's regime, Dostam was assigned to guard northern Afghanistan's mountains and desert around Mazar-i-Sharif, especially against the mujahideen leaders Masood and Hekmatyar.

But during the past few years, Dostam secretly went relatively easy on Masood while concentrating on obliterating Hekmatyar's rebels.

Chuckling with pride, Dostam said he clandestinely made friends with Masood and some other mujahideen to "prepare for our uprising and the toppling of the Najibullah government."

Dostam's own militia was comprised mostly of men from his Uzbek tribe but included ethnic Tajiks and Turkmen alongside Afghanistan's majority Pashtuns.

Collectively they guarded his fortress, the surrounding desert and nearby slopes of the Hindu Kush.

Indicating the diversity of his allies, Dostam tried to deflect allegations that he was a selfish, opportunistic traitor. He insisted his motive was solidarity with ethnic minorities who suffered under Najibullah, who was Pashtun.

"Najibullah was very much against the various nationalities of

Afghanistan."

In victory, Dostam then targeted Hekmatyar, also a Pashtun, as his priority enemy.

"Hekmatyar has cowardly tortured a number of Tajik, Hazara, Uzbek and other minority nationalities, and has taken away 60 to 70 civilians just because they were Tajik, Hazara and Uzbek, and put them in a shipping container and killed them.

"Hekmatyar has taken two innocent civilians and -- just because they were members of minority nationalities -- took them to the zoo in Kabul and cut their eyes out, and their noses off, and threw these pieces as bait for the animals in the zoo.

"In the past 13 years, because of my forces, Hekmatyar was not able to topple even one province of the country. That is why Hekmatyar is stressing the withdrawal of my forces from Kabul. Hekmatyar wants the continuation of war."

Earlier during the 1980s, America had played a decisive role against the Soviets by supplying Stinger missiles to the mujahideen. Washington eagerly handed out 900 to 1,000 shoulder-fired Stingers during the war. Mujahideen fired an estimated 360 Stingers, destroying about 240 Soviet and Afghan planes and killing thousands of people.

One of the Pentagon's post-Najibullah concerns was that a single Stinger in the hands of a disgruntled person anywhere in the world could destroy a commercial airliner packed with civilians.

After the Soviet withdrawal, hundreds of Stingers were still in circulation.

Alexander Vasilenko, general manager of the Soviet Union's national airline Aeroflot, grimly showed me the giant carcass of an Aeroflot plane rotting on a runway at Kabul International Airport in 1992.

"While the plane was flying at 8,000 meters [altitude], the Stinger hit here," Vasilenko said, pointing to a gaping, jagged hole in the Iluyshun-76 aircraft's left side. The Stinger's hole was just below the Aeroflot's official blue, hammer-and-sickle-and-wing logo, close to the pilots' cockpit.

"The hit began a fire. Twelve people were on board, delivering fuel to Kabul. It was July 1990. Where the explosion cut the pipes, hydraulic fuel leaked.

"The pilot couldn't use the wing's flaps, and he couldn't use other things. He switched off two engines because of the fire, so only could use the two other engines."

Vasilenko gestured toward the sky.

"The pilot began a big decline and appeared at the airport and used, we say, 'glide wing.' After touching the ground, without wheels, he landed on this safety runway. And the dust from the ground entered the engine and put out the fire."

All 12 Soviet crewmembers survived.

Vasilenko pointed to another wrecked Soviet plane at the edge of Kabul's airport, which had also been shot down by a Stinger, killing everyone on board.

"That plane was shot down in March 1990. Twelve dead. The black box was completely destroyed. We couldn't find any remains. Only parts of heads. And arms."

That was why the Kremlin, terrified of the Stingers, installed flares on all their planes flying in and out of Kabul in the late 1980s.

A rack with 192 flares was mounted outside on both sides of each plane's tail, 384 flares in all. A flare man perched in the very end of the tail, where he could watch the sky for incoming rockets and coordinate outgoing flares through a tiny, tail-mounted window.

Vasilenko drew a picture of a plane with little dotted lines to indicate the "hot gases" which its engines emitted. Stingers were heat-seeking, so the flares were designed to trick their homing devices.

"With the flares, we covered this shape," Vasilenko said, indicating an arc of heat which followed an airplane's engines while in-flight.

"When mujahideen fired, and if we could see their flash, we would begin to shoot these flares, and these flares saved many planes. It was very effective."

Vasilenko said the Russian flares worked only against the weapon's first model, which he called, Stinger One.

"If you use Stinger Two, it is impossible to protect these planes. It is more sophisticated and it never follows flares. There is a special calculator in the Stinger Two to fix at the level of the engine, and it knows this engine. And it never follows anything different from this temperature."

Aeroflots were especially unlucky because they were slow, lumbering aircraft.

"Remember, Stingers are designed against military planes at high speed. This plane is very easy to shoot down."

The following year, in 1993, Kabul's diplomats predicted Afghanistan's "nightmare scenario" had begun.

Dostam and Masood, unable and unwilling to share power in ruling Kabul, turned against each other.

All sides suffered.

Always treacherous, Dostam and his 20,000 fighters teamed up with arch-enemy Hekmatyar in the north and east against Masood's 10,000 mujahideen and other loyalists who were trying to govern the destitute country.

Afghanistan's long-awaited mujahideen government -- and Kabul itself -- were soon destroyed by assassinations, bombardments and retaliation.

INDIA'S KASHMIR

The mujahideen's dream of creating an Islamic nation ruled by the Koran was not confined to Afghanistan. Further east along the Himalayas stretched the mountains and valleys of Muslim-majority Kashmir. Pakistan controlled one-third of the disputed territory. India held Kashmir's wealthier two-thirds.

India's honeymooners and international hippies loved to live on houseboats and float on shikara gondolas across Kashmir's dreamy Dal Lake in the capital, Srinagar. Visitors also enjoyed hiking or riding on rented horses into Kashmir's forests and glacier-caked mountains.

Behind this thin membrane of peaceful illusion, thousands of people were being killed each year on all sides after the mujahideen's war erupted in 1989 in India's part of Kashmir. Every month, the death toll of guerrillas, security forces and innocent civilians increased.

Rivalry since 1948 between Pakistan and India, to control the entire region of Kashmir, was complicated by the more recent emergence of Muslim guerrillas seeking to snatch Hindu-majority India's Kashmir and make it part of Muslim-majority Pakistan, or achieve greater autonomy within India, or declare independence and create a new strategic Islamic nation.

Most of the rebels' low-level warfare erupted on India's side of the frontier, known as The Line of Control, which has been warily "observed" by monitors from the United Nations.

The most powerful Muslim guerrilla leader in India's Kashmir in 1992 was Syed Salludin, supreme commander of Hezb-ul Mujahideen, or Party of Holy Warriors.

Black-bearded Salludin's 15,000-strong mujahideen were the deadliest and largest of several guerrilla groups fighting against what they cursed as the "Indian occupation forces" in Kashmir.

America and other nations feared that the fight for Kashmir could one day escalate and unleash a nuclear war between India and Pakistan which had already fought three non-nuclear wars.

To interview Salludin involved traveling from the medieval ambiance of Srinagar, along a forested road into the Himalayas past Sopore town. Indian military convoys dominated the winding, mountainous route. They were searching for Salludin and any other Kashmiri insurgents they could find.

In and around Sopore, a spidery network of rebel safe houses lay hidden in the backstreets and forests. Inside each of their brick-and-stone main rooms, armed Kashmiri guerrillas sat in a circle, with their backs against the walls, on quilts covered in a clean white sheet and laid on top of carpets on the floor.

Sitting in a circle, we drank sweetened tea or ate together from a single, large plate of mutton, rice and vegetables while waiting for their spies to reveal if I could proceed to the next safe zone.

Salludin frequently changed locations.

Some safe houses also sheltered bleeding, bruised and bandaged young men who lay in beds, weeping while they spoke of beatings they suffered inside Indian army camps during lengthy interrogations.

All along the route, distraught residents in tiny villages described tortures inflicted upon them by Indian troops.

While riding in the car during the last section of our journey to meet Salludin, one young, laughing mujahideen sitting next to me in the backseat, held up a hand grenade for me to admire, as if he were displaying a delicious ripe apple.

The rebel proudly vowed, if Indian troops tried to stop this vehicle, he would throw the grenade at them.

Then we could all run away and escape.

Soon, a low-roofed house appeared, heavily guarded by a dozen mujahideen armed with AK-47 assault rifles, rocket launchers, walkie-talkies and hand grenades. The young mujahideen gently rolled his grenade back into his pocket, stepped out of the car, and dutifully took up a watchful position along a wall.

Salludin had confirmed by walkie-talkie that he would be waiting inside.

When he appeared, Salludin explained to me how he was leading a jihad, or holy war, to rip valuable Kashmir away from India, attach it to Pakistan and establish a fundamentalist Islamic society where true Muslims could be protected and dwell in peace.

"If someone does a theft, his hand must be cut off, so society can be saved," Salludin said in a voice which initially hid its gruffness.

"But we do not cut the hand of every thief. First, the government is bound to provide the necessities of life for every citizen. And we can't stone a person to death who is not married. It is a person who is already married, who rapes a woman and uses an illegal way for sexual satisfaction, and has brutal behavior. We want to save the society, so we want to give him a stern punishment."

Salludin's rebels also traveled to Afghanistan which was admired by Islamist guerrillas around the world as the best and most violent campus available to learn how to fight, because it offered sophisticated weapons training and proven, experimental insurgent tactics.

"More than 4,000 Kashmiri militants have received training in Afghanistan and, at present, more than 3,000 are there in Afghanistan now. That's a total of 7,000," Salludin boasted.

"As Afghanistan has done in winning, and the Soviet Union has disintegrated into so many pieces, India will also disintegrate if it does not recognize the self-determination of Kashmir's people.

"The Indian army kills the innocent masses. When we are going to hit a military convoy, we feel they will take their revenge on innocent people. In spite of that, we attack them. Then the people suffer. So, we try to hit them out of the population areas. But the people are ready for this cause, and tell us, 'Don't lose heart'.

"We hope to obtain a corridor along the border area," Salludin said, describing what he hoped would be the first-ever slice of guerrilla-held territory in Kashmir which could allow them to enjoy better supply links from sympathizers in northern Pakistan's part of Kashmir.

"It is in the best interest of Kashmir to become a greater Kashmir with Pakistan, and make a great Islamic nation."

As the fighting worsened, ardent Islamist guerrillas from other Muslim-majority nations sneaked in to help Kashmir's rebels battle India's army, which often appeared confused and poorly disciplined.

The most admired of these new, foreign combatants were battle-hardened Afghan mujahideen.

At another of Salludin's safe houses, one of his "battalion commanders," Mohammad Abu Nasar, 36, proudly introduced a handful foreign Muslim guerrillas who had clandestinely crossed into Kashmir and joined their fight.

From Afghanistan, heavyset Akbar Bai, 27, showed me his sinister "two-in-one" AK-47. He had the assault rifle customized with an additional, built-in, fat-barreled rocket launcher. Bai said he captured the rocket launcher from Soviet forces before they lost the war and withdrew, and he realized it could fit onto his rifle.

From Khartoum, Sudan, came curly-haired Yasin Salin Masood.

"I went to Afghanistan two years ago to fight, and came here to Kashmir one month ago," Masood told me.

"I came to share in the jihad. There are 300 to 400 Arabs here, from Libya, Algeria, Bahrain and other places. My organization in Sudan, the Akhwan Muslimeen (Muslim Brotherhood), first sent me to Afghanistan and then said: 'If you'd like to go to Kashmir, go'. They sent me for the experience. Here you feel the meaning of Islam and jihad."

Back in Srinagar meanwhile, victims languishing in the National Institute of Medical Science Hospital said they experienced a different feeling -- torture by Indian troops.

Some patients were beaten so badly by Indian security forces that their muscles had been pulverized. Tiny pieces of their smashed and broken muscle tissue had clogged their kidneys, causing renal damage and killing some of them.

Pointing to an agonized patient named Ali Mohammad, 22, the institute's Doctor Javed Rasool glumly told me:

"After they beat his muscle tissue, it broke down. When this broken muscular tissue gets filtered through the kidneys, it causes a block and leads to a severe renal problem. When it is renal failure, total blockage, they can die. It carries a very high mortality rate."

Mohammad the patient, struggling to speak from his hospital bed, said:

"I went to Friday prayers at the mosque, and there was an explosion half a kilometer away, and Indian troops cordoned off the area. Ten to 15 of us were taken and tortured. I was beaten severely on my buttocks, legs, face and chest. I don't belong to any militant group. I am a carpet weaver. I have nothing to do with them. If I was a militant, I wouldn't have undergone so much torture. I would have handed over any guns because I couldn't stand so much torture. They held me for four hours. They were yelling, 'Show us your gun! Where are the militants! Who are they?'"

P. M. Varadarajan, an Oxford law lecturer reporting in Kashmir for the Paris-based Federation Internationale des Droits de l'Homme (International Federation of Human Rights), told me with despair:

"The Indian security forces in Kashmir make the Guatemalan army of the early 1980s look like merciful angels. No one in the Kashmir Valley, young or old, male or female, is safe from their violence. If I were a Kashmiri youth, I would take to the gun without a moment's hesitation."

The Indian government insisted it was unfair to blame only the Indian security forces for torture and extrajudicial executions, because both sides were guilty of human rights abuses. They said rebels also kidnapped, tortured and assassinated victims, including innocent civilians.

When Kashmir's fighting grew serious in the late 1980s, tens of thousands of heavily-armed Indian troop reinforcements took up positions throughout the mountainous state.

In Srinagar, troops hurriedly built thousands of tiny bunkers using sandbags, rocks and rusty oil barrels, and draped the bunkers with dark green nets. Bunkers were installed every few hundred yards on busy streets and back lanes, allowing nervous Indian soldiers to continuously aim rifles and machine guns -- often with a finger on the trigger -- at pedestrians, traffic, shops, homes, animals and anything else they saw.

India warned the world that Pakistan's government was officially arming Kashmiri "terrorists" in a "proxy war" against

India and must be stopped, or else.

Insurgents freely admitted they traveled back and forth to the town of Muzaffarabad in Pakistan's Kashmir and other sites to replenish cash, weapons and ammunition. They insisted the supplies were given to them by Pakistan's civilian Kashmiri sympathizers, arms dealers and blackmarketeers -- and not the Pakistani government.

Pakistan meanwhile trumpeted the insurgents' demand for a United Nations-supervised vote on whether Indian-held Kashmir should remain with New Delhi or be allowed to break away.

When India gained independence in 1947 from the British Empire, the departing colonialists had hurriedly divided Kashmir between Hindu-majority India and Muslim-majority Pakistan when London partitioned the mammoth subcontinent, as part of an independence deal.

The British arrangement was clumsily finalized by an unelected Hindu maharaja, Hari Singh, who became frightened over a Pakistani assault to seize his prized piece of Kashmir. Singh had hoped his Kashmir would be an independent kingdom under his reign. Instead, in panic, Singh signed his Kashmir territory over to India's control without allowing Kashmiris to vote on his decision.

India and Pakistan fought three wars over the disputed territory. A cease-fire brokered by the UN at the end of the first war in 1948, included a promise by India's first prime minister Jawaharlal Nehru to allow a "final disposition" plebiscite on Kashmir's ownership. But that vote was never held, because New Delhi feared its chunk of Kashmir would opt out of India.

In 1989, it still seemed that most Kashmiri Muslims did not want their state to remain part of India. But many Kashmiri Muslims also did not want to join the Islamic Republic of Pakistan and preferred a third option: to form an independent country.

The Jammu and Kashmir Liberation Front (JKLF) led the demand for complete independence. It was a small, relatively weak guerrilla group. As a result of shunning Pakistan, it lacked the weapons and cash pro-Pakistani Kashmiri rebels received from across the border.

Pakistanis meanwhile despised the independence movement because the JKLF wanted to "free" all of Kashmir -- including a vow to "liberate" the part held by Pakistan -- plus Kashmir's former Aksai Chin region which China had seized after Beijing's victorious, three-week 1962 border war against India.

China kept glacier-covered Aksai Chin because it included the only highway connecting Tibet to Xinjiang, China's far-west, rebellious, Muslim-majority province.

One top JKLF guerrilla leader told me:

"We are not saying we'll fight a war with Pakistan. But how can we say Kashmir is free? It is also in the control of Pakistan. We hope when we get freedom for this part of Kashmir, they must leave Pakistan-occupied Kashmir. Also Chinese-occupied Kashmir."

He then placed his "lucky" Chinese-made gray pistol on a table in front of him at his Srinagar hideout and claimed to be a "liberal" Muslim and not a fundamentalist.

Salludin's pro-Pakistan Hezb-ul Mujahideen fighters meanwhile continued to gain strength and learned fresh tactics to fight an urban guerrilla war in Srinagar's tangle of narrow streets.

Akram Junid Sahil, whose narrow face accentuated thin lips and hyper eyes, was proud to be one of Salludin's guerrilla "platoon commanders" in the bustling heart of Kashmir's capital. Just 23 years old, Sahil's rapid, violent mutation into a skilled killer was, in many ways, the story of thousands of young Muslim men in the bloodied Kashmir Valley who had picked up guns in a quest to realize their dream of a Kashmir free from India's domination.

Sahil's told me about his life while we hid in a Hezb-ul Mujahideen backstreet safe house. Occasional gunfire echoed in Srinagar's nighttime streets.

"Hear that light popping? That is the Indian army's self-loading rifles."

After a long pause, Sahil said: "That heavier sound now is our Kalashnikovs."

A nearby muffled explosion whispered in the darkness.

"Hear that boom? A grenade. We militants are getting back at the Indian army tonight. I have personally killed about 15 to 17 Indian army men. I mostly use grenades. Now I'm commanding 200 guys."

Sahil said he became a rebel four years earlier.

"I decided to take up the gun when I was a student, 19 years old. There was a massacre in Lal Chowk downtown, where 200 people were killed by the Indian army. It was the first massacre, in 1988. I saw it and narrowly escaped.

"When I saw it was a massacre and they don't care who is a militant and who is innocent, I thought I am unsafe. So within three or four months, I took a gun to have safety for myself and for those who they massacre. I was reading the Koran where I found, in Islam, a jihad is our duty. To fight against cruel people is called 'jihad'. So I decided to fight against the Indian army who was making so much trouble for us, and burying us and burying Allah."

He scooped up dinner with a piece of unleavened chapatti bread.

"I joined the Hezb-ul Mujahideen because I saw their rules and regulations were good. In fact, they were in a jihad according to the Koran."

Wearing a traditional green Muslim cap -- the favored color of Islam -- and sporting a meager beard, the skinny, intense and sardonic Sahil said he had been wounded by three bullets in his foot, imprisoned, and was now on guard against "Indian intelligence" informants who tried to infiltrate rebel groups. But he and his comrades lacked enough ammunition and weapons.

"Only 70 per cent of our gunmen have their own weapons in Srinagar district. The Indian army is so big and has so many weapons. But when we are attacking them, they are firing back, but not directly at us. They are afraid. When they shoot, they keep their heads below their sandbags. That's why innocents are killed."

Sahil said his area of responsibility included Srinagar's Lal Chowk which was the city's prestigious busy center and included nearby shops, hotels, banks, travel agencies, restaurants, hospitals, bridges, apartments, government offices and newspaper bureaus.

His zone also included squalid food stalls which sold freshly hacked-off goat's legs on the hoof, which dangled above the streets' sewage-filled gutters. Lively bookshops offered Indian-authored tomes such as, The Sex Life of Hippies. Decrepit buildings, with elaborately carved wooden trim, leaned next to mosques hooked up to electric loudspeakers announcing prayers.

As guerrilla platoon commander, Sahil also decided which weapons to use to kill Indian troops. He liked the ease of hand grenades.

"When we are using Kalashnikovs, we fire and run away. But we have to carry the weapons with us back to the hideout. When we fire 30 bullets, only five or six will hit the army and some may hit the common man. With the hand grenade, after we pull a pin and throw, we don't have anything in the hand," as incriminating evidence.

"Or when we attack vehicles, we first use hand grenades, then guns. But in this locality here, we use mostly guns because the streets are crowded and people are rushing. If we use hand grenades, innocents might get killed."

Sahil was angry at the United States, Europe and other nations because they did not try to protect Muslim Kashmiris suffering human rights violations or support his fight to give India's Kashmir to Pakistan. But he was inspired by the Soviet Union's collapse which resulted in new nations being formed, free from Moscow's direct control. Sahil predicted the same fate for India.

"In Russia, they had to liberate some territories. Why? Because of the economy. India will have to face the same problem. Today, guns are firing in Assam, Punjab, and Bihar," he said, referring to long-running armed rebellions in three other Indian states by Hindus, Sikhs, Maoists and others. "A time will come when guns will fire in Delhi, Bombay and Calcutta."

Sahil's life was also grueling and dangerous.

"It is my duty to look after 200 guys physically and mentally. I have to watch my area and see if anyone will inform the government. I have to find out the area of the Indian army. Is my position dominating? Or do I have to increase my position?

"I have to produce my report to my commander every 15 days. I have to see how many of my guys are without weapons or other things. I have to see if any militant will tease the common people. If I am not successful, there is our Mujahideen Intelligence Wing who will tell our supreme commander."

THE LIBERATION TIGERS OF TAMIL EELAM

A much more devastating war was ripping apart Sri Lanka, turning its popular cliché of being a "teardrop-shaped island" into a grim reality.

"He deserved to be shot," an excited Tamil businessman said loudly, waving his hands at a limp, gray-haired corpse tightly roped to a lamp post in Jaffna city's central bus station in the early morning.

A horrified crowd gawked at the bullet-riddled body -- a grisly public warning not to inform on Sri Lanka's ethnic minority Tamil guerrillas.

"You see the sign next to his body?" a Tamil housewife angrily announced to the gathering crowd. "It says he informed to the army about the boys."

The dead man had been positioned and tied so he slumped upright, leaning against the lamp post. Bare-chested, he wore a blood-stained white cloth knotted around his waist.

His weight caused the thick coarse rope to squeeze into his chest under his arms and thighs. His bare feet rested, slightly splayed, in the gutter.

Alongside him was a big, taller sign which displayed a long message handwritten with blue paint in Tamil language.

It also showed three signed documents stuck to the sign with thumbtacks above an illustration of an elephant using its trunk to grab and lift a bicyclist off the ground.

A striped tiger -- symbolic of the guerrillas -- pounced on the elephant's head, drawn to resemble Sri Lanka's President Junius R. Jayewardene.

The big blue text said the dead man was Nirmalan of Chithankarni village on Jaffna's outskirts. He was executed by the Tamil Eelam Army, one of the smaller guerrilla groups among about 35 Tamil rebel organizations fighting for independence for northern Sri Lanka's Jaffna Peninsula and Eastern Province.

Frowning shoppers, workers and bus passengers jostled to get a closer look at the body and read the sign.

Many of the Tamil witnesses muttered that the man got what he deserved.

One shopkeeper, gazing at Nirmalan's corpse, said to me the killing was "correct because he put the lives of the militants in danger by informing to the army.

"We have not yet gained our independent Tamil nation, so we do not have our own police, courts and prisons to give the fair trials usually held in democratic countries for these people. So, though I do not like to see bodies in our streets, there is no alternative."

As he spoke, several men clustered nearby and angrily blurted: "Yes! Yes!"

A businessman insolently gestured at the body and caustically told me:

"We feel he has received a fair trial because the militants are well-educated university boys under strict discipline by their leaders. This dead man must have received warnings, and would not have been killed unless the militants were absolutely certain he was an informer."

The documents which the Tamil Eelam Army rebels stapled onto the sign included photocopies of two letters allegedly signed by Nirmalan, which he addressed to Jaffna's police.

In the typewritten, English-language letters, Nirmalan purportedly named several Tamil suspects who had been secretly handing out the guerrillas' leaflets.

A reply, allegedly from the authorities, confirmed Nirmalan's letters were duly received.

"He was either naive or stupid to write such letters," a British diplomat told me while eyeing the body. The envoy had hurriedly arrived from a nearby hotel where he happened to be staying during his brief official visit to Jaffna.

In 1985, these rebel death squad executions were called "lamp post killings."

A local Tamil political analyst, who asked not to be identified, told me:

"The government offered rewards to these informants. So these lamp post killings help the militants a lot, because it stops most of the informants, and the boys are free to move through villages and towns. The boys also killed murderers, rapists and robbers.

"Because of the general situation, there is a lack of the usual civil administration in the Jaffna Peninsula. The criminal element took the upper hand, and the police were not there to bring law and order. So the people don't mind these killings."

On the same morning, around the corner, another Tamil man's body lay in Jaffna's main hospital morgue.

Security forces said Tamil Eelam Army insurgents had assassinated C. E. Anandarajan, a Jaffna community leader and principal of nearby St. John's College, because he had arranged for his students to play a soccer match with Sri Lanka's army.

The principal's body was discovered in a lane near his home. Bullets peppered his face and chest at close range.

Unlike the vocal support random people at the bus station expressed for the lamp post killing, many of Jaffna city's Tamil residents condemned the principal's slaying as too severe. They considered his death as a loss to the local Tamil community.

The next day, many people in Jaffna hung black flags in several streets and on shops' doors, protesting the principal's execution.

On the following day, Jaffna's Regional Director of Education, S. Pillai, agreed to close the city's schools for 24 hours to mourn the principal's death. The request had been made by the associations of Jaffna Schools Principals, St. John's College Teachers, St. John's College Old Boys, and the Jaffna Citizens' Committee.

Tamil Eelam Army guerrillas had warned the principal not to play soccer with the army.

"The militants told him it is not time to play games," one Tamil rebel sympathizer said to me. "They told him the army has killed so many innocent youths."

Other schools declined the Sri Lankan army's offer to play, because it appeared to be a blatant public relations stunt. One community leader said the principal had been using his influence among the army -- which was fighting in Jaffna against various guerrilla groups -- to gain quick release for some of his students who had been arrested during the government's frequent round-ups of young male suspects.

"The principal was a great man. Educational standards will fail," a prominent community leader told me.

"But the army was able to use the game as propaganda and say, 'Look, if we had killed any innocent people, why would these youngsters have agreed to play with us?'

"The principal was caught between both sides, and that is a very dangerous here."

President Jayewardene used the death squads' activity to describe Tamil rebels as terrorists.

"Many organizations abroad, like Amnesty International, put out well-documented publications with photographs of civilians who die in the course of operations carried out by Sri Lankan Security Forces," but those organizations ignore lamp post killings, the National Security Ministry said in a glossy pamphlet illustrated with photographs of executed victims tied to fences and trees.

"Is it because Amnesty International and similar groups think that kangaroo court proceedings, which last a few minutes before the trigger is pulled, are not a violation of human rights?"

One government pamphlet, Lamp Post Murders by Tamil Terrorists, displayed a large black-and-white photograph of a dead young woman tied to a tree.

The caption stated:

"Tamil terrorists came looking for the brother. Since he was away, his sister Miss Amarasingham Yogarani, 24 years, was dragged out of the house, tied to a coconut tree and shot through the ear.

"Often the Tamil terrorists tie the intended victim to a lamp post and pump three shots into the head. A placard is hung around the neck branding him as a traitor or as one engaged in 'anti-social' activities. Here what is termed 'anti-social behavior' is nothing but giving information to the security forces."

Victims were "shot through the mouth, shot through the eye, shot through the forehead, tied to a lamp post, tied to a tree, tied to a fence post."

The pamphlet described such killings as "sadism of the worst type. Tamil terrorists do not believe in blindfolding their victims. They are sometimes forced to look at the gun being aimed, trigger being pulled."

The government said 235 civilians were executed by Tamil insurgents in 1984. Only 16 of those killed were not Tamils.

The National Security Ministry reluctantly said the military had killed about 100 innocent Tamils during the past several years. The government officially called those killings "excesses" by the "inexperienced" majority ethnic Sinhalese-dominated military. The only punishment for about 300 guilty military men was dismissals.

The biggest and most feared guerrilla group were the Liberation Tigers of Tamil Eelam (LTTE).

The Tigers' rigid one-party, Marxist ideology would never embrace democracy. In 1986, two of the Tigers' Political Committee members told me their future nation would not permit multi-party elections.

The committee members spoke while relaxing in the main room of one of their safe houses in Madras, in southern India's Tamil Nadu state where most of India's 55 million Tamils lived.

A portrait of the Russian Revolution's leader and first prime minister of the Soviet Union, Vladimir Lenin, was pasted on the wall.

The Tigers' Political Committee Member Dilip Yogi said:

"We will tell the people we want a one-party system. A multi-party system won't work. To bring a radical change, it is not possible in a multi-party system.

"In a one-party system, when you implement a program, the other parties cannot change it. If you have many parties, one might get only 12 percent of the vote and win the election. But he is not representing the people. We have seen throughout the world what these parties have done. They've never had radical changes. They've never helped the people.

"The Jaffna Peninsula is under our control. People know from the way we are running our parallel government, that once liberation is achieved and we have power, we will have an economically viable society which won't exploit one another. We want the working class people to have the power. So the power comes from the bottom.

"The Western world wants to save Sri Lanka because it is capitalist. They don't care about the Tamils," Yogi said.

Many war-weary Tamil residents however appeared willing to compromise with the government and drop all demands for independence. They said they would be satisfied with regional autonomy and political power similar to an American state or a Canadian province.

They knew if independence was not achieved, the civil war

would continue.

"You can usually tell who is a terrorist because of the way he looks. A terrorist looks dirty. After hiding in the jungle for a long time, he smells bad.

"You can also tell a terrorist because he has no occupation, no identity card and has marks on his body from handling a weapon."

A bit chubby in his uniform, but with his black beret at a sharp tilt, Security Forces Coordinating Officer Lieutenant Colonel Lakshman Wijayaratne was Sri Lanka's newest weapon in October 1986 against the Tigers on the island's increasingly violent east coast.

He and his men were now consolidating their gains, which they scored in a major offensive in jungles around Sambaltivu village.

Wijayaratne planned to secure the area and main roads, and keep them free of Tigers who had escalated their hit-and-run attacks, threatening the safety of nearby Trincomalee port.

"The terrorists' aim is to show the world they are in control of Trincomalee," Wijayaratne said.

Trincomalee was the valuable, government-held, deep-water port 15 miles south of here, which the Tigers claimed would eventually be the capital of their independent Tamil Eelam.

"As you see, it is all jungle around Trincomalee. It is all open to them."

During a day-long tour with Wijayaratne and his soldiers aboard a military helicopter above Trincomalee and nearby east coast, and in a heavily guarded vehicle and on foot at Sambaltivu, it became easier to understand the way the army sees its war.

Seen from a US-built Bell helicopter with two Sri Lankan machine gunners manning both sides, Trincomalee's area appeared as flatlands covered by lush foliage and edged by gorgeous beaches.

Houses with thatch or red tile roofs dotted the region alongside lagoons and roads.

"The Tamils have grievances, I admit. There has to be a cause they are fighting for," Wijayaratne said after the chopper landed at Sambaltivu.

He stressed the need for a peaceful political settlement and an end to racial discrimination by Sinhalese against Tamils.

During the tour, Wijayaratne tried to present himself as friendly, disciplined and concerned about the safety of both communities.

"We have to safeguard all our people. We are not fighting a foreign enemy."

He described how, during a military offensive at Sambaltivu which began on October 2, Wijayaratne and his forces invaded the area slowly over three days, to allow the mostly Tamil villagers enough time to leave and avoid any cross-fire.

"You see we have not committed a My Lai massacre here," he said, laughing and referring to the US Army's Vietnam War atrocity against innocent civilians.

Wijayaratne claimed his army killed 10 Tigers and captured 18 during the battle for Sambaltivu.

Community leaders said four civilians were also injured, and one of the dead was an innocent 16-year-old boy.

Wijayaratne said the fight was lopsided because the guerrillas enjoyed several advantages.

"We need radar, more patrol boats and mother ships to coordinate them."

Wijayaratne said separatists used high-speed boats to ferry themselves from Jaffna in the north where they dominate to Trincomalee in the east where they were trying to increase their presence.

While he spoke, Wijayaratne cautiously eyed nearby palm trees and undergrowth for guerrillas and their tell-tale land mine wires on the narrow road we walked toward Trincomalee.

A handful of rifle-toting soldiers nervously fanned out ahead and behind us, while an army man communicated on a backpack radio.

"The terrorists expected us to attack from the south, coming up from Trincomalee. They built a line of bunkers along these hills, all pointing south. So I ordered my forces to attack from the north and east. I moved men up there by navy gunboats."

A rugged, brown armored personnel carrier rumbled slowly down the road.

"We bought some of these APCs from South Africa. They are specially built to resist mines. If you are inside with your harness on when a mine goes off underneath, you will not suffer many casualties."

Wijayaratne said the fight to defeat the Tigers would be slow and tough, especially in rebel-held areas in the Northern Province's Jaffna Peninsula, and would involve advancing the military's hold on slivers of territory, piece by piece.

Western diplomats punched holes in his optimism and strategy.

"The military can't recapture the north, not even piece by piece," a Western diplomat told me.

"They don't have enough men, and they wouldn't be able to find enough well-trained men. And the soldiers they do have, don't know how to fight."

Wijayaratne said his immediate concern was the alienation of innocent Tamil civilians whose villages were suddenly invaded by security forces during battles or sweeps.

Residents were often hurriedly forced into makeshift refugee camps.

Male Tamils between the ages of about 15 to 40 were seized at random for questioning or detention without trial for up to 18 months.

"We dropped leaflets from the air before this latest offensive," Wijayaratne said.

The papers, in Tamil language, read in part:

"YOU HAVE BEEN SURROUNDED BY THE SECURITY FORCES. OUR OBJECTIVE IS NOT TO HARASS THE GENERAL PUBLIC, BUT TO DISARM THE TERRORISTS."

The leaflets told people to immediately evacuate.

"IF AFTER TWO HOURS, ANYONE OF YOU IS FOUND IN THE VILLAGE, YOU WILL BE RESPONSIBLE FOR ANY CONSEQUENCES YOU FACE."

"Even the textbooks say anti-terrorist operations cause a further erosion of public sympathy for the government," Wijayaratne said.

"That's why we have civic programs and psychological warfare, trying to win the hearts and minds of the people. We try to make use of the media for this purpose."

The majority Sinhalese who supported the government's attacks against the Tigers were often confused by the guerrillas' victories, he said.

When separatists staged a sensational raid or assassinated a senior political or community leader, "The Sinhalese think the whole world is lost. I tell them, 'No man is indispensable'.

"When the terrorists killed the assistant government agent in Morawewa recently, I told them, 'Don't worry, I'll give you another assistant government agent'."

Wijayaratne admitted security forces sometimes massacred innocent Tamil civilians in reprisals, especially after rebel land mines destroyed military vehicles, killing and wounding security forces.

"We could have court-martials every day for these people," but no one would testify against the security forces, he said.

More than 300 members of the security forces had been dismissed for massacres, but there had never been a court-martial.

Wijayaratne, a Buddhist, reflected on the irony that Buddha preached nonviolence and detachment from earthly problems, yet today many of Sri Lanka's powerful, saffron-robed Buddhist monks demanded tough action against the separatists.

"Buddha would have solved this civil war, I am sure," he said, chuckling.

"But Buddha lived 2,500 years ago. Buddhas isn't around these days to tell us how to deal with these terrorists,"

Wijayaratne said.

"Generally, the army commits retaliatory acts," a British diplomat told me.

"They don't have a policy of terror. They are basically a parade ground army, not a trained, disciplined army."

The escalating guerrilla war also worried President Jayewardene.

Sri Lanka's poorly disciplined army had been abusing a special legal provision which allowed it to shoot and cremate anyone without an inquiry.

No questions asked.

The guerrillas gained popularity among Tamil civilians every time the military indiscriminately killed more innocent men, women and children.

Unable to control his inefficient military, the pro-Western Jayewardene turned to foreign countries for money, advice, training and sophisticated weapons to deal with the insurgency.

By 1986, the civil war had attracted Israeli intelligence agents who secretly helped the Sri Lankan government collect information about the 2,000 or more Marxist Tamil insurgents.

A bunch of tough, beer-drinking British mercenaries had also been invited onto the island to teach the government's security forces how to hunt insurgents in jungles.

The Tigers had what government forces lacked: discipline, high morale and excellent guerrilla warfare training.

The Liberation Tigers of Tamil Eelam admitted the Palestine Liberation Organization trained them in 1972 in Lebanon.

The government meanwhile hated acknowledging when the military rampaged, burned innocent Tamils' houses and shot families as they fled.

Local news media was heavily censored to silence or sanitize such reports. But because of the frequency of the army's rampages, the government reluctantly began admitting the problem existed and offered explanations.

National Security Ministry Deputy Director Albert Fernando told me about a typical rampage:

"For example, the army goes berserk after a terrorist's land mine blows up under their jeep. The land mine doesn't kill everyone. Some army men survive and they stagger out of a vehicle half dazed and then keep firing at anyone.

"People get killed, even innocent people who are just going to the market, because the army men come out in a state of shock. It escalated after 1981. Since then, the maximum of innocent people killed must be 75 or 100. Maybe an equal number injured."

Tamils claimed the death toll of innocents numbered in the thousands.

Fernando said Tamil rebels killed about 500 innocent people during the past two years.

Amid the mayhem, the discreet Israelis were very busy.

Their office in the capital Colombo had no sign, no names, no official insignia.

The door merely said, "314" -- their room number in the nondescript Liberty Plaza Building. The door was watched by the their own closed-circuit video camera mounted above.

"The Israelis are helping with intelligence-gathering work," Fernando said.

"They're not involved in combat training. There were two of them, they've finished their assignment and gone back. They were here only for four months."

But at least two Israelis remained on the island during 1986, behind door 314.

They comprised Israel's new diplomatic mission. Sri Lanka had asked for Israel's help because of Mossad's deadly reputation. In exchange, Israel demanded diplomatic recognition, Western diplomats said.

Sri Lanka feared if it recognized Israel, that would anger the island's friends in Arab nations where many Sri Lankans worked to send valuable foreign exchange back home.

As a compromise, Israel officially opened an Israeli "interest section" in the American Embassy, the first of its kind anywhere in the world, though Israel had interest sections in other foreign embassies in Africa.

A senior US State Department official reportedly said he hoped the American Embassy's involvement "does not cause problems for the United States in Arab countries."

The Israelis "operate as a regular diplomatic mission independent from the US Embassy" which is several blocks away, a Western diplomat told me. "The Israelis have started issuing visas.

"Israel wants diplomatic recognition, they need as much international support as they can get. Israel wanted some high profile agricultural projects here which could be seen. They wanted a brass plate on the door which said 'consulate.' But they didn't get very far," the diplomat said.

Tamil rebels condemned Israel for helping the government fight against them.

"It is very unpleasant and unfortunate for the Israelis," the diplomat said.

"Israel has nothing against the Tamil people. The only thing the Israelis do is help anyone in the world combat international terrorism. If there is involvement by Israel it has to be seen in this context. These Tamils were trained by the PLO."

Sri Lanka's opposition parties were also outraged at the government's connection to Israel.

When Sri Lanka's foreign ministry announced in May 1984 that Israel would advise their security forces, former Prime Minister Sirimavo Bandaranaike said the invitation "may only lead to bringing the Arab-Israel conflict and all its violence to our homeland."

Bandaranaike, in 1979, broke relations with Israel to demand it withdraw from occupied territory.

The arrival of British mercenaries in Sri Lanka was equally problematic.

"Sri Lanka's national security minister hired a [British] company who he says are training his forces," a British diplomat told me in 1987.

"It is highly embarrassing to the British government to have a non-government force here. It implies Britain is involved in that kind of thing and they don't want to be. They don't think it will do any good. The situation is inter-communal, internal and requires a political solution.

"London feels if you only take on the terrorists, then the political solution doesn't come," the diplomat said.

"They have some experience about fighting terrorism," National Security Minister Lalith Athulathmudali told me in 1987, explaining why his government hired the Channel Island-based private security company Keeny Meeny Services (KMS) three years earlier.

"We made use of them primarily to train the police and create a paramilitary group, and our men have learned a lot of new tactics. They've brought areas where they are under fairly good control," Athulathmudali said.

KMS reportedly had provided bodyguards to a British ambassador in Beirut in the past. They were now training a Sri Lankan police squad known as the Special Task Force. The task force was comprised of young volunteers who had been policemen for one year.

Most KMS men were former members of Britain's crack Special Air Services (SAS). They also included Rhodesians, South Africans and other veterans of guerrilla wars.

They were a secretive lot.

Asked about his role in Sri Lanka, KMS Commander Ken White, an ex-SAS colonel, told me:

"We are employees of the Sri Lankan government, and I would ask you to listen to what the national security minister and the British High Commission have to say about us. More than that, I have no comment."

British High Commission press spokesman Jack Jones carefully choose his words when describing KMS to me:

"The British government views the presence of KMS in Sri Lanka as a matter between the company and the Sri Lankan government. There are no British servicemen in Sri Lanka.

"I understand some of them are former servicemen. It's not

for the British government to approve or disapprove of their presence. As far as I'm aware, it's a legitimate commercial company which has a legitimate commercial relationship with the Sri Lankan government in a strictly training role, and I understand that the employees do not take part in operations," Jones said.

Britain's Home Office Minister of State David Waddington said on a recent visit to Sri Lanka that KMS is "likely to be a good thing because it would probably improve the standard of training of the Sri Lankan armed forces."

Tamils were not so pleased.

They accused the mercenaries of turning the Special Task Force into a death squad that terrorized innocent Tamil civilians, torturing and killing them in the eastern part of the island.

Western diplomats compiled evidence of numerous massacres committed by the task force.

The London Daily News reported dozens of KMS men quit their $33,000 a year tax-free jobs in Sri Lanka after complaining that the Special Task Force troops they trained were out of control and committing atrocities against the Tamil population.

The Sri Lankan government and KMS denied the reports.

The paper quoted KMS commando Sammy Dougherty, who was still in Sri Lanka:

"Maybe there are atrocities, but not as many as there would be if we weren't here. Indiscipline cause atrocities. Scared, badly trained troops cause atrocities. But what I teach helps stop them. We're saving lives here. We're teaching self-control."

In Kalutara, near Colombo, a handful of brawny British mercenaries were meanwhile mingling with tourists at the Tangerine Beach hotel.

KMS mercenaries were playing tennis, swimming in the pool and dining at the posh supper club. A few miles away in Katukurunda, their colleagues were training Sri Lankans how to kill.

Although KMS was officially portrayed as training and

advising, the line between that and active involvement during combat was sometimes blurred.

For example, 35 KMS men trained Sri Lankans to fly Bell 212 and 412 helicopter gunships.

When flying over battle zones, "The KMS man sits in the co-pilot seat, so a Sri Lankan is captain of the aircraft," a source who asked not to be identified told me.

Problems occurred when there was ground fire by rebels at the helicopter.

"The Sri Lankan guy in the rear of the helicopter shoots back, and the KMS pilot takes control" because he has more flying experience dodging enemy fire.

The Sri Lankan government was also giving shotguns to Home Guards -- villagers with permission to kill any Tamils they decided were terrorists.

Asked to describe the Home Guards, National Security Ministry Deputy Director Fernando told me:

"Villagers are given shotguns."

The Tigers were unable to break the stalemate.

"The rebels are absolute rabble, you can't compare them with the IRA, the PLO or the Red Brigades," an analyst told me. "When they fight standing up against the army, they don't win."

Then one afternoon, literally out of the blue, Indian Prime Minister Rajiv Gandhi surprised everyone. He ordered the Indian Air Force to illegally airdrop supplies over northern Sri Lanka in June, 1987.

Four of India's sleek, gray French-built Mirage-2000 bombers took off from Yelehnka airbase about six miles north of Bangalore in southern India.

The fearsome Mirages screamed toward Jaffna Peninsula, providing escort protection for five of the Indian Air Force's Russian-designed Antonov 32s.

The nine secretive flights entered Sri Lanka's airspace at the westernmost tip of the Jaffna Peninsula.

While aboard one of the Antonovs flying over Jaffna, I watched black-booted Indian Air Force men release six tons of supplies out of our fully-loaded plane, starting at about sunset.

But our Antonov plane developed a problem.

Its back door successfully yawned wide open just before the scheduled drop. But the cargo compartment's slick wheeled tracks also opened, because an electronic magnetic release unit "malfunctioned," allowing all six tons of supplies to drop too soon, said the plane's Captain V. Wadhwa.

As a result, Wadhwa's load fell out of the plane one or two minutes early, causing it to parachute several miles from the targeted area, he said.

"This is Eagle Formation Mercy Mission from India," our Antonov's two pilots repeatedly radioed to Sri Lanka while flying over the island's territory.

"We are coming in with foodstuffs for the suffering people of Jaffna. Can you read me?"

The pilots said no one replied.

Asked about our flight's level of danger, Navigator S. C. Madan replied: "Medium risk."

Sri Lanka did not possess sophisticated anti-aircraft weaponry.

As each of the five Antonov's six tons of cargo slid out of the planes, the cargos' white parachutes billowed in the overcast sky, carrying a total of 30 tons of supplies onto the green and tan Jaffna Peninsula below.

Some supplies were attached to green canvas bags marked, "Ordinance Parachute Factory, Kanpur," referring to a city in India.

There was no independent public confirmation about their contents. The bags were already tied up when the flights began.

Navigator Madan said the supplies were "only some vegetables and rations, not much else."

Most supplies landed just north of Jaffna city near the villages of Kokkuvil and Chunnakam, which were reportedly dominated by rebels.

Our flight path continued east between Jaffna city and Palali village, which was also the location of a Sri Lankan Air Force base, the navigator said pointing at a map. The planes then veered north back to India at the Sri Lankan coastal town of Point Pedro.

We had flown over Sri Lanka for about 10 minutes at an altitude of 1,500 feet, the navigator said.

The airdrop was peaceful. It also appeared haphazard.

Neither the pilots nor navigators knew for certain which areas of the Jaffna Peninsula were occupied by Tamil rebels, Sri Lankan troops, or by civilians, said the navigator.

The distinction was vital. India had said the supplies were exclusively for civilians, and not for guerrillas or Sri Lankan forces.

Several days before the airdrop, Gandhi had said in a statement directed at the Sri Lankan government:

"Thousands of defenseless civilians in Jaffna are strafed from the air and repeatedly and systematically subjected to carpet bombing" by Sri Lanka's military.

Gandhi blamed them for the "massacre of unarmed noncombatant civilians," the "horrific loss of innocent life," and "calculated slaughter of thousands of Sri Lankan citizens by their own government...on the basis of only ethnic difference."

Sri Lanka denied the charges and said India exaggerated the number of casualties because Gandhi believed the Tigers' propaganda.

Western diplomats agreed. They said Sri Lanka's miniscule air force was incapable of "carpet bombing."

The US State Department said it had no evidence of widespread destruction of the Jaffna Peninsula by Sri Lanka's armed forces.

Gandhi's airdrop was presented as a way to temporarily relieve Sri Lanka's five-month-long economic embargo, which had been clamped on Jaffna Peninsula to weaken the guerrillas. Sri Lanka was unable to militarily protect itself against India's airdrop because the tiny island was no match against its giant neighbor.

Gandhi's airdrop came one day after he suffered an

embarrassing defeat while sending relief ships carrying medicine, fuel, matches, bread and other food to Jaffna.

Sri Lankan gunboats stopped those vessels in the Palk Strait, which separates the two nations by 25 miles of shallow ocean water. The Palk Strait snub made Gandhi appear unable to help stricken Jaffna Tamils, after publicly pledging to save them.

One senior Indian official involved in the airdrop said it was "to signal to Sri Lanka not to take us for granted," or expect India to remain uninvolved in the plight of Tamils in Sri Lanka.

"The supplies have been sent, we have made our point."

Sri Lanka had repeatedly claimed that India actively aided the guerrillas, providing them funds and allowing them to train and collect weapons in India, which were then secretly ferried across the Palk Strait into northern Sri Lanka.

India denied the accusations.

Ominously, Sri Lanka now warned it would build an air defense system with help from "friendly" nations, which it did not name. Diplomats speculated Sri Lanka might mean India's two enemies, Pakistan or China.

Shortly after the airdrop, Sri Lanka gained support from India's next-door neighbors Pakistan and Bangladesh amid a chorus of complaints against India's illegal action. Traditionally quiet Nepal also said it disapproved of India's tactics.

Gandhi was now seen by several nations as a South Asian "bully," using big-stick diplomacy against a smaller country.

Sri Lankan Foreign Minister A. Hameed told the United Nations that India committed a "violation of the country's sovereignty, independence and territorial integrity."

Sri Lanka condemned India for "naked aggression."

US State Department Spokesman Charles Redman said, "We regret the decision by the [Indian] government to drop the supplies by air."

Despite their differences, Gandhi convinced Sri Lanka to invite the Indian Army onto the island. Gandhi insisted he would protect Tamil civilians and convince the Tigers to accept autonomy and surrender.

Gandhi and Jayewardene signed an "Indo-Sri Lanka Agreement to Establish Peace and Normalcy in Sri Lanka" on July 29, 1987, which said in part:

"The President of Sri Lanka will grant a general amnesty to political, and other prisoners, now held in custody under the Prevention of Terrorism Act and other emergency laws, and to combatants, as well as to those persons accused, charged and/or convicted under these laws."

"Combatants" referred to the Tigers and other rebels who, after surrendering their weapons, would enjoy the amnesty.

A grinning Gandhi said of the Tigers, "I feel they will come along with us in implementing this agreement."

That didn't happen.

One month later, the Indian Army was patrolling Jaffna's streets to enforce the treaty.

All along the rubble-strewn roads, they saw larger-than-life color portraits of dead Tigers, standing like painted ghosts. The revolutionary folk art displayed men brandishing assault rifles and wearing berets atop serious, soulful faces.

The guerrillas' blood-red flags, branded with a snarling tiger's head in front of two crossed bayonets, flapped defiantly in Jaffna's arid, tropical breeze.

Jaffna had suffered heavily from the 15 years of warfare. Every street displayed rubble and skeletal remains of bombed buildings.

Bullet holes pocked the walls of homes and shops. Residents gazed from behind wooden doors and over fences made of dried palm leaves. As a result of India's military might, a nervous peace on stilts had been erected in across the war zone.

Dome-shaped automobiles made in the 1950s, and wooden carts drawn by twin oxen, were overflowing with the meager household goods of Tamils returning to the peninsula. They had been sheltering in several towns and villages scattered across northeastern Sri Lanka.

The lucky ones found their homes only slightly damaged, although usually stripped by looters, troops or rebels.

The unlucky discovered bright green, baby palm trees sprouting through cement rubble where their homes once stood.

Ornate Hindu temples, decked with wild-eyed deities, suffered bomb damage or neglect.

Schools, churches and Catholic nunneries lay deserted in the peninsula's rural areas where earlier fighting between the Tigers and Sri Lankan security forces had been the most severe.

Many of Jaffna's traumatized residents were desperate for peace and hoped the Indian Army would protect them from Sri Lanka's troops and the Tigers.

Amid the eerie landscapes, the Indian Army set up fortified positions throughout the northeast.

Newly arrived Indian soldiers eagerly smiled and waved at Tamil residents who often greeted them with smiles. But to ensure their domination, India installed 100,000 troops on the island.

The government and Western diplomats estimated 6,000 Sri Lankans on all sides had already died in the fighting during the civil war.

Students at Jaffna University meanwhile marveled at Indian Air Force helicopters landing and taking off from their campus, which included a large lawn close to the Tigers' political headquarters across the street.

Amid the temporary calm, Jaffna's streets bustled with bicycle-riding residents flocking to markets, commuting to work, and visiting friends.

Jaffna's residents were dynamic. Their squalid lanes bounced with loud, lilting music from blaring tape cassettes. Sari-clad women strolled alongside men wrapped in sarongs.

Daily life was still frustrating, with few basic services.

All of the telephones in Jaffna city and peninsula were dead because earlier fighting had damaged telephone exchanges and wiring. Telex lines were also extinct, leaving the city and countryside cut off from the outside world's telecommunications.

Damage to railway tracks had halted trains. Buses continued to run, but were dangerously overstuffed with passengers.

As a result, many goods were in short supply in a region which had always lacked the industrial development found in the island's south where most Sinhalese lived.

Jaffna city and district, populated by about one million people, also had no policemen.

Years earlier, the rebels had declared themselves Jaffna's guardians of law and order. Indian Army officers were now slowly setting up checkpoints where residents could air their grievances, but much of the city was essentially lawless.

The Indian Army was also inspecting villages for possible booby-trapped houses left by retreating guerrillas. Tigers however were cooperating with Indian troops and were showing them where rebel-laid land mines were hidden, so they could be safely exploded by experts.

Huge craters marred every road where rebels had earlier detonated mines under Sri Lankan military vehicles. Smaller craters were being filled with sandbags so vehicles could pass, but bigger craters forced drivers to divert across the rust-colored, dusty earth between palm trees.

"Many families built bunkers next to their homes to protect themselves from the government bombings," one elderly resident told me. "The first bunker I built, collapsed in the rain and my wife told me to build it again. It was expensive, it cost me 1,700 rupees ($60)."

Jaffna's once-busy Modern Market was flattened from the government's recent offensive, which included a bomb which decapitated a statue of Avvaipati, a Tamil poet, at the shopping mall's entrance.

Tigers were meanwhile wondering if they should completely disarm and submit to the Indian Army's domination, or prepare for the worst.

"You know where this machine gun is made?" a laughing teenage Tiger asked me in August 1987 while we rode in the back of the guerrillas' truck toward their political headquarters in Jaffna.

"Russia!" his young comrades cheered in unison, raising similar guns aloft while trying to remain standing in the open, bouncing vehicle.

"And this one?" another young rebel rhetorically asked.

His battle-hardened, chuckling buddies chimed: "America!"

"See that big hole," a short boy said, pointing to a crater in the road which forced our truck to slow.

"We set off a land mine there and destroyed an army truck. We killed six [Sri Lankan] soldiers."

These were Sri Lanka's children of war.

The oldest among them, in his early twenties, identified himself -- perhaps in jest -- as Captain Crazy. He watched with amusement while his comrades showed me their guns.

When I reminded them that they would have to surrender all their weapons under the new peace treaty, none of the rebels expressed disappointment.

"We will do it if we are ordered by our leader," Captain Crazy said.

While Sri Lanka slowly tried to recover from the agony and confusion of the LTTE's 15-year-long failed guerrilla war, the future of such boys and girls was now a fresh problem for the government and society.

Under the Sri Lanka-India treaty, all rebels, political prisoners and others involved in the war were to be given amnesty, to reintegrate as civilians.

For young guerrillas, it meant surrendering their weapons, leaving their fortified base camps, and going back to families and school or looking for work.

The journey back to normal life was not expected to be easy.

The LTTE claimed it had a total strength of 10,000. Western diplomats however estimated the LTTE now had 2,000 armed rebels. Another 3,000 belonged to other guerrilla groups. No one knew how many were adolescents.

"Not only will it be a problem for the young rebels to fit back into home life, but also for the boys, many of them innocent, who were arrested and jailed, and who are now being released under the amnesty," J. G. Rajendram, president of the Coordinating Committee of Citizens' Committees in nearby Vadamarachy told me.

His district had suffered the worst destruction during the entire war.

"I saw one boy released in June from [the government's] Boosa Detention Center, whose male organ was pulled with a pliers by his jailers," Rajendram said.

The government denied most charges of torture. Some officials said unfortunate, isolated cases of torture occurred during interrogation.

Many of the more than 4,000 Tamil youths now being released from Boosa and other facilities were believed to be innocent.

Under Sri Lankan law, they had been legally held without trial for up to 18 months on suspicion of supporting the guerrillas.

For many young Tamils returning home from battlefields or incarceration, the first task involved surviving in an economy shattered by war.

The Tigers had evolved into one of the most deadly insurgent groups on earth, and taught their fighters mostly how to obey, kill and commit suicide.

Alongside young boys, the Tigers also sent teenage girls to fight on the front lines.

Helpless Tamil parents had complained that their daughters would suddenly disappear, join the Tigers, and not be allowed to meet their parents ever again -- not even one final time to confirm that their startling overnight change was voluntary.

Tiger leaders insisted each new son or daughter was allowed to visit their family at least one last time after joining, to explain their motives. But when the new rebels' training began, the children would be not allowed family visits.

Guerrilla leaders said their units were constantly on the move, so it was too difficult to maintain secret contacts with the children's' relatives.

Many parents hated the arrangement.

In the front yard of one Tiger safe house in Jaffna in August 1987, a trembling father softly told me:

"We are here now asking to see our daughters. The rebels are holding our daughters and won't let us see them. All of us are parents whose daughters suddenly disappeared."

He discreetly gestured to seven other adults who nodded in agreement.

"Our daughters are all 17 years old and the LTTE haven't let us seen them since they went missing. It's been more than three months for me. One day, she went to school and disappeared.

"They say our daughters have joined the LTTE. All we want to do is talk to our girls and ask them if they are all right."

The guerrillas' Jaffna commander, Kumarappa, did not like such talk.

Kumarappa, a heavy-set, moustached man with a pistol on his hip and a hair-trigger temper, became enraged when guerrillas told him that the parents were complaining to me.

He grabbed a bullet-packed bandoleer, rushed out of the safe house, and stormed into the yard, shouting at the parents. They cowered under his curses in front of a garage.

Kumarappa lunged and forcibly twisted my notebook out of my hands while his men pushed me away.

One of the Tiger's political committee members, Dilip Yogi, ordered the parents to leave the yard.

While the parents were being pushed out of the gate, Yogi tried to soothe the atmosphere and told me:

"Now the daughters are with us. When they joined the movement, we allowed them to see their parents once. And the parents could talk with them.

"If the boy or girl wanted to go home, they could go. But once training has started, until training is finished, we won't allow visits.

"After training, they are allowed to go to their own houses. If they don't want to come back to us, they don't have to. We also talked with the daughters a few days ago. They said they do not want to go home.

"But we will make a decision on them in a few weeks time. We have told the parents to wait," Yogi said.

One father, being shoved into the street, shouted to me: "You see how they treat us? They are trying to intimidate us. We've never seen our daughters. Never, not once!"

Yogi glared at the gate and replied, "They are lying."

In August 1987 however, the LTTE's leader Velupillai Prabhakaran ("Vel-LOOP-uh-lai Prah-BAHK-uh-ran") was a broken man.

Trapped.

Betrayed.

Seething with anger.

Indian troops were demanding his rebels surrender all their weapons and finally end their war for independence.

"We are doing things which we don't want to do, so naturally we are bitter," Prabhakaran told a handful of journalists during our rare joint interview in a bleak Jaffna city safe house.

Prabhakaran's answers in Tamil language were simultaneously translated by Yogi, who appeared alongside him.

Wearing a blue shirt and slacks while flanked by five armed rebels, the surprisingly short Prabhakaran instinctively looked up at the ceiling when an Indian Air Force helicopter gunship buzzed overhead.

"We never started this war," Prabhakaran said.

"The war began because of Sinhalese politicians and Sinhalese people, who were racists and practiced racial discrimination. It was only because of racism this fighting was forced on us.

"If tomorrow the same racial hatred erupts, we will have to take whatever steps necessary.

"We are absolutely sure we will achieve an independent homeland nation, but the mode of our operation can be different and I am not going to reveal it to you."

Prabhakaran said he was reluctantly agreeing to the treaty,

which allowed the Tigers to try non-violent political ways of achieving their goals.

"Indian Prime Minister Rajiv Gandhi assured us that the Tamil people living in the north and east will be secure, and there will not be genocide against the Tamil people hereafter," Prabhakaran said as a nearby explosion suddenly echoed in the room.

He reacted with a startled grimace.

His rebels assured him it was their fellow Tigers publicly setting off a land mine to make a road safe for the Indian Army's vehicles, to prove the guerrillas were complying with the Indian troops' arrival -- for the time being.

Still jittery, Prabhakaran said if the treaty failed to protect the Tamil minority, Gandhi and his soldiers "will be responsible for the consequences.

"The Tamil people will hold us responsible for the happenings of the past several years, so they definitely will ask us why we are surrendering the weapons," he said, stroking his bushy moustache.

"We will have to explain how, and why, and what are our weaknesses. This struggle has been going on for more than 14 years. In these types of struggles, you can never stipulate a time limit.

"Even India fought for 300 years to achieve their freedom" from British colonialism, he said.

In response to the treaty's requirement for the rebels to disarm, Prabhakaran's LTTE began by surrendering five small Datsun truckloads of weapons.

The arms included machine guns, assault rifles, mortars and three anti-aircraft guns.

Some of the weapons and ammunition were rusty and outdated. Indian and Sri Lankan officials were confident that most of the Tigers' best guns would eventually be surrendered.

Prabhakaran refused to confirm how many rebels were in the LTTE or the number and type of weapons they possess. Western diplomats and Indian Army officers said Prabhakaran did not want to disclose the exact number because he secretly did not want to surrender all their weapons -- in case he decided to fight again.

One LTTE leader, who used the code-name Raheem and acted as a spokesman, said the rebels would give up about 5,000 weapons. He refused to describe the arms.

For the past five years, Prabhakaran had depended on India's support. The Tigers enjoyed sanctuary, base camps and illegal access to fresh weapons in nearby southern India's Tamil Nadu state.

Prabhakaran now said Gandhi betrayed him by agreeing with Sri Lanka to kick the Tigers out of India, and use the Indian Navy to stop the smuggling of arms across the Palk Strait into the Jaffna Peninsula.

Prabhakaran did not want to fight Indian troops, because he needed the Indian Army to protect his rebels and the Tamil minority from attacks by the Sri Lankan military.

Some Tigers told me they were worried because India's forces could crush the LTTE, especially because the guerrillas lacked ways of smuggling ammunition from India.

"It is true India is a major power, and we don't want to oppose the Indian government or Indian people without any reason," Prabhakaran said.

"But I, and the LTTE, are doing these things [agreeing to the treaty] not because we are militarily weak or can't confront their forces. We have a supreme sense of sacrifice and, along with explosives and special suicide teams, we could harass and oppose even their major forces."

Prabhakaran personally boycotted the August ceremony marking the official start of the LTTE's surrender of arms, which was attended by other senior Tigers.

Instead, on the day before, Prabhakaran made a rare public appearance and addressed 100,000 Tamil residents who gathered at a Hindu temple in Jaffna.

He explained to them:

"If we refuse to hand over our arms with which we defended

our people, there is the danger of a confrontation with India, a country we deeply love and respect."

But the India-Sri Lanka treaty was deeply flawed.

It called for Sri Lanka's Northern Province which included the Jaffna city and peninsula -- the Tigers' stronghold -- to be joined with the island's much more strategic Eastern Province which the Tigers also wanted.

The two united provinces would enjoy an interim administration with limited autonomy.

But the treaty said this arrangement would last only one year.

After one year, elections would be held so the Eastern Province could determine if it wanted to permanently remain with the north, and create an autonomous Tamil zone.

"I will not hold any posts" in the interim administration, Prabhakaran said in the safe house.

"I'll remain leader of the Liberation Tigers of Tamil Eelam. The administration will be given to us," he said, indicating he expected the LTTE to dominate the temporarily united Northern and Eastern Provinces.

The treaty however did not detail who would sit on a vaguely defined interim board.

The rebels previously indicated they would stop fighting if the two provinces were permanently joined under Tamil autonomy. They disliked risking the loss of the Eastern Province in a future election.

Tamils formed nearly 100 percent of the Northern Province, but comprised only 42 percent of the Eastern Province.

If the election went against the provinces being united, Prabhakaran would have to suffer his territory shrinking to just the northern part, which was mostly arid and poor.

To achieve a viable, prosperous nation, he needed the valuable real estate in the east, especially its priceless deep-water port at Trincomalee which could turn his Tamil Eelam into a major international import-export zone and military powerhouse.

The Sri Lankan government was obsessed with never letting

"Trinco" fall under the Tigers. That's why the treaty had an escape clause for the east.

And that's why Prabhakaran despised it.

Under the treaty's official amnesty, Prabhakaran and his LTTE were also set to walk free from the killing fields.

His new untouchable status confused many frightened Sinhalese.

For the past 15 years, Sri Lanka had told the world that innocent men, women and children were being butchered by a bloodthirsty terrorist named Velupillai Prabhakaran.

Sinhalese believed their government-controlled television and radio, and censored newspapers, which also reported the Foreign Ministry's claims that Prabhakaran was financing his guerrilla war by international heroin smuggling.

National Security Minister Athulathmudali had described the LTTE as "terrorists...the most brutal and unreasonable in the world."

Prime Minister Ranasinghe Premadasa called them "murderers" responsible for "atrocities."

Among Tamil civilians, Prabhakaran was still viewed with a mixture of worship, respect, fear, and hatred.

Many Tamils had been convinced Prabhakaran and his "boys" were their only protection against Sri Lanka's undisciplined security forces, who were comprised mostly of Sinhalese.

He was their last desperate hope at ending the discrimination they suffered in education, employment and language rights under Sri Lanka's racist laws and policies.

They shared his dream of a Tamil homeland free from Sinhalese domination, where innocent Tamils would not be targets of the security forces' revenge attacks.

Other Tamils perceived him as the reason their homes were bombed by the Sri Lankan army. Some Tamils did not understand, or failed to agree, with his dialectical Marxist theories. They simply wanted to live quiet, normal lives.

Prabhakaran, born November 26, 1954, grew up facing

Sinhalese racism, which twisted him into a hardened, committed idealist willing to die for a separate Tamil homeland.

It was said that as a four-year-old, he witnessed the 1958 race riots, and grew up on stories describing brutalities committed by Sri Lankan security forces against the Tamil population.

By the age 16, he was reading Karl Marx and creating a Revolutionary Youth Federation.

One year later, he was hurling hand grenades and firing revolvers.

In 1972, he formed the Tigers and declared himself chairman of its central committee, and commander-in-chief of its military wing.

Prabhakaran once told India Today magazine that his first foray into big-time killing "was in 1975, when I shot and killed the former mayor of Jaffna, Alfred Durapiappa."

That was nothing compared with Prabhakaran leading an ambush against a military convoy in 1983, which killed 13 Sinhalese soldiers and triggered the worst carnage in Sri Lanka since the nation gained independence from Britain in 1948.

Within hours of the ambush, angry Sinhalese -- backed by officials revealing lists of names and addresses of Tamil residents -- unleashed anti-Tamil riots throughout the island, killing an estimated 400 innocent Tamil civilians and leaving 100,000 homeless.

Indian Prime Minister Indira Gandhi, fearing possible large-scale Pakistani, Chinese and American military support for Sri Lanka's vulnerable government, decided to help the Tigers.

Her government allowed the Liberation Tigers of Tamil Eelam to establish rebel training camps in southern India, but she expected them to obey her advice.

Prabhakaran meanwhile told Tamils that his guerrillas would save them from murderous Sinhalese.

"We are not terrorists," he once said. "We are the representatives of people who want to get out of the clutches of state terrorism."

He appeared well on his way to establishing a separate Tamil

Eelam when his rebels seized control of most of the Jaffna Peninsula in 1985 and set up a loose civil administration.

They collected taxes, held trials for criminal and civil offences, licensed slaughterhouses and restaurants, and ran factories which churned out simple domestic items such as fruit juice and plastic chairs.

Sri Lanka's government put up "wanted" posters showing photographs of young LTTE suspects.

The posters promised:

"Any person giving information to the nearest police or security forces camp, that will lead to the arrest of these Tiger terrorists, will be amply rewarded."

The LTTE counter-attacked with propaganda, newsletters, press releases, record albums, tape cassettes and posters showing mauled corpses of innocent Tamils allegedly slaughtered by security forces.

Prabhakaran also discovered new enemies.

Smaller Tamil rebel groups emerged with a similar Marxist ideology, led by men with different strategies.

The LTTE eventually killed off enough rivals to become the largest and deadliest of them all.

Now Indira Gandhi's son Rajiv was telling Prabhakaran if he refused to surrender his most valuable weapons, Indian troops would forcibly disarm the LTTE.

During the first few weeks after the treaty was signed, the civil war turned topsy-turvy.

On a hot afternoon in Jaffna city, a car full of teenage LTTE rebels slowly cruised past a group of Sri Lankan soldiers who were bound by the treaty not to shoot them.

The guerrillas defiantly rolled down our vehicle's windows and mockingly grinned at their newly restricted enemies.

The soldiers could only glare back.

The rebels loudly laughed in their faces and floored the accelerator.

The Tiger driver told me:

"Now they know we're not afraid of them."

Elsewhere in Jaffna, a Tiger knowingly gazed at a rifle held by an Indian soldier at a checkpost. The unarmed rebel sneered, flicked the casing which insulated the rifle's barrel, and said with superior gesture of dismissal:

"It's plastic."

Nearby at Point Pedro on the Jaffna Peninsula, a Sri Lankan army officer showed newly arrived Indian Army officers a huge crater in the road, created by the LTTE's favorite weapon -- land mines.

The Indian officers listened, warily eyeing the evidence of a blast which had hurled a South African-built armored personnel carrier into the air.

The strange, peaceful lull lasted only three months.

By October 1987, full-scale fighting had erupted between the Indian Army and a disgruntled LTTE.

Near Jaffna city, a young skinny Tiger silently unreeled a thin brown-and-blue spool of electric wire and carefully laid it, hidden among the trees and grass.

He was also lugging a massive, Tiger-built land mine powerful enough to hurl an armored personnel carrier, fully packed with troops, into the air.

He bent forward while he walked, unreeling the twined wire and arranging it like a seemingly endless snake in the wild grass.

He unreeled the spool further and further. The wire crossed a black ribbon of narrow asphalt road. It meandered over a barren patch in the jungle. And onto a nearby wider road.

He was quick.

Nimble.

Reaching a choice spot, he dug a shallow grave next to the road near two trees.

He placed the land mine in the hole and connected his lengthy wire. A skilled electrician, he made minor repairs. Satisfied with his handiwork, he connected a trigger.

He buried the wired bomb.

A handful of other Tigers silently fanned into the jungle, crouching close to algae-covered walls of abandoned village homes. They waited in sultry heat.

The Tigers hoped they could ambush and destroy an approaching convoy carrying enemy Indian Army reinforcements.

That Indian convoy was rumbling towards the rebels. The Indians wanted to encircle and assault nearby Tiger-held Jaffna town.

Suddenly, a Tiger opened fire with his AK-47 rifle. His loud staccato piano of bullets blasted the silence, to lure the Indians towards the concealed land mine.

Despite a few more bursts of bullets, no Indian troops appeared.

So the 10 disappointed Tigers gingerly dig up their mine, connected its wire to the unused length on the reel, and slowly carried their bomb closer towards the convoys' suspected position while unspooling the electric snake.

The Indian Army cleverly waited a full 45 minutes before making its move.

We barely heard the two puffed whispers from twin Indian mortars coughing in the distance.

"Down! Down!" screamed a young rebel who, moments before, proudly showed off a big decal on the stock of his AK-47.

The decal displayed a map of Sri Lanka with a bright red northeast chunk ripped out of the island amid shafts of glorious yellow light. The red chunk was to be their independent Tamil Eelam. A leaping tiger also appeared on the decal. Fearsome and brandishing saber tooth fangs, its long-clawed front paws brought the tiger's head through a sunburst illustrated with 33 big yellow bullets laid in a circle, set in front of twin black blades from crossed bayonets. The decal evoked the bright yellow tiger's head at the center of the Tigers' red rebel flag.

Two deafening explosions from the Indians' mortars suddenly hit the nearby red earth.

As soon as the thunder of the explosions cleared, the rebel frantically shouted, "Move! Move!"

Everyone ran along winding, dirt lanes, retreating through the jungle towards Jaffna Lagoon.

After several minutes, we heard the distant whisper of two more mortars firing.

"Down! Down!"

All of us dove for cover just before two blasts exploded with a more frightening intensity, much closer than the first pair.

For the next 30 minutes, twin mortars alternatively whispered and exploded. After the blasts of each double volley, the rebels ran terrified until someone heard another set of faint shots. Then everyone cowered in the dirt, waiting in sweat and prayer as the two shells flew closer, seeking its targets with seemingly devilish glee.

The insurgents eventually rushed into an abandoned, one-room home. One rebel refused to go in. He said being inside an easy-to-spot building may be more dangerous than hiding outside, because it was an easy target for the helicopter gunships now approaching.

"The walls will collapse if it is hit!" he shouted.

So everyone rushed out of the house and squatted amid a clump of palm trees, deciding which way to run next.

"Move! Move!"

Everyone ran.

"Dive! Dive!"

Everyone dove.

Amid the labyrinthine lanes, a small cinderblock shed appeared with a 14-year-old Tiger sitting at the entrance. Inside the shed were two hand grenades, an AK-47, a coconut, a box of Britannia cookies and an empty plastic bucket.

Jaffna town was now being cut off by several Indian Army units advancing across the nearby lagoon's jetty.

A breeze off the lagoon brought a low droning sound which became noisier and noisier.

Sri Lanka's tiny air force was helping the Indian Army by sending helicopters to strafe the lagoon, and cut a narrow pedestrian causeway which crossed its water.

These usually languid lanes near Mirusuvil, 18 miles east of Jaffna city, were rapidly becoming a tightening, life-or-death maze.

The onslaught of mortars stopped.

Waving his hand, the 14-year-old Tiger whispered, "The Indians are coming."

The Indians were sending hunter-killer teams on foot to probe rebel defenses.

The insurgents strained to hear the Indians' approaching movement in the surrounding jungle.

The Indians fired a few rounds of machine-gun fire as they closed in from the east. The teenager grabbed his hand grenade and assault rifle and ran towards the shooting. Other Tigers pondered their fate. Some collected coconuts from nearby trees and got bananas from a shy Tamil boy on a rusty bicycle who was passing by.

A few nervous villagers emerged. A Tiger heard on his walkie-talkie that Indian troops had sealed off a nearby highway. Jaffna city was being overrun by the Indian Army. More Indian reinforcements were coming in from Elephant Pass, including the ones advancing on us.

This large-scale Indian offensive on Jaffna would kill more than 500 innocent Tamil civilians, according to senior Sri Lankan military, intelligence and administration officials.

Indian High Commission diplomats in Colombo reluctantly admitted 300 to 400 innocent civilians died during the October onslaught.

Bombing and machine-gun fire by both sides also displaced 500,000 Tamils who fled their homes in Jaffna and the surrounding peninsula, officials said.

Among the Tamils who remained behind during the fighting was 56-year-old R. Ponniah, a writer.

At the gate of his home in Neerveli village, four miles northeast of Jaffna city, he cursed the Indians.

"If India wants to kill us like Hitler, let them put us in gas chambers and kill us, because now they have been torturing us much worse by bombing us with mortars and all," he told me as we walked by.

An 11-year-old boy named Thananchagan, who fled into a Hindu temple at Madduvil several miles away, held up three fingers when I asked how many people in his family died in the offensive.

"I'm scared of the Indian Army because of the shelling."

He broke into tears and began crying.

"Momma, momma..."

His mother had perished in an Indian mortar attack during the assault.

The Hindu temple overflowed with more than 3,000 panic-stricken people who fled the attacks.

A cowering mathematics teacher, V. Ponnampalam, told me:

"We thought the Indians were our saviors but now they are killing us. Indiscriminate shelling on every side of our house. We fear the Indians may still massacre us here, but this is the last place we can go."

In Point Pedro Hospital, an 18-year-old female Tiger lay sprawled with a bullet in her leg.

"I killed six Indian soldiers," she told me.

"I use an AK-47 when I fight. The Indian soldiers are not very good fighters. When we shoot, they run away."

The girl, code-named Kema, looked at her leg.

It was bandaged toe to thigh.

"But then the Indians come back," she said sadly, staring at her red-splattered gauze. "And then they shot me with a rifle at Urumpirai."

Kema said she had been a Tiger for the past two years. She was undergoing treatment at the hospital, now controlled by the Tigers, on the jutting, northernmost tip of the peninsula.

Doctors at the dilapidated hospital told me the bullet hit her leg bone, but she was strong and would recover.

"They took my cyanide away," Kema said with dismay.

Her rebel colleagues had removed her poison vial when they found her.

A guerrilla at Kema's bedside told me, "We take the cyanide away from Tigers when they are wounded because the pain is so bad they might eat it and commit suicide."

Every male and female Tiger wore a capsule containing the powder in a tiny glass vial dangling below their throat at all times.

The brown, leather, thong necklace was as silent as a noose.

Delicately knotted for a personal apocalypse.

Tiger leaders said hundreds of guerrillas had killed themselves by biting their vials and swallowing its bitter, white dust.

Most of those suicides were described as rebels devotedly obeying the Tigers' doctrine -- trapped insurgents must commit suicide rather than be captured, so they could not be tortured into betraying comrades.

Earlier, near Elephant Pass, I met a burly Tiger who wore two tiny cyanide vials lashed together on his leather necklace.

I asked him for one.

To test and prove it contained cyanide.

He refused.

Why?

"I need two. In case one isn't enough."

The battle where Kema was injured, in and around Urumpirai, was one of the toughest the Indians had fought on the island.

This was the fight where Tigers had earlier unreeled wire to plant a land mine, and retreated when the army advanced. Indian soldiers, backed by mortars, artillery and air attacks, seized Urumpirai several days later.

Tiny Urumpirai, two miles north from prized Jaffna city, straddled a key junction on the path of the Indians' onslaught.

Kema said she personally knew about 100 Tiger girls defending Jaffna against the Indians. At least six female Tigers died in the fighting, she said.

Tiger leaders boasted there were more than 1,000 female Tigers in all. That number may have been an exaggeration or included females who performed only medical tasks or lugged equipment. Females were rarely seen in public among the Tigers.

Kema and other girls who joined the Tigers were known in Tamil language as Sunthanthira Paravaigal, which can be translated as "Birds of Freedom." Females were said to undergo the same rigorous training as males -- handling assault rifles, hurling grenades, and planting land mines and booby traps.

The Tigers enforced strict discipline.

Rebels were forbidden to drink alcohol, smoke, or make love. To monitor each other's behavior and conversations, insurgents usually traveled in groups of three or more. Their anti-vice conduct was admired by many Tamil adults.

In some cases, girls eagerly joined the rebels after Sri Lanka's security forces brutalized their relatives during the war, the Tigers said.

Dharsha, a pretty 22-year-old Tiger in a simple brown dress adorned with a white-leaf pattern, told me in the hospital:

"Some girls use weapons, but others help. For the past two weeks, I've been in real battles, looking after the injured. I have experience dressing wounds. I've helped nine wounded Tigers.

"I joined the Tigers three years ago because I want freedom for the citizens of Tamil Eelam. I don't want to marry. If I got married, I wouldn't be able to continue with my military activities.

"I know 12 Tigers who killed themselves with cyanide. It was an act of bravery."

Dharsha said she already received weapons training, but had not yet fought. She enthusiastically insisted she would fight if ordered by her leaders.

Dharsha's comrade Joha, 20 and plump in a purple dress, told me:

"I also don't have a boyfriend. I've been a Tiger for one year. If I am asked to, I will fight. I'm never afraid."

A third woman, Daya, 21, stiffly nodded, but remained silent.

Asked if any of them would like to lead the Tigers after

Prabhakaran passes from the scene, Dharsha diplomatically replied:

"I met Prabhakaran. He's a great leader. No one else is capable of taking us forward to liberation and Eelam. He will never be gone."

She paused and thoughtfully added, "I don't want to be the leader. There are others to replace him if he passes away in the future."

Near Dharsha's cot, civilian Tamil women lay bleeding and grimacing in pain.

Flies fed on their bullet wounds.

"The Indian soldiers just walked into my house. They shot my mother, shot my father and then shot me," Mrs. M. Kanageswary, 28, told me while a doctor and nurse stood by her hospital bed.

"My father died on the spot. Our house wasn't the only one chosen by the soldiers. I don't know why they came to my house."

Mrs. Kanageswary gnashed her teeth while the doctor inspected her wound.

"The Indian Army came in a chained [tracked] vehicle. I was shot in the leg by a short, fat soldier who looked like someone from Nepal," she said, perhaps describing to one of the Indian Army's ethnic Gurkha soldiers.

In a metal cot alongside Mrs. Kanageswary, her next-door neighbor Mrs. T. Rasamalar, 35, lay wheezing and emaciated.

"The Indian soldiers came into my house. They killed my husband and killed my three children" aged ten, five and two, Mrs. Rasamalar told me.

Mrs. Rasamalar's head was swathed in heavy bandages, including a bandage wrapped underneath her chin where a bullet had entered.

Both women said the Indian Army attacked them on October 20 in Urumparai village.

Indian troops eventually seized and held Urumparai after heavy fighting. The junction enabled the Indians to surround

Jaffna city while Tigers desperately tried to defend it.

Officially, all female patients in Point Pedro Hospital were described by medical staff as "civilians with direct gunshot wounds."

Most civilian and rebel deaths during the fighting were killed by the Indian Army's mortar and artillery shelling, hospital staff said.

Indian officials refused to estimate civilian casualties.

Tamil officials in Jaffna issued a joint statement which said "almost 700 innocent civilians are believed to have died" in India's October offensive.

Nurses meanwhile wheeled another civilian woman into the room after she underwent surgery.

She was sitting upright on a gray metal trolley.

Nurses had draped a sheet over her body, but the cloth slipped to reveal huge bandages criss-crossing her chest.

"I was alone and returning from a funeral when the Indian soldiers shot me on the road," Mrs. N. Rajamaney, 62, told me.

"I had put my hands up, but they shot me anyway. Two Indian soldiers."

Mrs. Rajamaney said she was shot for no reason at Vayavilan village, 10 miles west of Point Pedro near Palali, the main airbase for Indian troops on the peninsula.

Indian soldiers were flying from India to Palali and then moving in convoys to junctions on main roads leading into Jaffna.

Tamil civilians and insurgents also described deliberate attacks by the Indian Army including rapes, point-blank executions, using civilians to walk ahead of troops to clear mine fields, and other atrocities.

Their reports could not be independently investigated because the peninsula was rapidly falling under India's control and other witnesses could not be immediately found in the chaos.

New Delhi dismissed all such reports as LTTE "propaganda" and accused the Tigers of the same allegations -- which the insurgents also denied.

"Most of the casualties coming in from the war are civilians, old women, children, those sorts of people," Doctor S. Thiruchelvam told me in the hospital. "In the past two weeks, about 200 civilians have been treated here."

He pointed to two small children sharing a cot.

"They were hit by Indian mortars."

The boy, Yogaranchithan, aged four, and his sister Selvaloginy, nine, were injured by shrapnel in Karaveddi village three miles southwest of Point Pedro, their father told me.

Their mother slowly waved a straw fan over their faces to keep flies away.

About 25 Tigers were also being treated in the hospital.

They included a senior rebel, code named Captain Krishna, who stared dully into space while a tube drained a chest wound caused by artillery in Jaffna city.

The Indian Army had initially been greeted with appreciation by many Jaffna Tamils who believed they would bring peace.

But when this latest fighting erupted, India unleashed 20,000 soldiers against Jaffna. It took them two weeks of heavy mortar, artillery, air and ground attacks before Indian forces dominated the impoverished town.

Most Tigers escaped with weapons and ammunition. Many civilian survivors were again hailing the Tigers and hoping they would avenge the Jaffna assault by staging hit-and-run attacks throughout Sri Lanka's northeast.

"They are good boys," a businessman told me.

"They don't drink, they don't smoke and they don't take women. They are protecting us with their lives."

Others said they were saddened and helpless because the Indian offensive destroyed their hopes for peace. Independence for a Tamil Eelam again appeared as the only path, they said. In many of the worst-affected areas, it was virtually impossible to find any Tamil civilians who supported the Indian Army.

Instead, residents said they would actively help the guerrillas defend the Tamil community.

Jaffna General Hospital was now struggling to treat about 600 civilian casualties from the fighting despite a lack of blood, oxygen, medicine and other items due to India's blockade of the city, officials said.

Indian troops had also overran guerrillas sheltering at the hospital and kept it under the Indian Army's control.

The Tigers said Indian troops "killed 150 patients and 100 civilians" including five doctors while seizing the hospital, and raped nine nurses.

LTTE Political Theoretician and Chief Spokesman Anton Balasingham said the executed patients included about 100 Tigers who had been wounded in battles.

New Delhi denied the allegations. The Indian High Commission said guerrillas killed two doctors while retreating.

Doctors who fled to refugee camps to escape the bombing said other casualties were being treated in people's homes without medical supervision because several hospitals were cut off by advancing Indian troops, or supplies and staff had disappeared.

Tigers behind the Indian Army's lines at Neerveli village near Kopay North, three miles northeast of Jaffna, displayed one such victim -- an elderly farmer who they were transporting to a safe house for treatment.

The farmer had been hit by a mortar blast, the guerrillas said, indicating a crumpled and bleeding man on the floor of the Tigers' white van.

Indian officials said their October offensive intentionally moved slow, to avoid civilian casualties. They claimed any dead civilians had been unintentionally "caught in crossfire."

Western diplomats however said the Indian Army was responsible for "atrocities," rapes and revenge killings against innocent Tamils during search-and-destroy missions.

About 1,500 Tigers remained in the northeast's jungles, purged from most of their strongholds but still delivering deadly hit-and-run attacks against the Indian Army, according to Western diplomats.

"I believe the Indian troops want to get out. It's like America in Vietnam," one Western envoy said. Unable to defeat the Tigers, the Indian Army withdrew from the island in 1990.

By then, more than 1,200 Indian soldiers had perished and 2,500 were wounded, vainly trying to control the Liberation Tigers of Tamil Eelam. During the Indian Army's 1987-1990 presence on the island, more than 5,000 Tamils and other Sri Lankans also died.

One year later, on a sweltering May 21, 1991, a female Tiger named Dhanu assassinated Rajiv Gandhi in southern India with a suicide bomb, also killing more than a dozen others.

Indian investigators said it was a revenge killing meticulously orchestrated by Prabhakaran because of Gandhi's military intervention, and to stop Gandhi returning to power as prime minister in an upcoming election and possibly sending India's army against the Tigers again.

With a bomb hidden under her clothes, Dhanu approached Gandhi at a public campaign rally. A police officer stopped her but Gandhi told the officer, "Let everybody get a chance."

Dhanu then placed a garland around Gandhi's neck and bowed to touch his feet, as if she were honoring his greatness. When he bent down to raise Dhanu up, she set off her explosives.

In 1998, a court in India convicted 26 people, including several Tigers, the LTTE leader Prabhakaran, and their Indian supporters, in the conspiracy to assassinate Gandhi.

The Tigers denied involvement.

"The main reason why Dhanu became a Tiger is that her brother was a well-known cadre who had died and she was carrying on the family tradition," said Mia Bloom, an author who researched the assassination.

"Allegations of Dhanu's rape [by Indian troops, prompting her to become an assassin] have never been proven, and sources within the Indian government assert that she was still a virgin at the time of her death.

"Although such sources have cause to lie, in my interviews

with the Tamil Tigers, they too do not think she was actually raped. There have been questions raised about whether her mother might have been the victim of sexual abuse by the Indian Peace Keeping Force when they intervened in the country in 1987-1990," Bloom wrote.

"It should be emphasized that checkpoint rape on the part of Sri Lankan military in Tamil areas -- for example, on the east coast -- has certainly mobilized female Tamils, encouraged abused women to join the organization that would provide safe haven, protection, and acceptance, and provides evidence of the government's cruelty."

Bloom was responding in a letter to a New York Review of her book, Why They Do It, in which reviewer Christian Caryl alleged that she wrote that Dhanu was gang-raped.

"My apologies to Ms. Bloom. I did indeed overstate the case in my paraphrase of her description of Dhanu," Caryl replied.

"It is by no means a firmly established fact that Dhanu was gang-raped by Indian soldiers."

India meanwhile had mixed feelings about their army's intervention in Sri Lanka.

"On 9 February 1999, the first memorial service dedicated to the 1,248 [Indian] officers and soldiers who fell in Sri Lanka was held in Bhopal [India] under the aegis of the 21 Corps, born out of the Sri Lankan expedition," wrote Ashok K. Mehta, a former Indian Army major general and founder of India's Defense Ministry Defense Planning Staff.

"Ironically, on the same day, Indian Army's eminent thinker and the army chief who launched the IPKF [Indian Peace Keeping Force] in Sri Lanka, General K. Sundarji, died.

"In a sense, IPKF was Sundarji's brain child which he later lived to silently regret."

CHAPTER 4 ~ SEX

PERI, A NEW YORK STRIPPER

How does 24-year-old Peri earn a living?

"I take off my clothes in public," she tells me, winking.

It all started when she needed a part-time job to help pay for college. She stepped onto a strip club's stage. Since then, she's done shows in Mexico, Las Vegas, Boston's Combat Zone, and Manhattan's Playboy Club.

Leaning her heart-shaped face towards a round, magnifying mirror so she can put her false eyelashes on straight, Peri insists she is more interested in jazz dancing than stripping.

"I didn't like being poor and I wanted to dance. I found out strippers could dance, they could do anything they wanted. The only stipulation was, you had to take your clothes off."

Peri flutters those eyelashes to make sure they're glued. She is preparing for an audition and prefers to dress at home, so she can take her time.

She reaches for rouge.

Recalling her first audition at a very elegant, private club near her campus, she says:

"First, I tried stripping in front of a few boyfriends. I saw how it went with the opposite sex, and if it went over."

She coyly chuckles.

"And it did."

During her first day onstage there, a producer walked in, watched her dance, and asked her to be in one of his shows.

"Where again, I took my clothes off. But I had fancier

costumes."

She left college and went with the show to Mexico.

"I worked at this very plush club which catered to Mexican aristocracy and rich Americans. It was called El Tapa Tio. On the highest mountain in Guadalajara."

The show ran into difficulties with its Mexican agent, so she left and went on her own to Las Vegas.

"To call Vegas sophisticated or elegant makes me throw up. It's one big blaring fake."

But she found a lot of jobs. Especially burlesque where Peri saw the seamier side of a showgirl's life.

"A lot of times, casino people want a girl that'll do whatever they want. Like either go with the casino manager, or with a big money gambler. In Vegas, that's what many of the showgirls are like."

The Vegas money came fast, but she spent it just as rapidly. Her average time onstage was 10 to 15 minutes. Usually, she danced three shows a night. Six nights a week.

Some places made a girl dance 20 minutes each show, kicking and gyrating. It all depended upon the showgirl's act. Elaborate costumes took more time to display. Sometimes she had to change costumes five times for each show.

"The most tiring part is the dressing and undressing before and after each number."

Peri twists her neck so her profile reflects in the mirror like a mug shot.

The rouge is OK.

She strides towards her closet and thinks for a few minutes about what's best to wear to audition her act tonight in Manhattan. She learned in Las Vegas, the best strippers perform acts.

"You could come on as a gypsy lady. Or as a little girl and become a woman. Or pretend you're Little Red Riding Hood."

She grins mischievously, enjoying how she can manipulate an audience's fetishes.

"The girl creates her own act. The only stipulation is that

you've got to have no clothes at the end. Whatever else you do to get there is your decision."

Rapport with viewers is vital.

"I need everybody's eyes," she says, poised in a dancer's stance with feet at right angles while she gazes at her wardrobe.

"I seduce with my eyes. That's why I have to have eye contact. If there's nothing to look at, I can't seduce it."

Her favorite costume is The Leopard Lady. A leopard skin cape and a little, ragged, black and yellow striped skirt.

To turn her audience on, she dances sexy, crawls towards them, and purrs.

"I hide false fangs in my mouth and then do a somersault, landing an inch from somebody's face in the audience. I open my mouth and go, 'GRRRRRROOOOOOWL!' Somebody in the audience freaks every time! It's fun."

She says men enjoy her concept of the "American Male's Ideal Woman, a combination of Mae West, Marilyn Monroe, and a little bit of Woody Allen."

From her closet, she lets a robe slide onto her shoulders, and holds a pair of pants to her waist.

"How did a nice girl like me get this way?" she asks her full-length reflection.

"I always liked men. I feel sexy before I go onstage. I have to prepare myself that way mentally. I get very involved in making movements seductively onstage. That's my specialty."

She says stripping is a power trip. She loves it. Peri doesn't feel exploited by stripping, she says, because she finds value in her work.

"Nobody approves or disapproves," she says harshly, suddenly defensive.

"It just makes no shit to me. I'm more independent than any other lady I've met."

She makes good money. And her shows allow her to perform jazz dancing.

"If you were going to take off your clothes, wouldn't you rather get money for it if you could?"

After ferreting a blouse from her drawer, she straps on a red bra and dives into a silky, rose-patterned shirt. She pins a red beret at a tilt.

"I don't do anything offensive to get a reaction. Some strippers rub their crotches. There's no need for that. I get offended. It's not sexy. It's crude.

"I love nudity. We all have that in common. We can all be naked."

Magazine advertisements portraying glamorous women speckle her walls. Above her make-up table, a painted wooden sign reads:

Burlesque Show Live Onstage Every Hour On The Hour.

"Now I'll talk like a stripper and you'll hear what she's like."

Turning her voice into thick Brooklynese to satirically sound the part, she slurs:

"I go out there and I move around to the music, doll face, and I take off my clothes. This guy slipped me 20 bucks under the table for a blow job, and I'm so mad at the boss because he wants me to go with another customer over there who bought a 200 dollar bottle of champagne."

Laughter cascades out of her lipsticked mouth.

As she stuffs a jar of cold cream into her purse, she says she enjoys doing burlesque much more than just stripping. Burlesque has an act which goes beyond peeling off clothes. In Las Vegas, she also designed her own costumes.

"A burlesque queen is like the Statue of Liberty of Ziegfeld Follies. Very American."

She used to dance in Las Vegas for eight months, then travel. She frequently returned to Vegas, using the city as base to contact producers and choreographers.

If she couldn't find a job, she stripped in less extravagant surroundings.

"I worked for about two weeks in this place in Boston's Combat Zone. It was the sleaziest joint you could find. The Peek-a-Boo Club."

Peri was thankful when the Playboy Club in Manhattan

recently hired her for Minsky's Follies.

"I love the Playboy Cub. They treat you like gold. They make sure newspapers write you up, and you get fantastic photos taken of you for advertising. You're built up. You're glamour."

She hopes to find another dancing job in the city. Or dance in France, where her cousin lives. She peers at her watch and says she must leave for her audition stripping at a New York dinner lounge.

Her audiences at lounges often include married couples. Women in the audience are usually more critical of her act.

"Men are sold right away," she says, then talks bass, mimicking them: "Yup, she's all right, heh, heh."

She insists she doesn't want to sexually arouse women, but then adds, "I do not like frigidity in women. Even though I might not be turned on to them, I'm a stripper. There's a reason why you take off your clothes. It's an expression of sensuality. It's like doing a dance."

Peri tiptoes between sex and sensuality.

"Like when I do my 16-count split. I'm simulating, uh, I don't like to say 'lovemaking' because I'm not pumping the floor, right? Or playing with myself. But..."

She searches her feelings while putting on her coat and counting bus fare.

"I'm just showing what I feel making love is like. As a stripper, you're arousing people to that. Being sensual. Feeling sexual. It turns me on to know I can turn all those people on."

On stage, after Peri took off her camouflage of clothes, she was naked. But not many people would pay the price of a dinner show to see her simply standing undressed.

It was only when her body danced -- merging into music, toying with a costume's illusion and nature's passionate drama -- that people would watch with awe.

Peri and other strippers displayed a thin slice of the experiences and struggles nightclub dancers and sex workers endured in 1978 in New York.

Elsewhere in the city, down-market venues offered much

raunchier, exploitative performances where the women were in no mood to indulge in the belief that they were expressing themselves in an artistic way on stage.

MICHELLE, IN PEEPLAND ON 42ND STREET

"I used to be a prostitute," Michelle tells me.

"I used to work in a peepshow as well. 42nd Street. In 1993. How can I describe Peepland? Peepland is a peepshow. It's a peepshow on 42nd Street.

"It has two floors. It has been there for quite a while. It's a landmark building. Up front, where you walk in, there is a huge eye and lots of neon lights. Has a carnival atmosphere to it.

"You walk in and you buy your tokens. And then you have a selection of porno films from all over the world, because Peepland's owners enjoyed collecting them. Some of the films were very bizarre.

"Then you go downstairs and that's where the girls are. There are six stages. They have a lot of loud music and there are some guards down there. It's quite dark, with lots of colored lights.

"The stages are surrounded by booths, and the guy goes into the booth, he puts in his four tokens, and then the window goes up. And then he chooses a girl.

"It has these glass mirrors. They are really distorted, kind of like fun house mirrors. And you have, like, these bright pink or very, very dark red carpets, and then you have about three girls to a set.

"So you ask the customer if he's tipping. Tipping means, 'Are you touching?' So if he gives you money, it's obviously not just because he wants to just stare at you, it's because he wants to touch.

"Then you go up to the window and, depending on how much money he gives you, you know what he wants, because you weren't allowed to quote prices.

"Sometimes you would have DTs who came in and they would, like, bust us. DTs are detectives.

"In the back, you have the girls' dressing room and general hangout place. We worked like 15 minutes on each stage, so it's 30 minutes for each set, and then girls would come to relieve you, and then you would take another half an hour off. So it was a very easy job.

"I mean you always had bizarre experiences with customers, and the back room was always pretty weird because the girls were all very different. I think the freakiest thing was watching Alison get stabbed.

"I was on Stage One. She was on Stage Three. And it was not too far from Thanksgiving, and there were not too many girls there because it was a Sunday afternoon. I was alone on stage and I was making pretty good money. What you could do is, you stood on the little coin box that's in front of each booth. And then you could look over the partition and see, like, the other stages and the guys.

"And when I was standing up there, because usually we call guys in that way, I saw Alison on the other stage and she bent over. It's like she took the money. And she bent over. And all of a sudden, this guy just took a knife and stabbed her in the butt.

"And then she just screamed like it was an unbelievable sound. It all happened very quickly. She fell. So another girl grabbed her, someone yelled for security. There was one [security guard] who came inside on stage to see what happened. And the [customer] guy was still in the booth, so the security guard went and basically held him inside.

"I didn't see him after this, but this is what they told me -- he was crouched down on the ground like he was in shock or something and, um, they just locked the door and called the cops.

"Alison was pretty bad. There was blood everywhere.

"I wanted to stay off stage because I went there to see how she was doing and, um, basically they told me to get back to work because they didn't want to leave the stage empty, because there were still customers there.

"It was truly bizarre because you had security guards screaming holding this guy, you had Alison screaming with blood everywhere, and you had all of these customers who just continued to go into the booths and um, you know, wanted to, um, ha, ha, just, you know, continue working business as usual. And it was funny, because the money was very good too. It was like just the fact that the place was in such disarray, there were people screaming, it's like it turned them on, they wanted to spend more money.

"And then the cops came and they were all over the place.

"They came into the booth, and they asked me if I wanted to go out. They tipped and touched me and asked me for my phone number and they were totally like no one had cared that this girl had just gotten stabbed. They just carted her away in the ambulance and dragged the guy up from the booth, kicking and screaming. He was really freaked out, yeah. So I guess that was one of the freakiest things.

"Alison stayed away for several months. She went on to marry her pimp.

"It seemed like the guy [with the knife] had been there before. He was regular customer who just lost his mind. It was the first time I realized the real threat that there is, when you are working with a customer.

"They would have things, like, guys who would do stuff. Like, they'd put something on their hands that would burn you. I don't know what the substance is, but a customer is touching you between your legs and he has something on his hands or on his gloves. There were guys who used to come in and they would wear these kind of surgical gloves. If you were not really watching a customer, he has access, he can do anything to you. So if he put some ammonia on his fingers, or some liquid that was alcohol-based, he would try to put his fingers in your pussy to burn you.

"So that stuff happens. Then you have to be careful of guns

and hypodermic needles because we were on 42nd Street and all of the locals would come down. I mean these guys were basically drug dealers and gang members and, of course, pimps. Like these are the guys you didn't want to piss off because you always had to walk back outside again.

"I had a customer and then, after work when I was leaving, he followed me out of the building and was trying to talk to me. But because I was outside, I became myself again and I wouldn't talk to him. I was ignoring him.

"And, uh, he freaked out on me and he screamed at me when I was half-way down the street:

'You stupid bitch. You think you're too good to talk to me, but I just touched your pussy for five dollars.'

"It was mortifying. Because it was like, you know, when there's a scene, everybody watches you. So all of a sudden there are dozens of people who all turned to look at me because of his screaming and carrying on. And now they know I work in a peepshow.

"There was one particular who used a flashlight and he would want you to kind of, like, you would have to hold onto its handle and you would have to spread your legs because he wanted to see inside. He spent a lot of money. He was a regular customer. He always did this. He always brought his flashlight and his surgical gloves. He was black, in his 30s. Very serious. He wore glasses. I mean he looked like a regular guy. And that was his trip.

"He'd just say things that he wanted you to do like, 'Spread them. Contract your pussy muscles.'

"He would always be upset because you wouldn't bend down far enough. You were like leaning because you were holding onto a handle and you had your leg raised on this thing and you were standing, so that's how he would peer. And he would keep trying to spread your thighs apart so he could see."

[Michelle, who were some of your female colleagues at Peepland?]

"Lotta Top. She's from Oklahoma and she was probably in her mid-50s. She used to be a very popular porn star and made films in Germany and Australia and all over the place. They called her Lotta Top because she had huge breasts. They were supposedly the largest natural-sized breasts at that time.

"And she was really cute because she had this kind of blonde Barbie doll kind of hair, and she put little pink ribbons on top. And she would always look like a freak. Or she was a freak.

"She is also famous for having the longest clit in the world. It's not like she's a hermaphrodite or anything. It wasn't a penis. It was just a very long clit. It was about this long, about two inches. The customers used to like it when she put it between her fingers like this [gestures with two fingers twisting in the air] and play with it. They were really into it. But she herself, when you looked at her, she was actually a freak. She was like a character out of Katherine Dunn's book, Geek Love. She was really like that.

"When you spoke to her, she was really sweet and really normal and that just made her seem extra bizarre because she was actually just a freak. You could see that she was probably very, very pretty, when she was younger. And she had all of this very, very roller-curled blonde hair, yeah, and she'd keep it up like this with a little ribbon. She kind of looked like Baby Jane or something. Isn't Baby Jane from Bette Davis?

"And then when you go, like further down, it's like she had no neck and she was just, she had like these breasts which were huge, like transcending normal bra size. They were like each breast itself looked like it had three breasts in there. But because she was older, they began to sag. So she had this weird kind of pulled skin. It would be flat like this, and then there were her breasts here. They kind of gathered around her stomach area. And then she had that clit thing.

"And then she opened her mouth and she had this real kind of ditsy Oklahoma farm girl accent. She would always behave as if she was just like this very middle America-type person. It just made her seem very, very bizarre.

"Especially when you see some of her films. There's a film called Dogs in Love. It's a German film. I think she had done a version of that. I've seen it. It's like an orgy of Lotta and a guy and two dogs. German Shepherds or whatever. She, um, does everything with the dogs. It eats her pussy. She has sex with it. That's basically what it was."

[And your other female colleagues at Peepland?]

"Roe Roe. She's a really together dominatrix. Yeah. She took me to The Vault [a sadomasochism club in Manhattan] one night. She showed me what it was all about.

"She used to do this trick when she was pregnant. She would, because she was pregnant, overweight and whatnot, she would get guys who would say, 'Do you got milk in there?' And so, for 10 dollars, she would squirt her tits. And shoot milk. Milk would come out. She was very much into the psychology of submissiveness, and passive-aggressive, and this whole, like, sadomasochist trip. She used to be a slave herself. In order for, as she would put it, 'to be a good dominatrix,' she would have to learn how it is, how it feels to be a slave and to turn your will over to someone else. She said it was exhilarating.

"I used to watch her onstage with her leather get-up and she would -- remember I told you about a guy who wanted to have his face kicked in with the heel of a shoe? She used to do that.

"And she would always talk to her customers. And some of them would give her 50 or 100 or 200 dollars just so that she could verbally abuse them. She was very good at it. She would play on their guilt by saying things like:

'You know the only reason why you came here now is because you're a little shit who really wanted to fuck his mother, but never had the nerve to.'

"When we were at The Vault together, it was Good Friday, and they had a huge wooden cross in the middle of the room and they had like these old men who were dirty and had ragged clothes on, and they would be chained to like a pole or something. And their penises would be hanging out. And they had other strange things, like people with whips and paddles. She told me to wear a leather jacket that had spikes in it. That way they would know I was dominant and not submissive.

"So you'd have guys coming up to you and they would follow you all around all night very meekly, begging you on their hands and knees, pleading with you so that they could suck on your toes. Or that you could like slap them every time when they tried to masturbate. They wanted you to stop them. The more you would refuse, the more desperate they became and the more excited.

"They had a thing that night where they tied me to the crucifix with this rope, with all these elaborate knots. Nude, except for my G-string. And then they beat me with palms. You know, Palm Sunday, and you get the palms. Palm leaves. It was very funny because they had people pouring hot wax on me and beating me with those leaves. I'm sure it was quite a vision for somebody sitting at the bar. The Vault was a pretty wild place.

"They had, what do you call those things that you put your head in, and your arms? A stockade. She would put someone in there. She would get a slave and she would beat him and throw things at him, and he would be begging her to spit in his face and she would refuse. Finally after a long session, she would let him out and allow him to masturbate. And then tell him he can't come. And then start another agonizing session. Just basically a lot of degrading things. She would degrade them. Make them walk around on all fours. Eat dog food.

"She is Italian. I think her first name is Roezella. Roe Roe was her stage name, her nickname.

"I was Coco. I got into the business, working the peepshow, when a friend introduced me to Peepland. I created this personality who is Coco, who is the one who was able to get up on stage and do everything. I chose the name Coco from a television commercial for Coco Chanel, the perfume. It had this girl who was kind of, I don't know how to explain it to you, free-spirited and in control but at the same time she was a little bit manipulative. That was how they presented her in this commercial. And I decided that I was going to be Coco. I just liked the way it was presented, this image, or this fantasy, of Coco.

"I have a friend named China and she had been in and out of the sex industry for many, many years and she began telling me about it and how much money she was making.

"At that time, I was down to 108 pounds, so I looked very good. I'm about 5-foot 4, or 5-foot 3. So she says, 'You are going to make so much money.' She says, 'You're going to love this. You'll have the best time of your life.' And she told me, 'You can do what you want.'

"I was hesitant at first, but she wanted me to go with her to work and just check out the place and see it.

"So while she was getting dressed, she said, 'Why don't you come up for one set and try it?' A set is 15 minutes.

"She said, 'Just take off your clothes. You don't have to do anything but just stand there, and you can ask them if they're tipping or just let them point to you.'

"At first we were just laughing and goofing off about whether I should do it or not. And I did.

"I just stood there, awkward and uncomfortable. Someone pointed to me, put some money in my hand and told me to, 'Bend down' because he wanted to feel my breasts. Anyway, 15 minutes later, I had something like 50 dollars, 50 or 60 dollars. That was exhilarating. I couldn't believe how easy it was.

"I hadn't been working there too long and this was on Stage One I remember, early in the evening, and there was this young guy, early 20s, and he asked me if I would pee in a cup for him. He looked so, I don't know, I felt sorry for him. At first, I told him no. And he said, 'Please, I'll give you 50 dollars.'

"And I thought, well, you know, 'Hmmmmmmmm, OK, 50 dollars, I can pee in a cup for 50 dollars.' He had the cup with him, right? I didn't know what I was supposed to do with it. He said, 'Just do it right here in front of me.'

"And the girls were laughing and yelling things like, 'I'll do it for 50 dollars.' Things like that. Anyway, I did it. And I gave it to him. He gave me the 50 and then he started drinking it and I became revolted and I turned away and the window went down. But he was really well-dressed. He looked like the typical Long Island guy. Real sweet looking. But I guess, you know, it's not like he can ask someone else.

"Usually you would have to bend down to see the man in the booth. The man walks inside the booth. When he inserts his four tokens, the window [a flat, plastic yellow curtain] would go up. It didn't stay up for very long. Maybe like a minute. It wasn't that long. Then it would come down.

"When the girl is on stage and she sees the window, she would have to bend down in order to see who's inside. If she's standing in front of the window, he's basically looking level at her pussy. It's strange because I've only been in the booths once or twice and we look very strange from the booths. Because first, the man sees all the windows and all the other girls through the reflection of a mirror. Or some girls working with some guy's hands sticking out. And all the man can see is the hands sticking out.

"If a girl comes up to his window, all the man sees is you have your major body parts in his face, like your ass or all that can fit into the window. Your ass or your pussy or your tits. There is no glass. When it closes, it just shuts down. When the time's up, the yellow plastic comes down.

"Everything else inside his booth, the partition, is black. On our side, there is a black coin box. That's where their money goes into, which activates the yellow window to go up. On his side, there's a slot so that he can put his tokens in. They are like quarters. You need four. A dollar.

"It had a kind of carnival atmosphere about it because you had the lights, the colored lights, the distorted mirrors, and the girls who were usually looking pretty flamboyant or whatever."

[What other women worked there?]

"Baby Doll. No one liked Baby Doll. We all hated her.

"She was very young. Little. We would have probably referred to her as white trash who thought she was very, very cute, but she was not really. She did make a lot of money. She turned a lot of tricks. But she kind of had this attitude on stage where she would portray this pseudo snottiness. No one could stand her after a while. Because she was making money, and she was favored by the owners, she became kind of arrogant. She started feeling that she had weight, that she was carrying weight in the place.

"What she had done, which is what a lot of new girls do, is they underestimate the old girls. Or rather the ruthlessness of the old girls. Because if they have it in mind to get rid of you, eventually they will. Doesn't matter how much the owners love you. She was obnoxious.

"You know what she used to wear? She'd get that really cheesy, long, see-through lingerie, the kind that some old middle-aged woman would wear when she's trying to seduce her husband, and these kind of very frilly little teddies underneath this. So she always looked like she was walking around her boudoir or something. She always had this baby doll voice that she would use on the customers.

"She was really disgusting. She would kiss the customers. That was like the one thing if you do, that would really upset all the girls. Tongue-kiss a customer. Yeah. Most people would see us as being pretty loose, because we allow people to touch our breasts or our ass or in between our legs, but the limit is you don't allow anyone to finger you. No one is allowed to put their fingers inside of you. These were the girls' rules. It was not management which said this. It was a code of conduct for the girls. It was looked down on. That and kissing. To actually kiss a customer was seen as really disgusting.

"The same goes for a guy eating a woman's pussy, but that was much more accepted. Some girls felt like it was the most disgusting intimate thing, and that you shouldn't allow a stranger to do that, otherwise you were really a slut, a whore, a prostitute. Because if you had boundaries, there was this false sense of saying like, 'OK, I'm a dancer.' It's like this denial. You would call yourself a dancer when you were actually never dancing, right?

"You would say, 'OK, I have these high ideals' -- even though you're a prostitute -- 'and so I'm going to set my boundaries.' And this is what will separate you from the really, like uh, the real prostitutes, the real 42nd Street whore. But the truth of the matter is, as Patty would say, 'Every bitch in here is a ho.'

"We would define a whore as different than a ho. It's very subtle. A slut is a girl who degrades herself out of a sense of low self-esteem. She can't help herself. She just degrades herself. And probably will feel worse after doing it. A whore is the girl who loves what she's doing. She loves the sleaziness. She gets off on it.

"But the prostitute is the same as the hooker, is the same as the ho. She's a professional. She's a detached individual who is basically just doing their job for the money. Sometimes these things cross over.

"China beat the shit out of Baby Doll. I can't remember all the details, but I think that Baby Doll wanted China off her set. China wanted to go up on her set, and Baby Doll didn't want the competition.

"So Baby Doll reacted by screaming and yelling, going to the manager. And China just grabbed her by the back of her hair and threw her into the lockers and wiped the floor with her. Totally scared the living daylights out of Baby Doll.

"We were all gathering around, all the girls gathering around, cheering and laughing and glad to see Baby Doll get beat up. She was humiliated. We realized that Baby Doll didn't know how to fight. Baby Doll was helpless. She didn't know how to fight, period. Eventually she left Peepland.

"We've had girls named Tequila, we've had Tamara who is now dead, she was killed. We've had Ebony, Chastity, Ivory.

We've had Venus, Roxanne, Eve, Burgundy, Moet. And the Hungarians. We just clumped them together. The Hungarians were known as the Hungarians.

"There were maybe 30 Hungarians. We called it the Hungarian Invasion, which basically had to do with one of the guys who worked there. What he did was, he had a scam going. He would go to Hungary and ask women if they wanted to work in the States for like three months or six months. He would get the visas for them, bring them over, have them work for a period of time. While of course taking money from them too. And then send them home with like 2,000 or 3,000 dollars, when we all know that they made something like 20,000. We called it Pimping Hungarian Style.

"Customers adored the Hungarians. They loved them. While the Hungarian girls were at Peepland, they were the only ones who clocked. It's an expression when you make money like this [she snaps her fingers repeatedly, very quickly]. No one could compete with them. They had this accent and most of them were quite pretty, though it wasn't that. I think it was their foreignness. But even that was no explanation because, like the French girls didn't make much money.

"You know what it was? Partly it was like their intro. They would have their accent, which is quite cute and sexy, the Zsa Zsa accent, and then they would do something that not many of the other girls did. They would touch the customers. Like they would touch his hair, touch his chest, or touch his face. I think that had something to do with it. They were open. And the rest of us were just more detached.

"Now you're talking about months and months and months of women who were coming in every day, on both shifts, and where the management favored them because they brought in money. So they would allow more than three girls to a set, so sometimes you would have five girls on a set, or six girls on a set. That would be all of us. So you could not work without a Hungarian because there were so many of them.

"That means if you were working with six other girls, and

three or four of them were Hungarians, you could leave that whole day with only 30 dollars, when previously you could leave at the end of the day with 100 or 500 dollars or more, depending on the girl. So when you talk about that kind of a cut in money for everyone, you've got a problem.

"A girl's gotta eat. She's gotta pay her rent. So in the interest of everyone, someone called Immigration. And Immigration came down and busted every single one of them. Took them way. Sent them home. Because it is illegal for them to be working on those visas."

[Who else did you work with?]

"Angel began working the peepshow quite young. She was underage, working in this peepshow at Peepland. There was Angel, Blade and June. Blade was really young when she started. And June began when she was really young, 14. These girls had a different kind of transition. They all ran away from home, or were thrown out, whatever, and ended up on the streets. By the time they turned themselves on to Peepland, they were so wise and so hard, jaded, addicted.

"But not June, because June had Patty and other older women who were there to protect her and take care of her. They all took care of June because she was the baby, she was so young. They would save money for her so she wouldn't spend it all and go crazy with the money she made, so she could save up to get an apartment and things like that.

"But Blade and Angel were on their own. They had been out there. They had to hook on the streets. They were on heroin. And God knows what else. The last time I had seen Angel, I was sure she was on crack.

"These girls became old, you know what I'm saying? They were pathetic because they could never get their shit together. You could see that whatever happened to them out there on the streets, aged them to the point of no return.

"Angel was a very thin, big-breasted girl. Really short. Very,

very skinny. And she was half Asian. And I think she's half black. She had tattoos on her body. She was into this hard rock thing. The heavy duty Lower East Side thing. Guns N' Roses and all that. She was also into things like black magic, The Necronomicon, which is the title of a book by the Mad Arab, I forget his name [Abdul Alhazred] and it's very ancient and it teaches you how to conjure evil spirits.

"Angel, the last time I saw her, she was still working in Peepland. She still had a habit. Supposedly she got married. She lives on the Lower East Side.

"Blade was interesting. She had a very beautiful face. There was one of our girls who OD'd in a hotel off of 42nd Street. Blade was in the apartment with her. They had done some bad heroin, some bad dope. When this girl shot herself up, and just laid there and started turning blue, Blade freaked out. She didn't know what to do.

"The girl had died. Blade did nothing. She just sat there. She freaked. She ended up leaving without calling the police or the ambulance and just abandoning the situation. That's how you begin to react to things when you've been out there on the streets too long. They did find the girl's body and I'm not quite sure how Blade took it. I mean, everyone knew she was there.

"China, she had been in the business for a very long time. She was originally from Georgia. She had a really crazy lifestyle. She was addicted to everything. Money, sex, -- oh, not so much sex -- she used to do heroin, she used to do coke, she used to do acid.

"She had taken 21 hits of acid in one evening, it was a suicide attempt. She basically ended up in the Psyche Unit for a very long time. She told me, the guy she copped from totally flipped out when he realized she had taken all of the blotters. He immediately called for an ambulance. She was fine at that point but things became hairy when the two medics showed up, understanding that she was on acid, but they overreacted. She flipped out. They put her in a straightjacket and she ended up in Roosevelt Hospital.

"When they were trying to interview her, while in the hospital, and they kept trying to get her to drink something -- I don't know if it was an antidote or something to make her vomit -- she said that the whole place became totally warped. Whatever liquid they were going to give her, didn't seem like liquid so she wouldn't take it. They tried to force her. She ended up strapped to a bed. And that's how she basically tripped for God knows how long. She told me all about it.

"Peepland was a way for her to kind of act out, but I think it was that way for everyone. She was like the Diva of Peepland. She was having an affair with one of the owners. So she managed to get her way in everything, she could take any set she wanted, and take extra sets when others couldn't. There were a lot of girls who really didn't like her. She was described as a 'doctor's wife gone mad' or something like that. It had a lot to do with the way she looked, which was pretty much very conservative and kind of upper middle-class.

"She was fired from the place. There was an incident with a customer. She used to piss off the customers a lot. One even pulled a gun out on her when she called him a nigger. But in this particular case, it was a dispute about the way he had touched her. He was obviously pretty rough.

"Then, I don't know, he must have said something. So she got off the stage and went outside, picked up a bucket that the cleaning men usually use, so it was filled with semen and water. You know they clean up the booths with the mop and the customers jerk off in there. She picks up the bucket and she flung it at the customer, simultaneously wetting about 10 other guys in the place. It was kind of like a scandalous action. So they fired her and threw her out. But she was pretty.

"She discovered she was dependent on the sex industry. She never took care of any of the other areas of her life. She used to make a lot of money. She could make, sometimes, a thousand, eighteen hundred dollars a night. But she never saved. She never did anything with it. She never had a bank account or anything substantial. So all of a sudden, her cash flow stopped.

She had a nervous breakdown.

"She was dating a lawyer who was really abusive to her, and he left, and she couldn't handle it. She ended up having like thousands of dollars of plastic surgery when she didn't need it, and ruining her body. She had liposuction which had them suck fat from her buttocks. Actually, no, it was right here, what do you call this part? Somewhere between her thighs and her buttocks.

"What happened later was part of the fat from her ass resettled and fell, leaving a kind of indent where she shouldn't have one. She had her nose tipped. You know, when you have it made slightly pointed, a little bit of a ski jump nose. She had fiber put into her lips so she that she could have fuller lips. She had her breasts done.

"The problem with her breasts is that they were perfect to begin with. And they were large. But she had them enlarged twice their size and the whole thing was a catastrophe. It was silicone. One of them became very hard. The other one was like marginally natural.

"Also she had her eyelids kind of, you'd call it a tuck. None of these things she needed. But she felt that her boyfriend left her, she had low self-esteem, she was fired from Peepland, she had to start go-go dancing alongside 18-year-old girls, and she was like 34. It didn't take too long before she began using drugs again.

"But then she stopped. She met a man. They went out for ice cream. She got pregnant. Three weeks later, they got married. This guy turned out to be a total maniac. 'He's the Husband From Hell,' she said. They were separated after their first six months and she started dancing again.

"Now he's back and she's still dancing. She has him in a 12-Step Program and maybe they will live happily ever after. That's China.

"There was one other girl, she was really odd. Oh, what's her name? Shit, I forgot her name. She used to be heavy into the punk scene and squatting in the Lower East Side and all that.

Then she started working for an escort agency and working at Peepland at the same time. She was an ex-heroin addict.

"I didn't realize how strange she was until she told me this story one night about this guy she was living with. She's asexual. She hasn't had sex for a very, very long time. But there was this guy. His name was Spike. He was kind of like pimply faced, and wore like really tight, tight jeans when he was a little bit overweight. Most of the people in her crew, most of the other punks, used to make fun of him. He couldn't take care of himself very well. I don't know how this happened, but he ended up living with her.

"She was telling me there was something really strange about him. Like they would go to a restaurant and order the same dish. And he would always get upset because he thought that she had more food than he did. He used to eat and drink her out of everything.

"She had a cat who was terrified of him. One morning she woke up and he had his pants down. He had the cat in his hand and he was stroking himself with the kitty. It was horrifying. Especially for the cat. Before she caught him, she couldn't understand why the cat was so afraid of him. He was stroking the cat against his penis. The back of the cat. The cat was struggling. When she woke up and caught him, he let go of the cat. He was petrified.

"She told him he had to leave.

"He was very, very upset. He was very embarrassed. Before this, she had realized he had been spending a lot of time in the bathroom and she used to think it was because he had problems getting dressed. She had to teach him about some very basic things, about personal hygiene and choosing clothes. Like you don't just go into a store and pick up a pair of jeans. You try them on to find out what your right size is.

"Anyway, it turns out that he was masturbating in the bathroom with her very expensive hair conditioner. Nexxus. It's like 26 dollars a bottle. It's very, very good. When you are working at Peepland, you can afford that kind of stuff. I think she walked in on him. So she had to explain to him that it was alright to masturbate, but in the future he should use KY Jelly. And she went and bought him some KY Jelly to use.

"So it dawned on me that this guy was retarded because she told me that he used to always talk about this place where he had worked. He ran away from home and he had worked in this place where there were retarded people. He would clean the floors and do things. But the more she spoke about him, I realized he ran away from that home and he was actually a retarded person.

"She felt very bad about throwing him out. She felt guilty because he had no place to go. So when she put him back on the streets, she was basically leaving him to all those bad elements.

"I couldn't believe that she hadn't realized before that he was retarded. I told her that she should inform his probation officer. I know that those guys won't notice things like that, but if she goes to them and explains to them that he indeed is slow or retarded or whatever, they can get him help. I don't know if she ever went about this or not. But I stressed it because I knew what will happen to this guy.

"She was a really odd person. Very pleasant and honest in an unknowing way. She wasn't self-conscious. That's what made her seem so odd. She used to dye her hair pink sometimes and carry it off very well. She wasn't a very happy person. She didn't like the work. She sensed life was basically a drag and that no one wanted to be where they were. Her dream was to take off with her best friend and go to London or Paris or something like Eve had done.

"Eve was another girl at Peepland. I showed you her picture. With red hair. Eve was a nice Jewish girl from someplace in Middle America. She was weird. Her father was like a doctor. She had moved to New York so that she could go to school and make a record with some people. They were going to get money together. So that's when she started working at Peepland. She'd been there far longer than I had.

"She was kind of crazy. She was really into black Afro-American men, Afro-American culture, and immersed herself in it. She was a Rastafarian groupie for a while and knew all the history and read all the books and was quite arrogant about it. But at the same time, she had a lot of condescending feelings towards Afro-Americans, especially if they were from the ghetto. I mean she was fairly well educated, working on her MFA, a Masters in Fine Arts. She was dating a graffiti artist who was actually quite famous. You know, 'It wasn't graffiti, it was art'. They would have shows for him in Soho.

"She kind of felt, or she had this vision, that she was doing something eccentric, immersing herself in this subculture of Peepland and being bizarre, having what she considered an avant-garde lifestyle. Because she was an intellectual. An artist. And working at Peepland among all these other very real-life characters. I think she really wanted to detach herself from her background and from her Middle American lifestyle.

"She considered herself to be very hip which means that she's a lesbian, she's bulimic and she's like, oh, she's Burroughs-esque. You know, like William Burroughs. She's really, I think, she's trying to fashion her life out of existing on these marginal lines.

"She's in Paris now. She was working in a peepshow there for a while and sculpting. Now she's discovered that she's actually very good, that she's talented and her work is in a gallery there. Probably not an important one. I don't know if she's sold any of her work yet. She sculpts 'functional art'. She says Amsterdam wants her. That's what she says.

"Then there's Leah. That's her real name, not her stage name. Leah and I became very close. Leah was an incredibly creative person. She used to change, literally, everything about her, every six months. She used to be in a Christian commune, a devout Christian. Then she left that. Then she would go from things like that, to writing screenplays. I have one. I think it was a great effort, but I don't think it was very good. She sent it into Sundance and they rejected it.

"But she's an incredible poet. I mean seriously so. Very natural. It's not something that she has to work at. They're beautiful. She should write verse more than prose or anything like that. She was in a rock group for a while, a lead singer. She wrote the lyrics. She played at The Bitter End, CBGB's and then she dropped out of that. Moved to Florida. And entered into nursing school. But her life was kind of like that. Always dropping in and out of things.

"She used to do heroin. Her hangout place was 8th Street and the Lower East Side. She would shave her head one day, end up in some acting role, and then end up in the hospital the next week for manic-depression. All along though, she was always questioning God. She felt guilty because she didn't know whether God would forgive her or not.

"She was always on a Jesus trip in a sense. Wanting to be saved and live according to the Bible. 'According to The Word,' as she said. But always drifting into these, um, kind of, uh, weird milieus. She'd just go into all of these dark crevices of life and looking for something and then having a nervous breakdown. She was extremely sensitive. Hyper-sensitive. Much more than I am.

"She had a weird relationship with her family. I think she resented her mom for being overly enthusiastic about her. And for stealing her boyfriend. But her mother is very devoted and supports her financially and emotionally. Leah was always surprised when people would not stand by her. She was always very disappointed in people. She was always looking for some depth, some true feelings, some meaning, and would come up empty.

"That's why she decided to become a nurse. To simplify her life, get out of New York, live in sunny Florida, get away from heroin, get away from all of the smiling, lying friends from the Lower East Side.

"A really weird incident happened with her. She joined a group that was really weird. It was like therapy. They call it meta-reprogramming. But what they do is they alter your thinking through a brainwashing exercise that puts you in a position of complete freedom, power, and self-insight and control of the universe. She went to their meeting. I was supposed to go but I didn't.

"She decided she wanted to join the course. They told her it would cost 1,500 dollars. She said she didn't have it. So they told her to get it. She said that she didn't know where to get it so soon, because they needed it right now to join the course. Like if she wanted to join the course for the next day, she'd have to pay them now or go and try another time.

"So she went and asked this guy who was in the room, another guy who was planning on joining, didn't know him, asked him for 1,500 dollars and he gave it to her.

"So now she's doing this thing. What they did was they locked you up for several days and they had like coordinators or facilitators who were there to break down your mental resistance. She said it was the most bizarre experience in her life. There were people who were screaming, crying, rolling on the floor, begging to get out, but they won't allow you to leave.

"She told me it was a little bit like an acid trip. Whatever it is, there's more that happened to her in this session, because when she got out, she disappeared for two days.

"They found her naked in Tompkins Square Park. Either she said that Jesus was coming or she was Jesus. I can't remember which. The cops grabbed her, threw her in the back of their car, handcuffed her and she ended up in Bellevue. Bellevue Hospital. The Psych Unit. She's another one who was strapped to her bed for a while.

"She said that that night, she had met Richard Gere and that he was with his bodyguard, and she met him around Washington Square Park or University Place. She said she had her head in his lap and she was talking to him. They were hanging out. She wanted to go home with him. He didn't want to go home with her.

"Or he just played it off. She said they began walking together and, this is weird, he picked her up and he sat her down on top of a pole. It was very high and she couldn't get down. When she did, she left, she went to Tompkins Square Park. She doesn't remember everything.

"She does remember taking off her clothes. She remembers the cops picking her up. I think that entire evening was a hallucination. They did pick her up. She was naked and they did pick her up. I don't believe she met Richard Gere. She probably met someone, but I don't believe it was Richard Gere.

"The main thing about Leah is that she could never find anything that could solidify what she believed to be reality."

Printed in Great Britain
by Amazon